ABOVE SCOTLAND

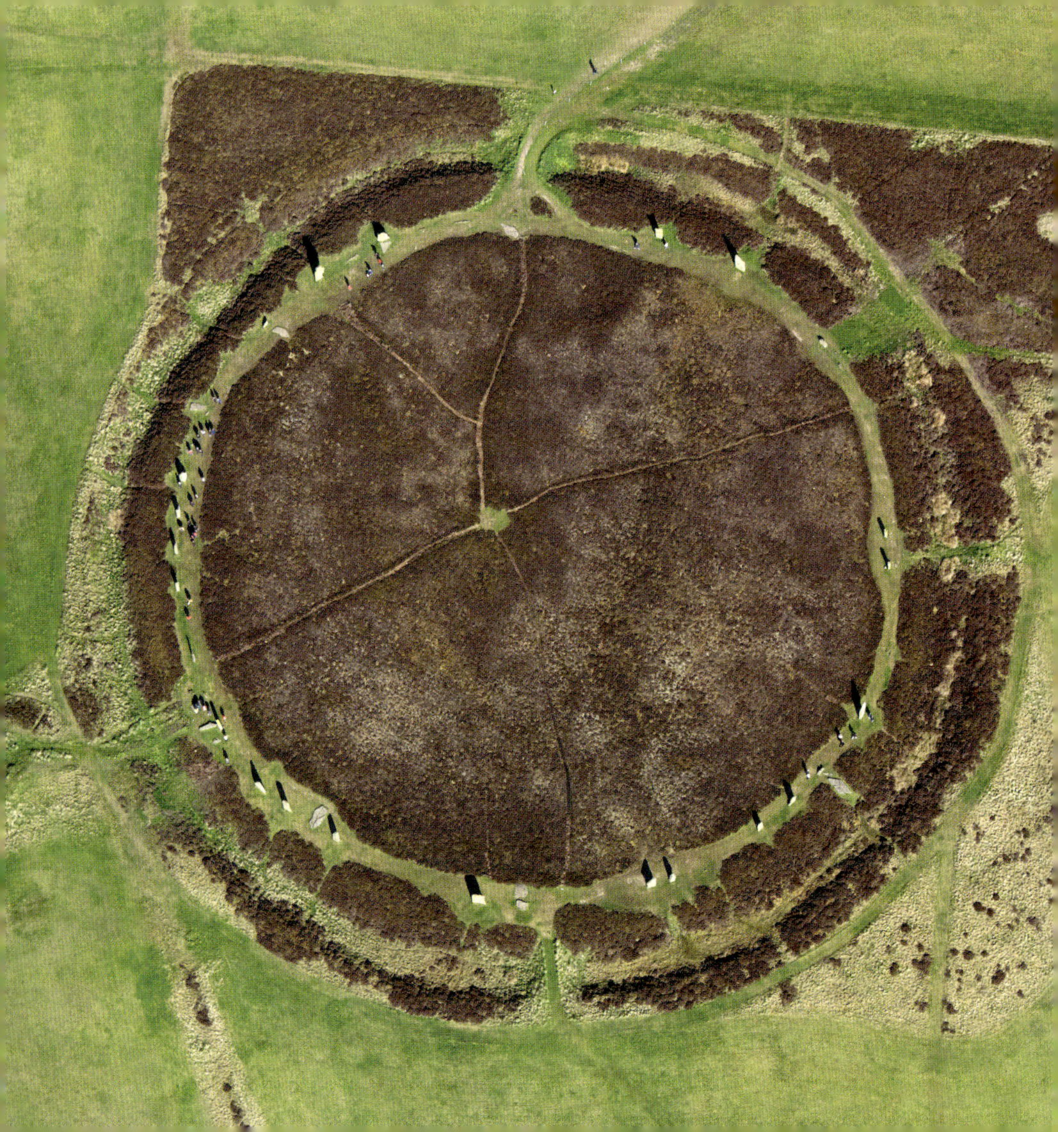

ABOVE SCOTLAND

Introduction by James Crawford

Published in 2024 by Historic Environment Scotland
Enterprises Limited SC510997

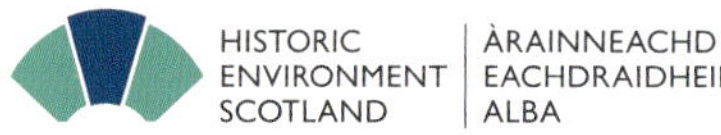

Historic Environment Scotland
Longmore House
Salisbury Place
Edinburgh
EH9 1SH

Registered Charity SC045925
British Library Cataloguing-in-Publication Data. A catalogue
record for this book is available from the British Library.
ISBN 978 1 84917 332 2

Frontispiece – Ring of Brodgar, Orkney HES DP058594

Typeset in Gotham and Gill Sans
Printed and bound in Italy by L.E.G.O. S.p.A.

contents

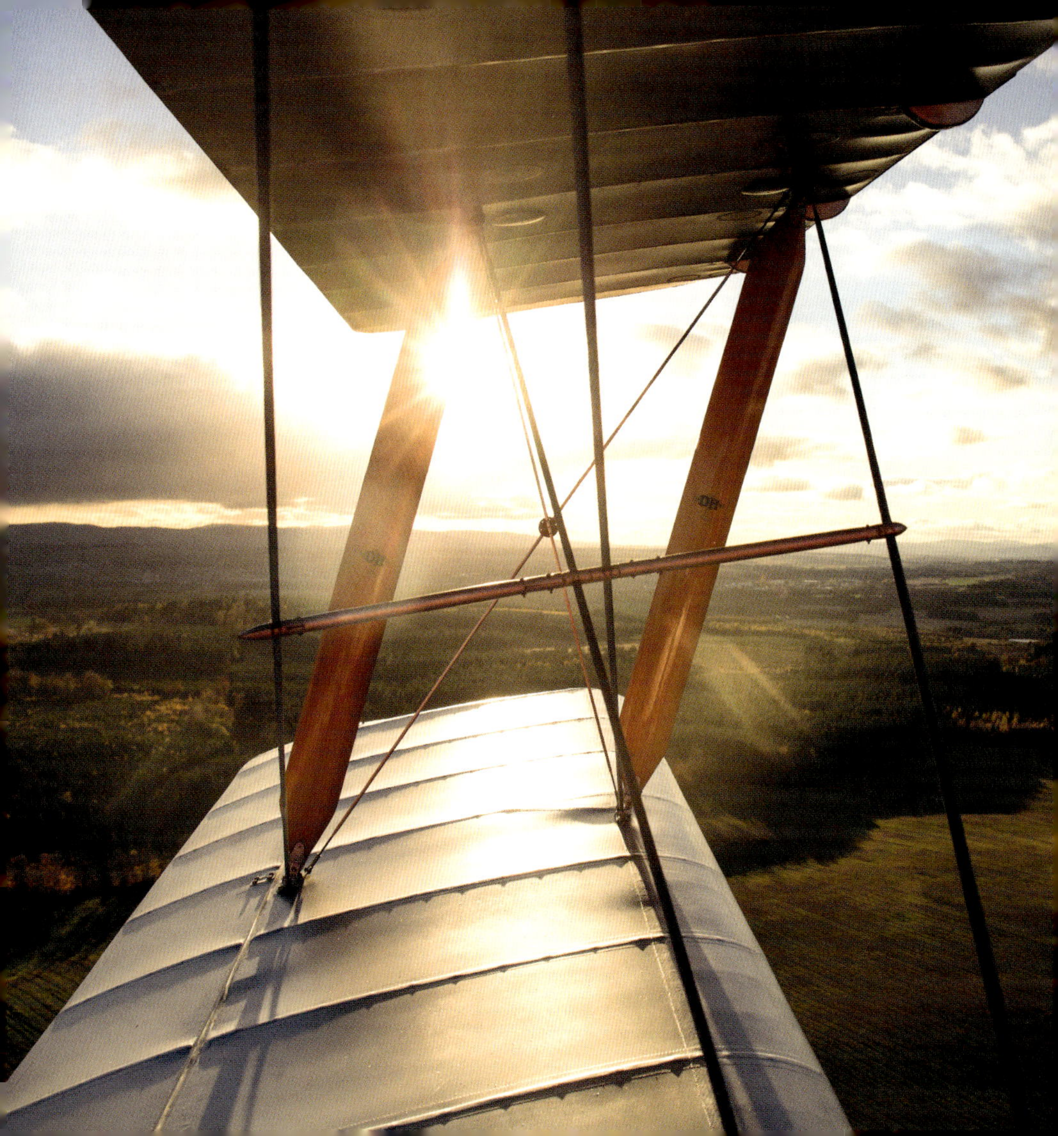

INTRODUCTION

Whenever you leave the ground in an aircraft, there comes a distinct moment where the world changes. On take-off, your body feels the urgent tug of gravity. But, at least for those first few seconds of flight, as you look out at the buildings, roads and people beyond your window, things are still clear and familiar. Then you climb higher. With every second, the view is shifting. People become dots, houses recede to tiny boxes, roads thin to fine lines unfurling into the distance. The horizon rushes away from you, hills and mountains ripple upwards. At some point in your ascent the moment comes, like a switch is being tripped in your brain: the landscape beneath you is transformed. Fine detail is overwhelmed completely by scale. If the sky is clear you can see for hundreds of miles, until the earth bends away. Look down and it is like you are looking at a map or a model. It doesn't feel quite real anymore. And it is mesmerising.

I've experienced this moment on many occasions, whether peering through the porthole window of a commercial flight, or out from the bubble of a helicopter cockpit – or even leaning over the side of a vintage biplane, with the wind rushing all around me. I like to savour it, to concentrate on feeling the exact instant of that delightful, lurching flip in perception. Try it yourself the next time you are on a flight. And, when you do, think about all those who have tried it before you.

Above Scotland in a vintage 1942 Tiger Moth, near Scone

Almost 250 years ago, at 3.45pm on 5 October 1785, an Italian called Vincenzo Lunardi lifted off from the gardens of George Heriot's School in Edinburgh in what he called an 'aerostatic machine' – what you and I would know today as a hot air balloon. He rose rapidly to 1,100 feet in order to clear the buildings of the city around him, and then he began to drift northwards. Not that he really noticed where he was going.

At this elevation I spent some time in contemplating the beauties of the scene below, which were indeed beyond description! Especially to those who have never been in a similar situation! The hills about Edinburgh appeared like small mounts raised by art, and the extensive labours of the neighbouring farmers as so many gardens, divided into little plots. The city of Glasgow I could plainly distinguish, and also the town of Paisley, as well as those on both sides of the Forth, the meanders of which, with the highways and rivers in the adjacent country, had exactly the same appearance as if laid down on a map; indeed every object seemed to lessen and recede from the eye.

Vincenzo Lunardi ascends in a hot air balloon, beginning his 'voyage' from Edinburgh
1785 etching by John Kay. Florilegius / Alamy Stock Photo

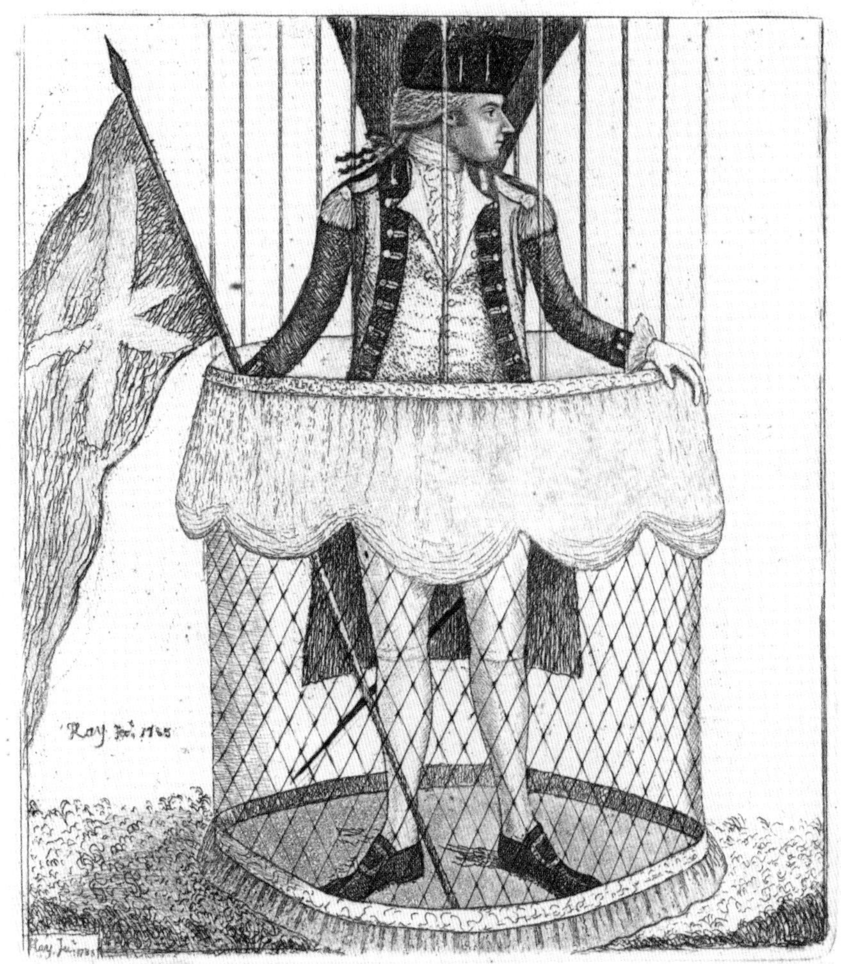
Ray fecit 1785

Even for a pioneering aviator like Lunardi, whose survival relied on his skill and attention in piloting his balloon, the view could be transfixing. He suddenly found himself drifting 'perpendicular over the Firth of Forth: I had been so immersed in contemplation that the balloon had ascended 2,000 feet without my perceiving it; and, had not the barometer been suspended as high as my head, I might insensibly have soared totally out of sight'. The wind continued to carry the balloon north and east. Lunardi flew in and out of clouds, he passed over the island of Inchkeith and met the shores of Fife at Lower Largo, coming to land in a field alongside the little village of Ceres. A modest plaque can still be found there commemorating the journey – 46 miles, 36 of them over water. As the inscription puts it, 'This was the first aerial voyage in Scotland.'

It is ironic, perhaps, that a view that was once the privileged experience of Lunardi alone, now greets millions of visitors to Scotland each year. When coming in to land at Edinburgh airport, you arc in over the wide mouth of the Forth estuary. To the north you can see the compact little harbour towns of Fife, clustered around the bright curves of beaches. To the south is the city of Edinburgh itself, the port of Leith leading up to the rigid geometric grid of the New Town. Beyond that the looming volcanic plugs of Arthur's Seat and the Castle Rock. And all cradled by the surprisingly muscular arms of the Pentland Hills. Just before landing, the Forth

Bridges come into view – a startling sight, perhaps, for the unprepared. Three crossings of the same stretch of water. Three time-stamps from history, each radically different in appearance, but all coming together to dominate the surrounding landscape.

There were no bridges over the Forth when Lunardi made his flight. No railways, or motorways or cars or power stations. Parts of Edinburgh's elegant Georgian New Town – which, today, is a World Heritage site – were still a messy construction site, bordering open fields leading down to the coast. But, all the same, what Lunardi saw from the skies above Scotland over two-hundred years ago is exactly what you will see today: a landscape in flux, breathing in and out, where old and new live side by side.

This is the essence – and the power – of the view from above. When you look down on Scotland from the sky, time at once compresses and unravels. The land becomes a captivating, ever-changing jigsaw, made up of interlocking and overlapping fragments of the past and the present. It holds the story of what we've done, going back some 14,000 years, all the way to end of the last Ice Age – the story of the buildings we've erected, the soil we've farmed, the industries we've created, the wars we've fought. Down on the ground, it's hard to see the pieces or to spot the joins. But, take to the air, and all that changes.

Look down from on high, for instance, and you can understand castles not as the picturesque ruins they are now, but as the looming – terrifying even – expressions of power they were when they were first built: dark thorns of stone surging up out of the earth. You can see ancient stone circles staring up like unblinking eyes, and grasp, in an instant, how these structures must have served as the centrepieces for arcane rituals honouring obscure, forgotten gods. And you can trace the incredible endurance in the land, some two millennia on, of the Roman war machine – preserved in earthworks left behind by roads, forts and a vast 36-mile-long wall that once marked the final frontier of their great Empire.

More than anything else, the view from above shows you just how much history is all around you, all of the time. If you are looking for ghosts, then perhaps the best place to find them is within the landscape of Scotland itself, where the lives of people long gone linger so powerfully in the marks that they have left behind – even down to the simple action of sinking a spade into the soil, hundreds or perhaps thousands of years ago.

This book, then, offers a journey into – or rather, *above* – Scottish history. It invites you to drift, just as Vincenzo Lunardi did all those years ago, over cities, hills, countryside and coastlines. In the photographs that follow, you will see Scotland from a whole new perspective. The familiar will be made unfamiliar, from the geometric maze of cityscapes, to the abstract, poignant beauty of abandoned crofting townships. You will travel to every corner of the country, over lochs, moorlands and mountains, and across the sea to even the most remote islands. You will see Scotland as it is today. But, at the same time, you will see how history everywhere breaks through the skin of our modern world. How the stories of the past are written into the land. And how, sometimes, the only way you can truly read those stories, is from the sky.

James Crawford

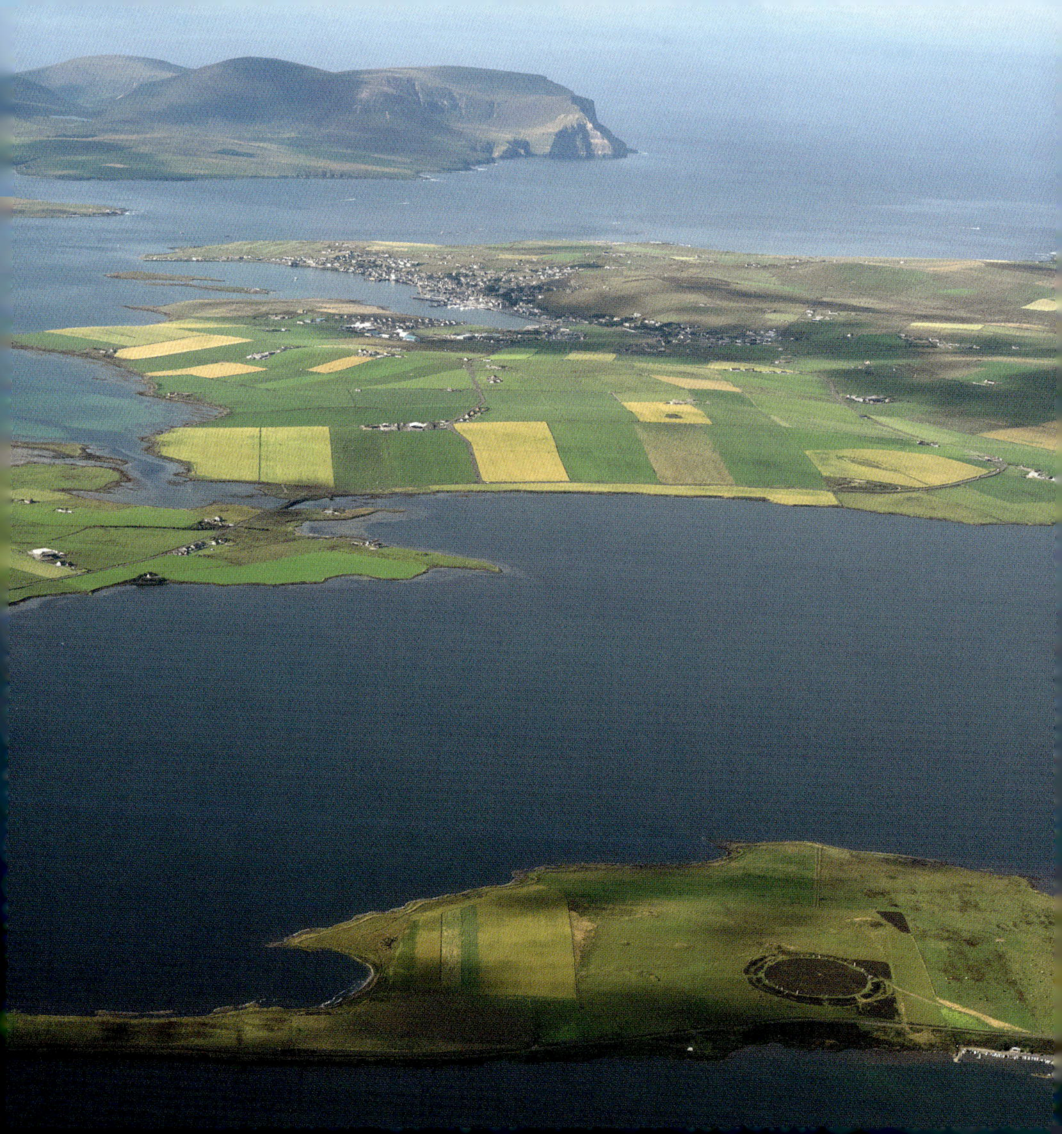

3,000 million years ago, the oldest of the rocks which underpin Scotland – Lewisian gneiss – was formed. In contrast to this geological foundation, evidence of humans transforming the land now known as Scotland stretches back only 7,000 years.

Little is known of these people, but archaeology and aerial photography illuminate what they have left behind. Sometimes this is revealed in small fragments, like discarded hazelnuts or flints. Sometimes, however, the evidence is truly monumental. Hill forts, standing stones, brochs, crannogs – these remaining features reveal a complex society: ceremonial, social, defensive. Slim ridges of prehistoric agriculture can also be found on patches of land inhospitable to modern development, places where human hands first began to mould the Scottish landscape to fit the needs of their communities.

While the language, faith and social structures of these people remain remote, what is known brings them tantalisingly close. We still share the same land, and even after millennia their presence has not been entirely erased.

Ring of Brodgar, Orkney
Surrounded by sea and sky, this vast stone circle at the Ness of Brodgar drew people together for ritual and worship thousands of years ago. Of the original 60 stones, only 36 survive. It is now one element of the ancient landscape which forms the Heart of Neolithic Orkney World Heritage Site.
DP083285

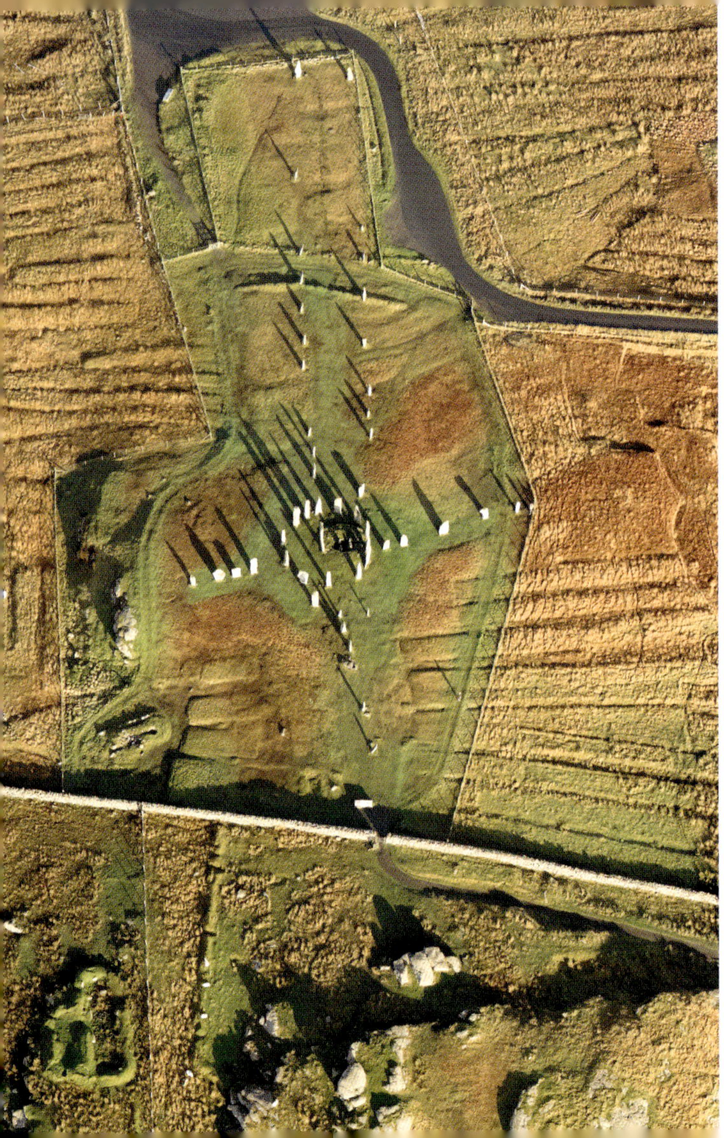

Calanais Standing Stones, Lewis, Na h-Eileanan Siar
The stones of Calanais radiate out in four lines from a central ring, alongside the marks of settlement and agriculture. Dating to c3000 BC, Calanais is one of the oldest monuments of its kind in Scotland and was a focus for ritual activity over a period of at least 2,000 years. Although its original purpose is lost to memory, the site has long been associated with astronomical events.
DP110867

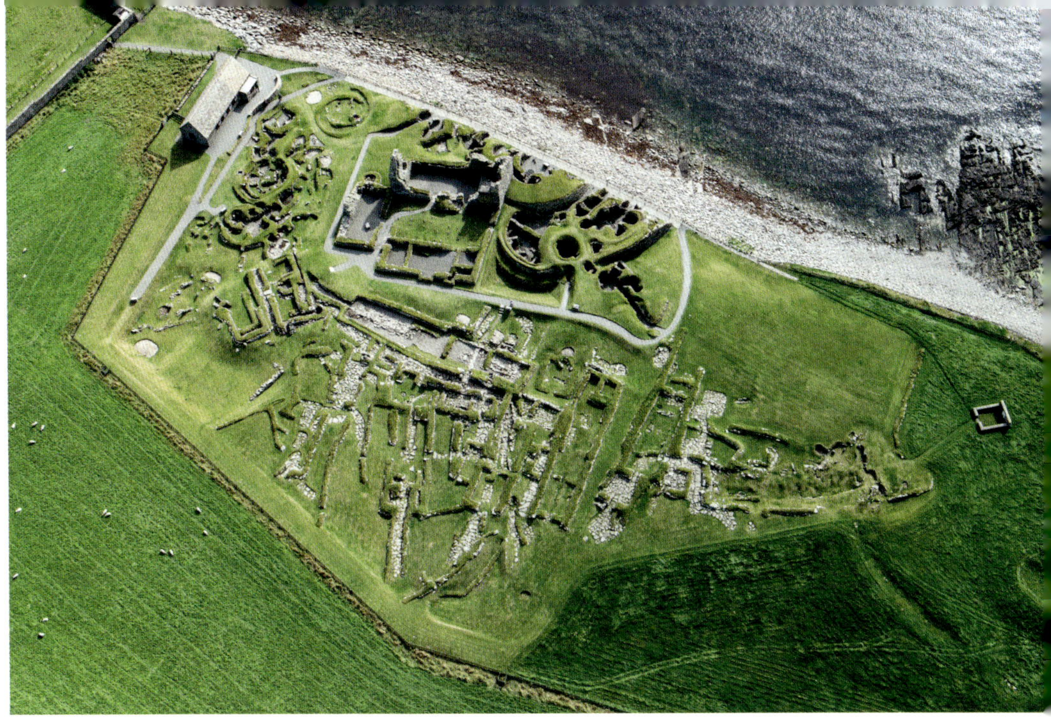

Jarlshof, Shetland

Overlooking the West Voe of Sumburgh, Jarlshof is a complex
site which was settled from around 2700 BC. With the remains
of Neolithic dwellings, Bronze Age houses, an Iron Age broch and
wheelhouses, Norse longhouses, a medieval farmstead and a laird's
house from the 1500s, the layers of over 4,000 years of habitation
are evident in this one place.

DP260624

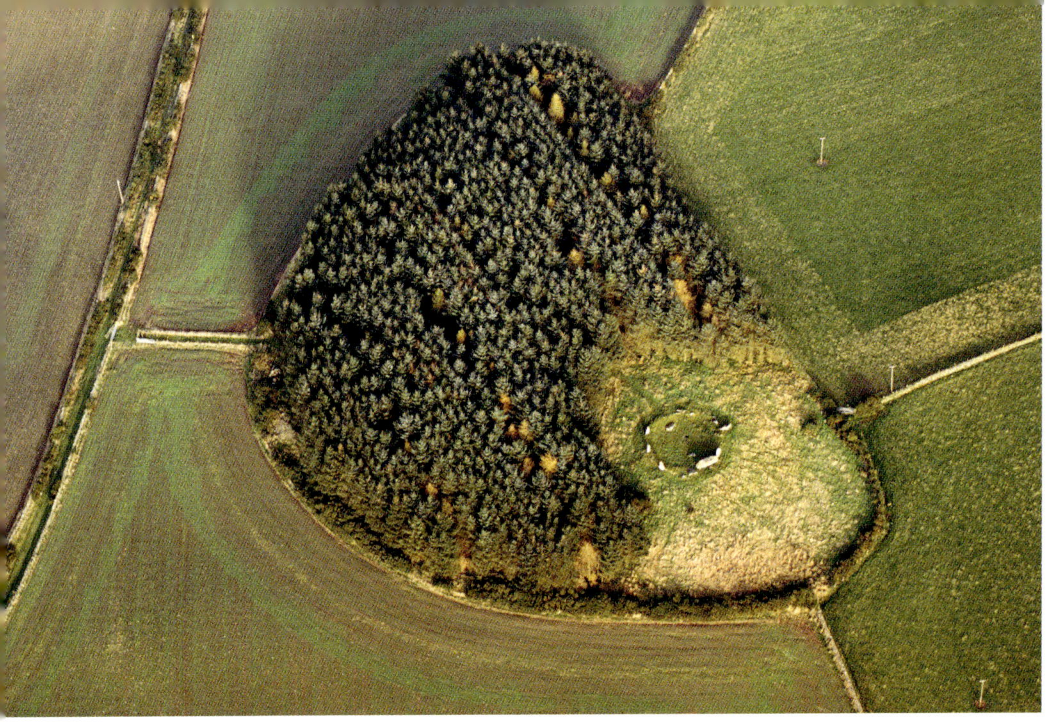

Aikey Brae Recumbent Stone Circle, Aberdeenshire
This hilltop stone circle is in a style found only in Aberdeenshire, with one massive slab – the 'recumbent' stone – set between two flanking pillar stones. It would have taken huge effort to move these giant stones into position around 4,000 years ago, with some being over 2m in height.
SC958377

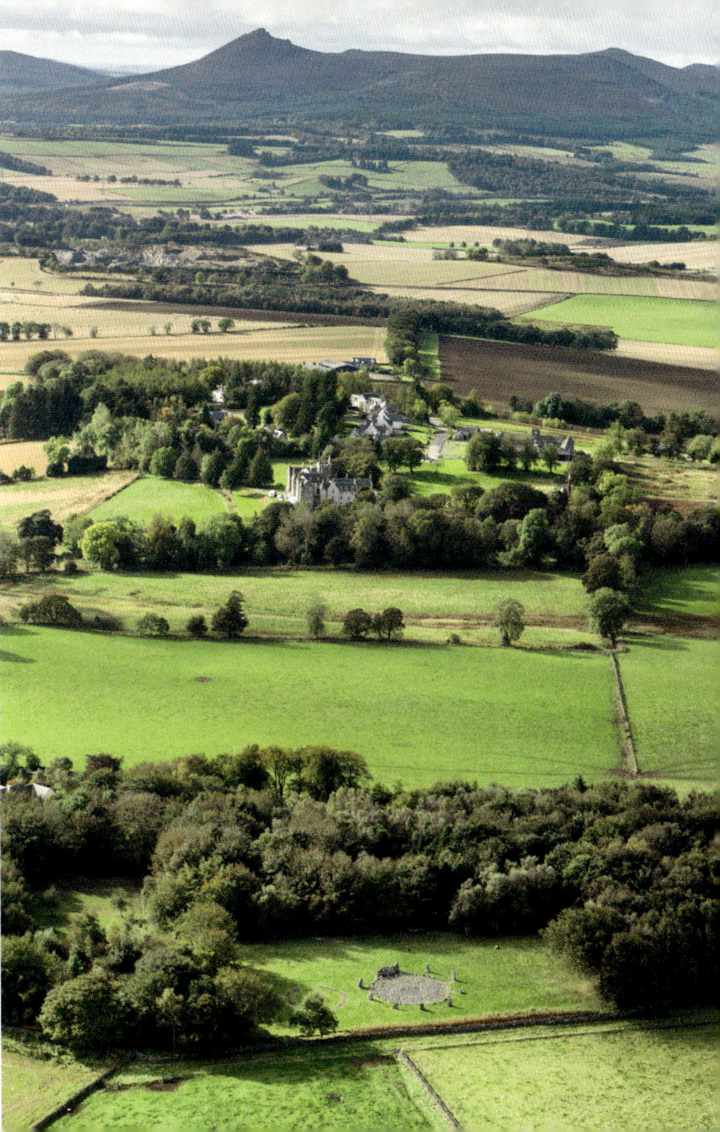

Recumbent Stone Circle at Loanhead of Daviot, Aberdeenshire

Archaeological investigations at this recumbent stone circle revealed charcoal and fragments of human bone, implying that this was once a place where funerary pyres were lit to cremate the dead. One of the oldest known structures in Scotland, this stone circle was constructed around 4,000 years ago, with the cairn predating the circle by approximately 500 years. DP082981

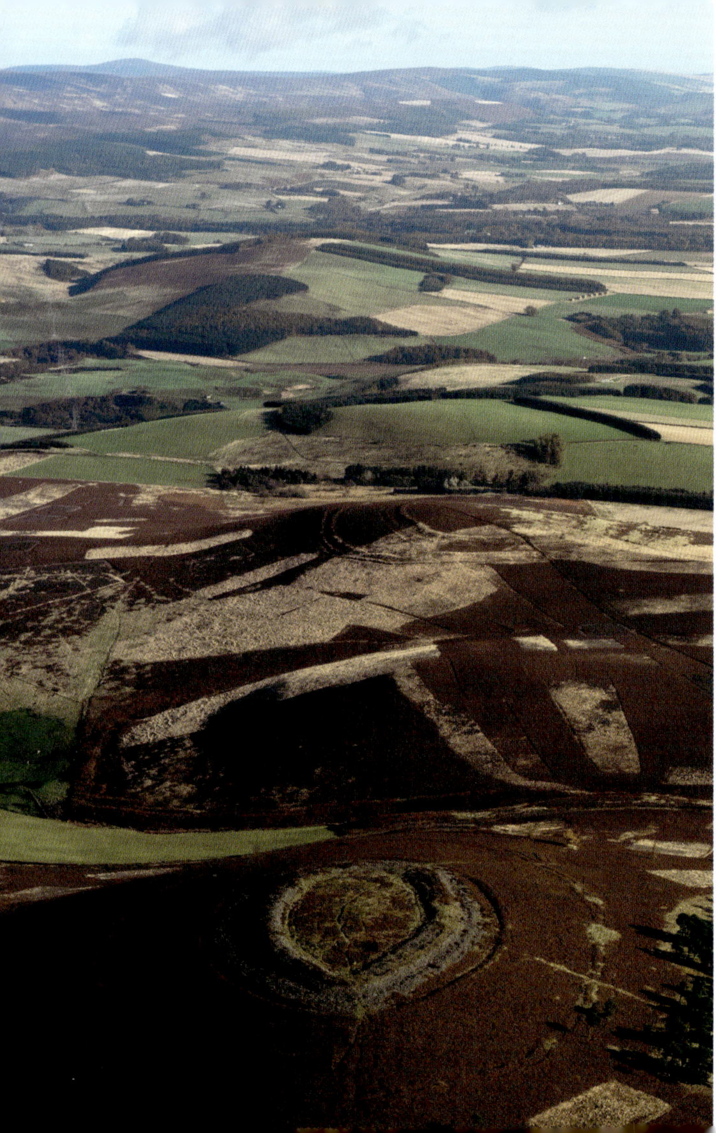

**Brown and White
Caterthun Forts, Angus**
These two massive prehistoric
hill forts sit on either side
of a shallow valley, ancient
fortifications preserved in the
collapsed walls and earthworks
of their once towering
ramparts and gates.
DP056577

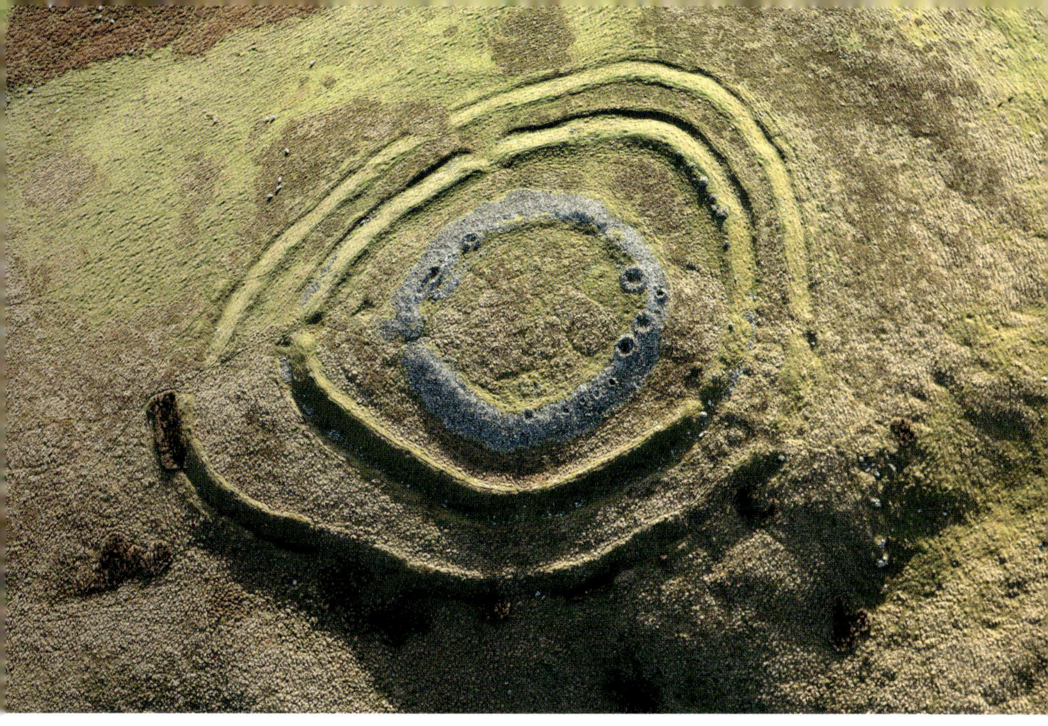

Arbory Hill Fort, South Lanarkshire
This huge structure, some 80m long by 70m high, stands as a ruined
sentry on the summit of Arbory Hill, almost 500m above the M74 as it
passes through a deep valley carved by the passage of the River Clyde.
DP208956

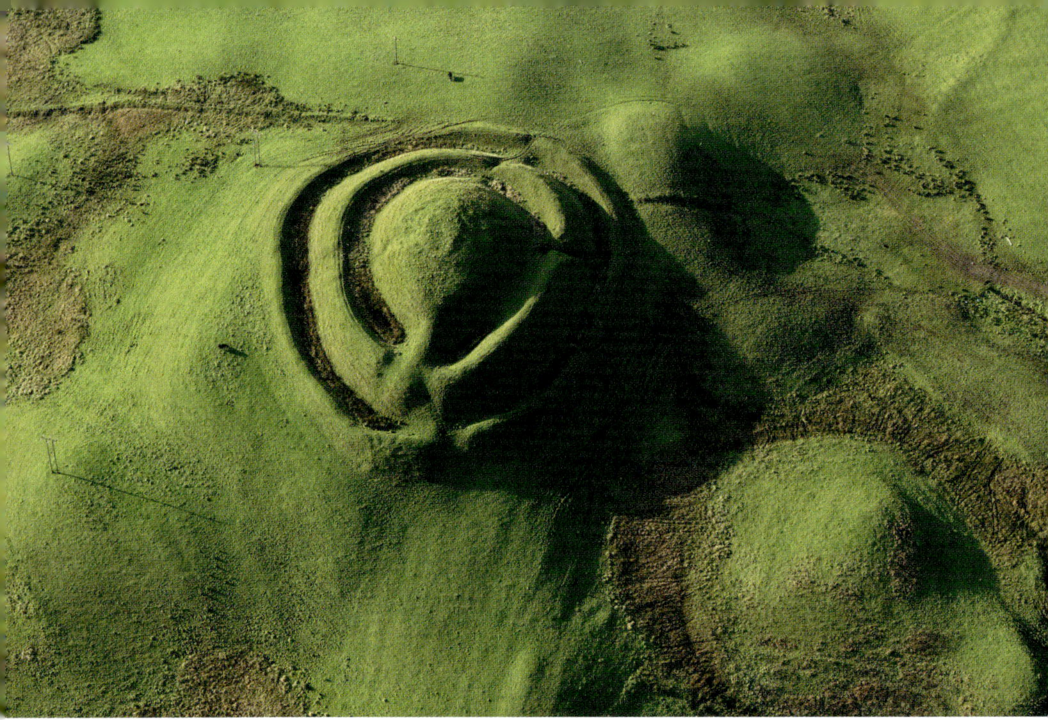

Dinvin Motte, Ayrshire

This motte, which would once have been topped by a timber castle, is one of the most striking medieval earthworks in Scotland. The deep surrounding ditches with external banks would have greatly enhanced the defences of the commanding hilltop position.

DP052214

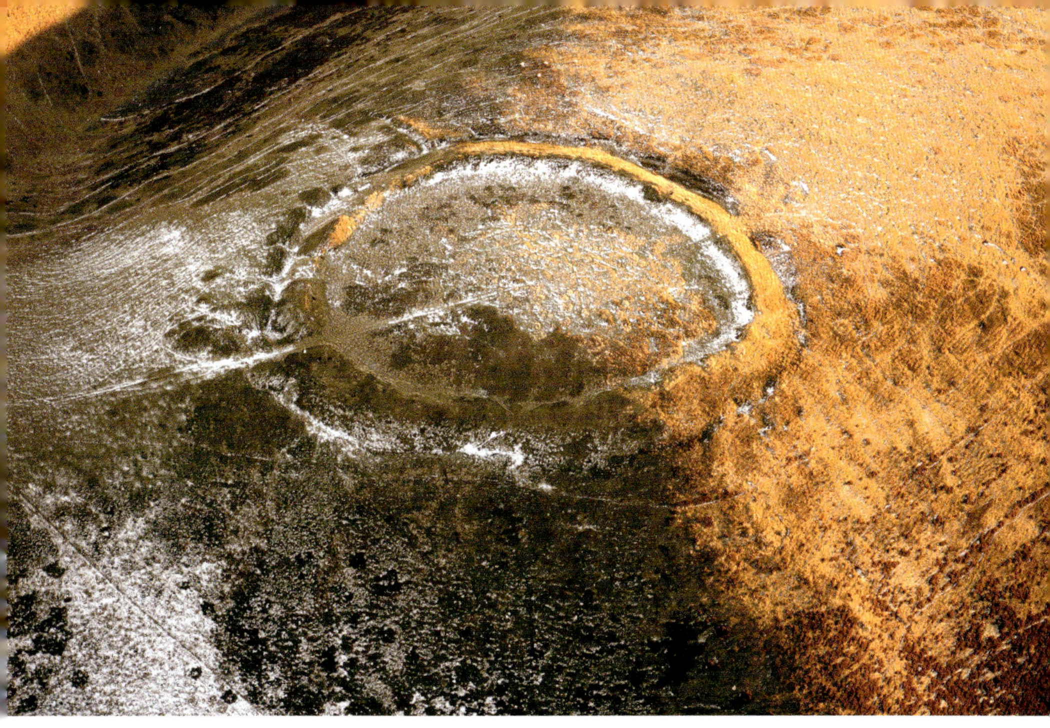

Blackbrough Hill Fort, the Scottish Borders
This small ancient fort allowed for the surrounding landscape to be monitored from atop a steep slope in the Cheviot Hills, ringed by a defensive earthwork enclosure.
SC677302

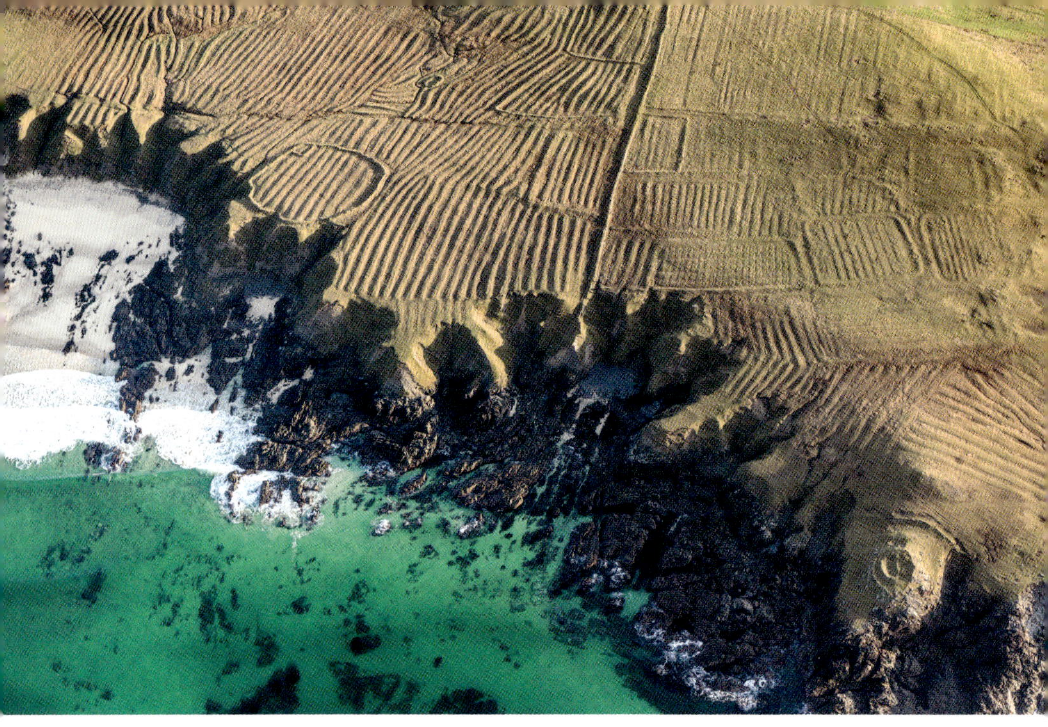

Dun Mara, Lewis, Na h-Eileanan Siar

The remains of this prehistoric fort sit at Carnan Thangadeir,
with traces of agricultural lazy beds and enclosures extending
right to the cliff edge.

DP109583

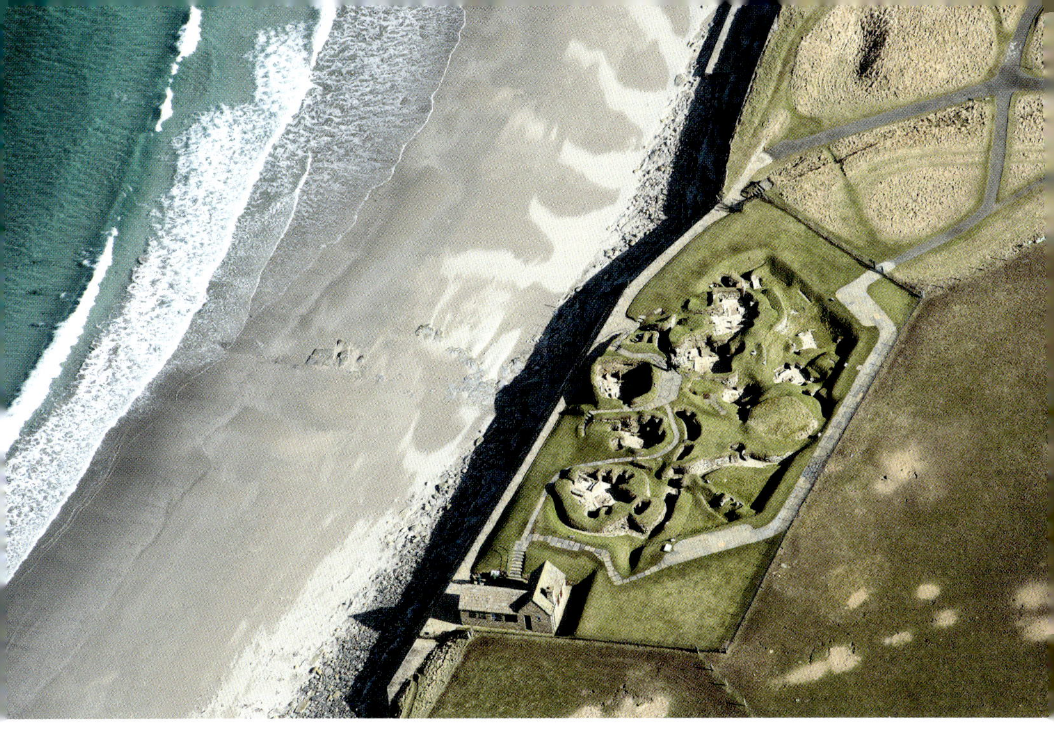

Skara Brae, Orkney

Re-emerging from beneath the sand during a storm in 1850, the astonishingly well-preserved Neolithic village of Skara Brae was in use for around 400 years before being abandoned – for reasons that remain unclear – in c2500 BC. The village was once larger, as an unknown number of structures have been subsumed by the sea.

DP273476

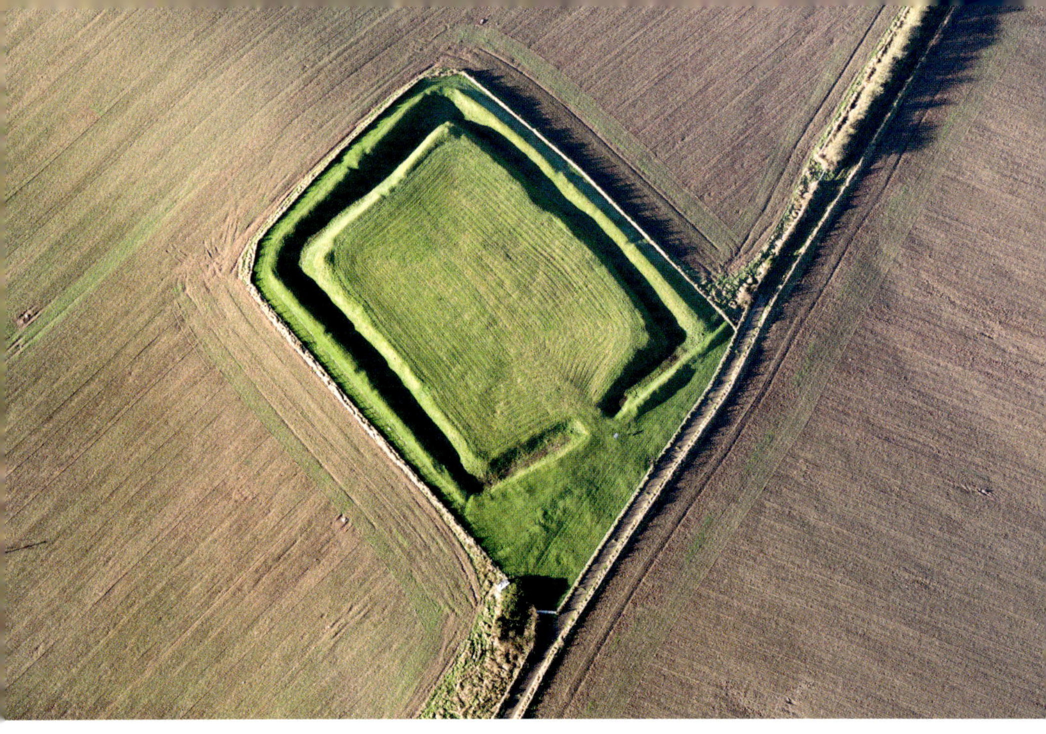

Rispain Camp, Dumfries and Galloway
Once believed to be a medieval manor or a Roman fort (the name Rispain 'Camp' being a result of this earlier theory), these rectangular earthworks are older – the remains of a fortified farmstead dating to c150 BC.
DP147963

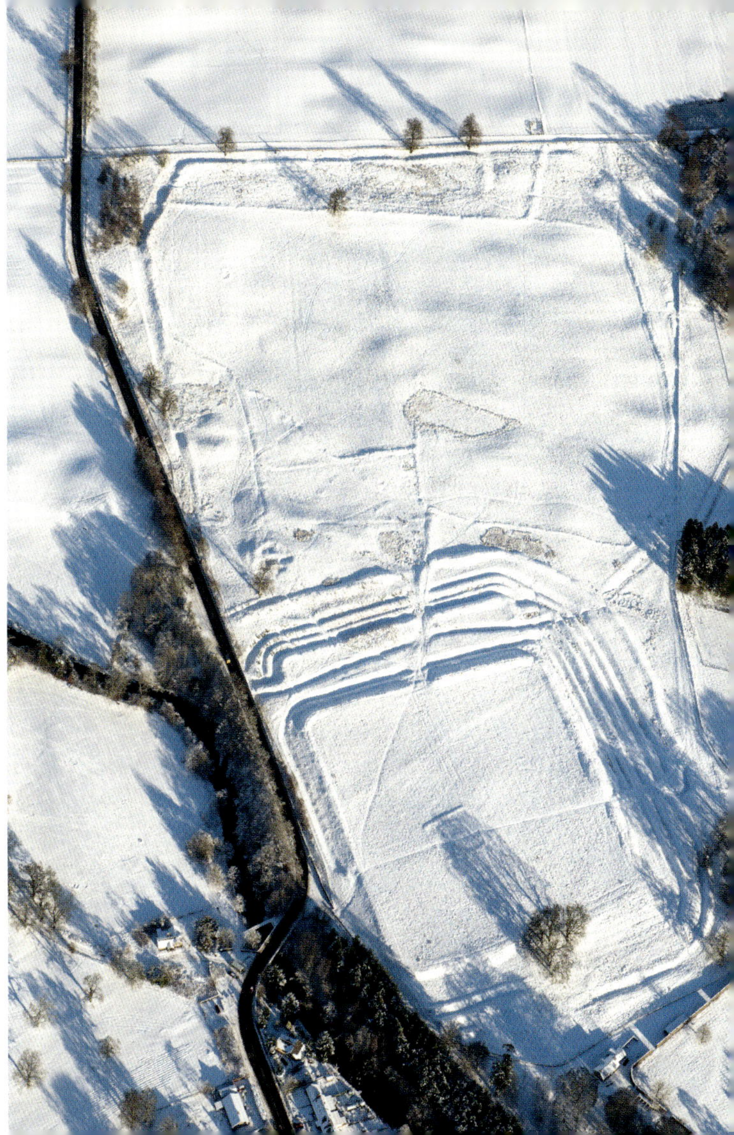

Ardoch Roman Fort, Perthshire

The fort at Ardoch is one of several that can be found along the path of an old Roman road. Originally constructed in the first century AD, its extensive floorplan is still deeply inscribed on the earth.

DP229035

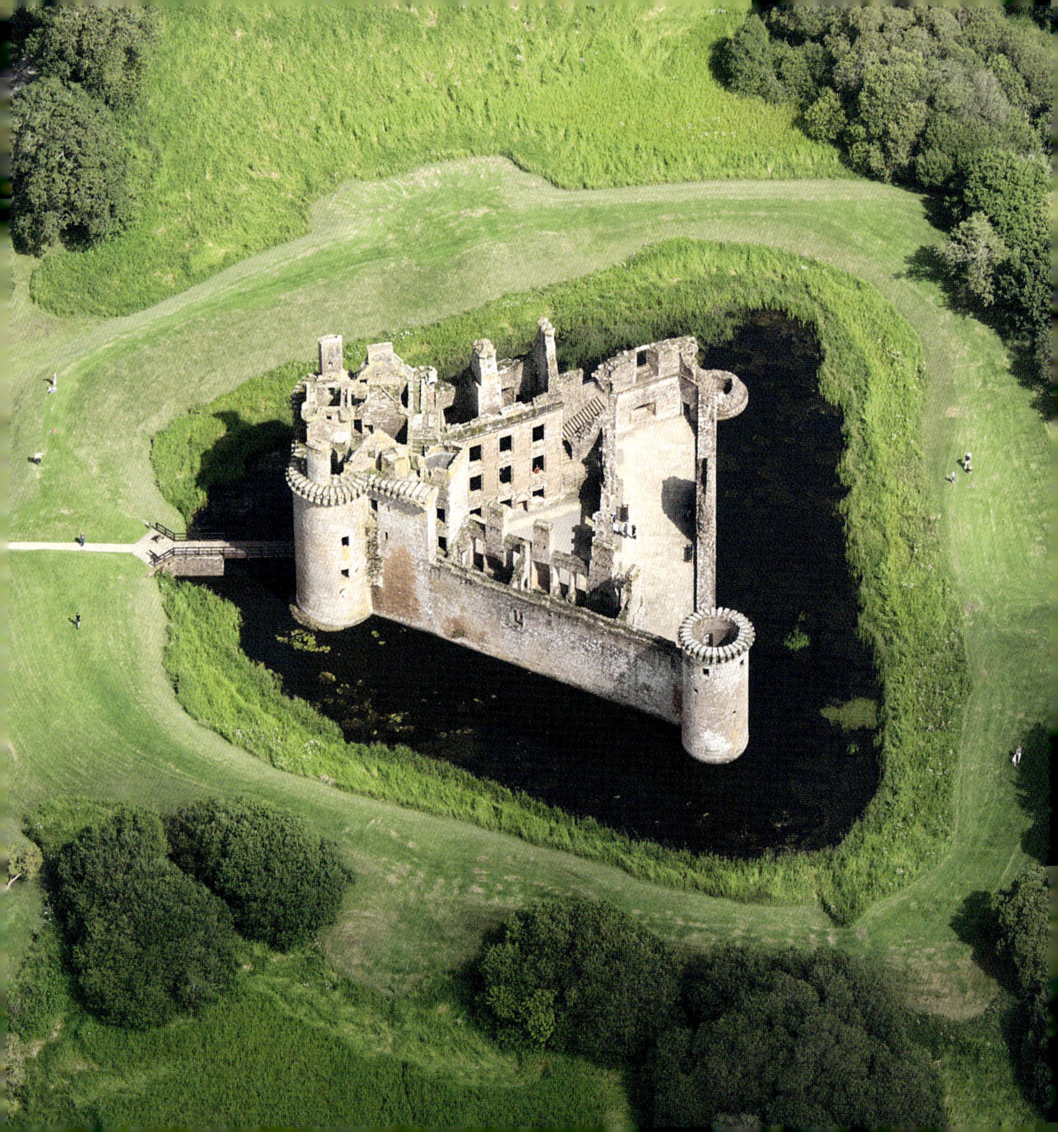

Clans once played a central part in Scotland's political life, particularly in the Highlands. These ancient family groups created powerful bonds, with allegiances forged in kinship and family ties – as well as rivalries which led to longstanding feuds. The clans also stamped their legacies on the landscape, and many of their territories came to be dominated by stone castles. These imposing structures, which began to appear in Scotland from the late 1100s, were not only for strategic and military might, but also for the administration and control of estates. Some castles, such as those at Edinburgh and Stirling, were built on existing hill forts and later became prominent royal residences.

In both the Highlands and Lowlands, by the 1700s, noble families were turning their backs on these older fortified residences. Defences were no longer needed and the luxuries of bespoke country houses emerged as the new status symbols of wealth and influence. As with castles, these eminent homes have adapted, fallen or thrived over the years as they found their place in an ever-changing Scotland.

Caerlaverlock Castle, Dumfries and Galloway
The distinctive triangular shape of Caerlaverock Castle, constructed of red sandstone, is unique in Britain. The castle's position in the south of Scotland resulted in it being embroiled in many border conflicts, including a siege by Edward I of England's soldiers in 1300 and the final siege in 1640, where the castle garrison fell after 13 weeks.
DP108243

SEATS OF POWER

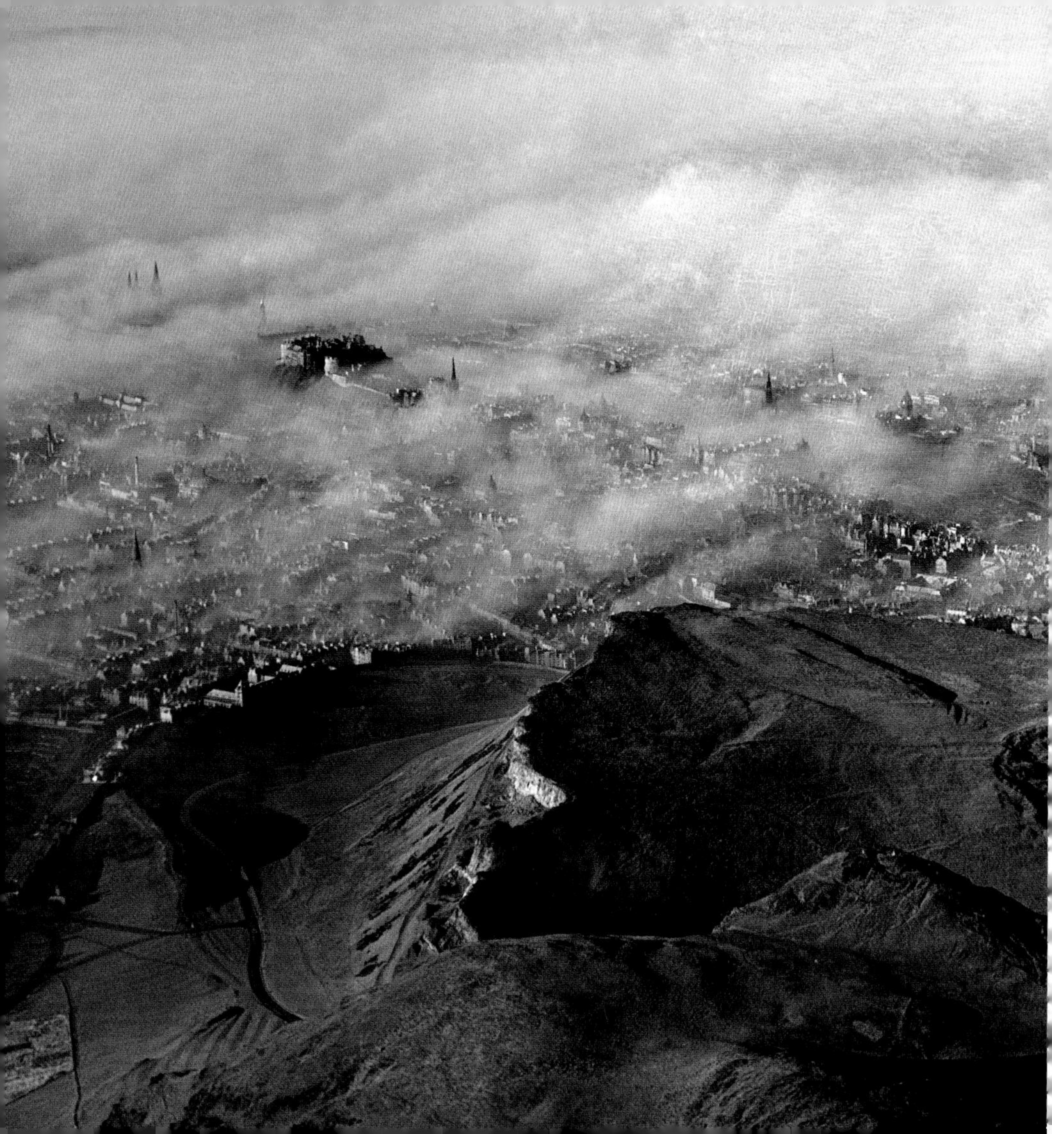

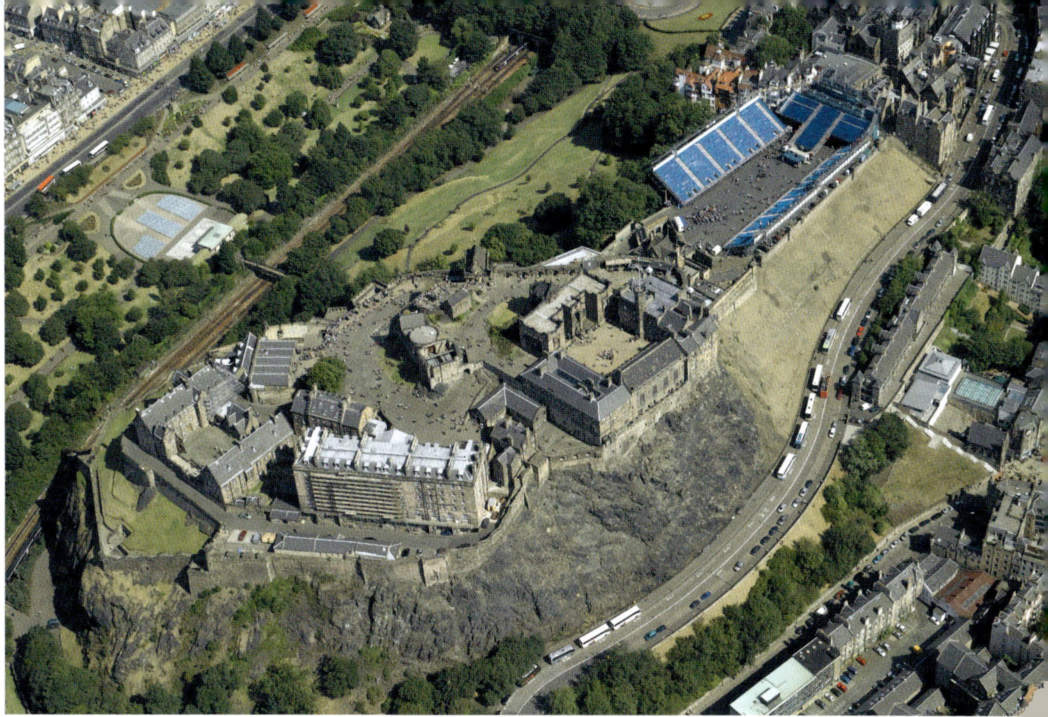

Edinburgh Castle

Edinburgh is dominated by its volcanic past, and nowhere more strikingly than with its castle. A fortification for nearly 3,000 years, it rises high above the city on an imposing surge of dark basalt rock. The castle began as an Iron Age fort, became an early medieval fortress and seat of royal power, held prisoners of war during the Napoleonic Wars and, today, is a garrison and tourist attraction.
SC1437830 (1949), DP012635

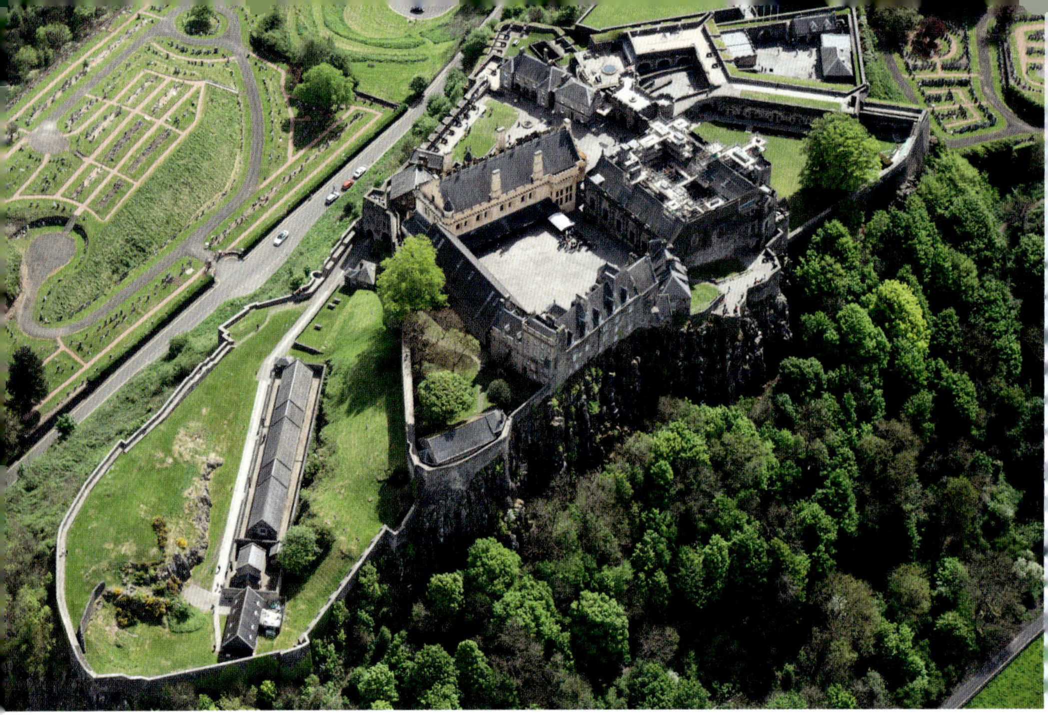

Stirling Castle

As with Edinburgh Castle, Stirling Castle sits on top of a volcanic crag which has likely been fortified since ancient times. The castle's position was of utmost strategic importance, making it the focus of nearby battles such as William Wallace's victory at the Battle of Stirling Bridge in 1297 and Robert the Bruce's defeat of the English Edward II at Bannockburn in 1314. It has been the home of many Scottish royals, reaching the height of its prominence in the 1500s, at which time James V drew on Renaissance ideas for the design of his new palace within the castle.

DP258885

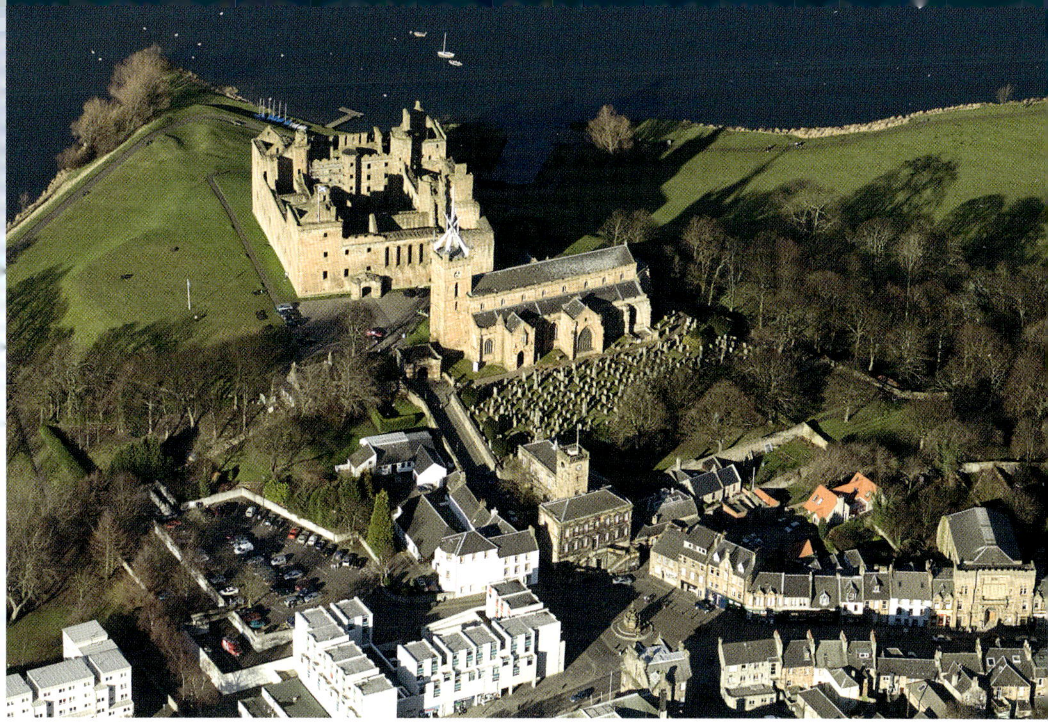

Linlithgow Palace, West Lothian

The first royal dwelling at Linlithgow, conveniently located between Stirling and Edinburgh, was built in the 1100s by David I. The roofless ruin that survives today is the remnant of a palace begun by James I in 1424 and later used as a nursery for Mary Queen of Scots. With the removal of the royal court to London after 1603 the palace deteriorated and was eventually gutted by fire in 1745.

DP013242

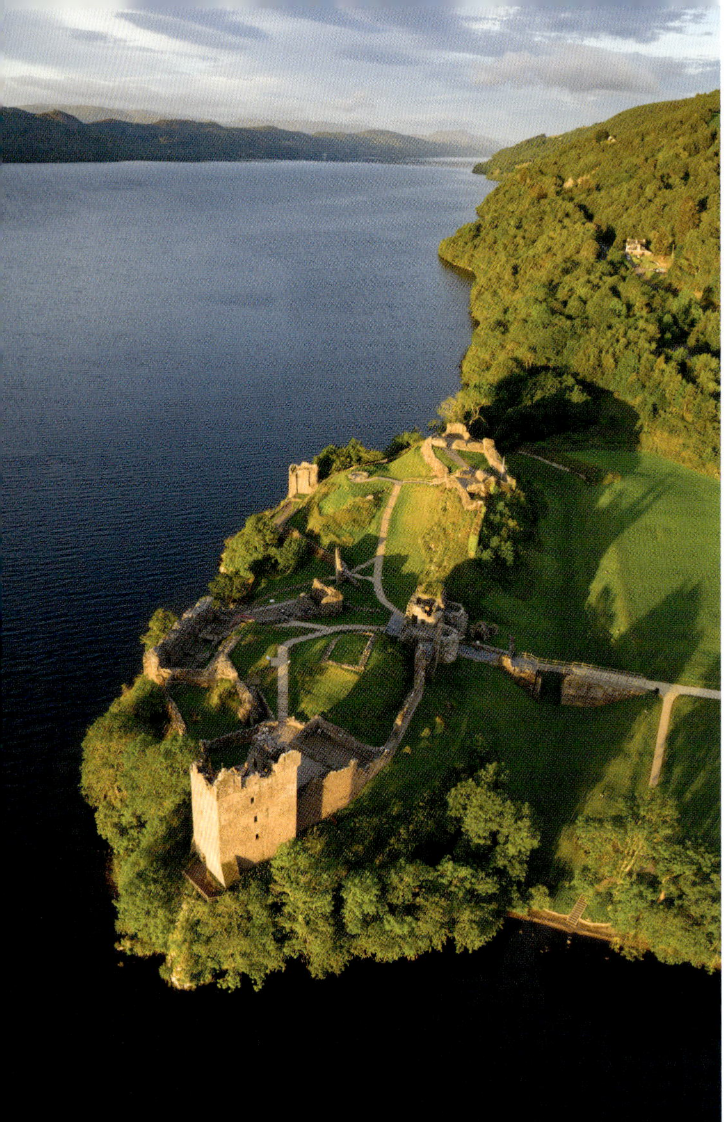

Urquhart Castle, Highlands
Positioned in the Great Glen overlooking the waters of Loch Ness, the now-picturesque Urquhart Castle has a turbulent past. The castle passed between English and Scottish hands during the Wars of Independence, was raided by the Lords of the Isles, and was besieged by the Jacobites in the 1689–90 Rising. However, this famous stronghold was left shattered by departing government troops in 1692, who, by blowing up the gatehouse behind them, abandoned the castle in a weak and defenceless state.
HES

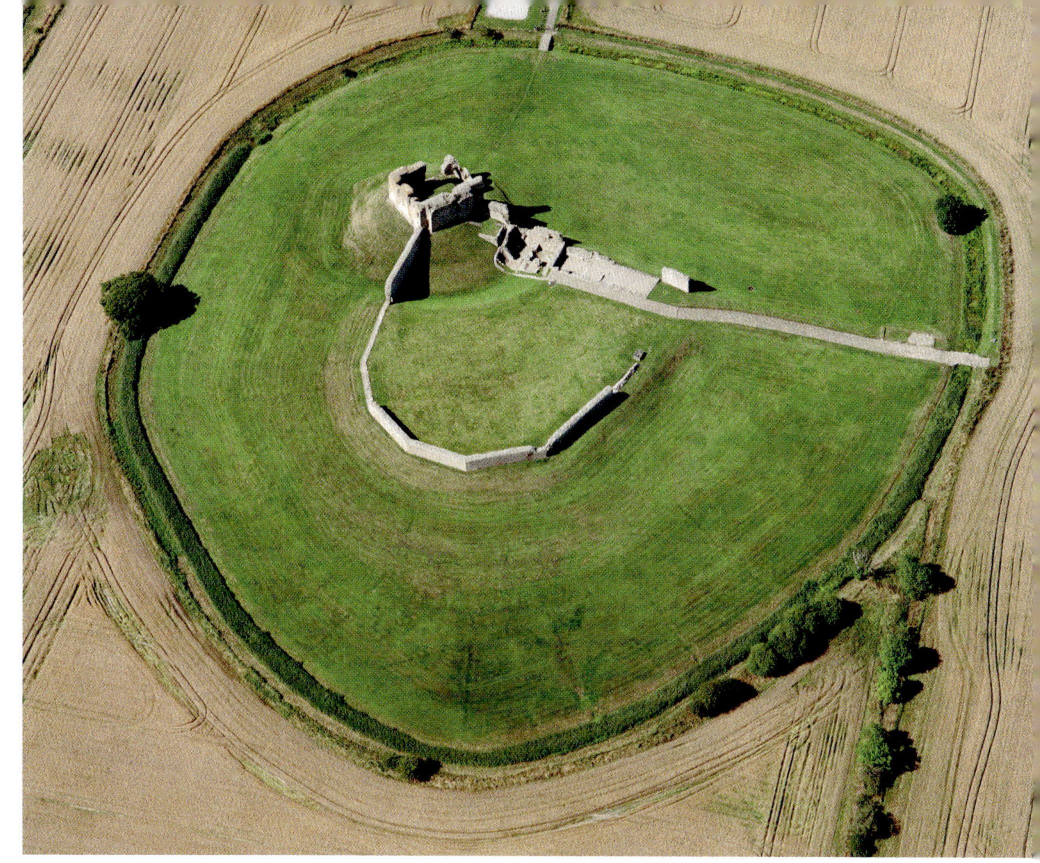

Duffus Castle, Moray

Surrounded by regimented modern farming, on land that was once
the shore of Loch Spynie, the stone castle at Duffus sits like an ancient,
abandoned island in the Lossiemouth landscape. Dating from c1300, it was
built on a motte that originally supported a twelfth century timber castle.

SC752247

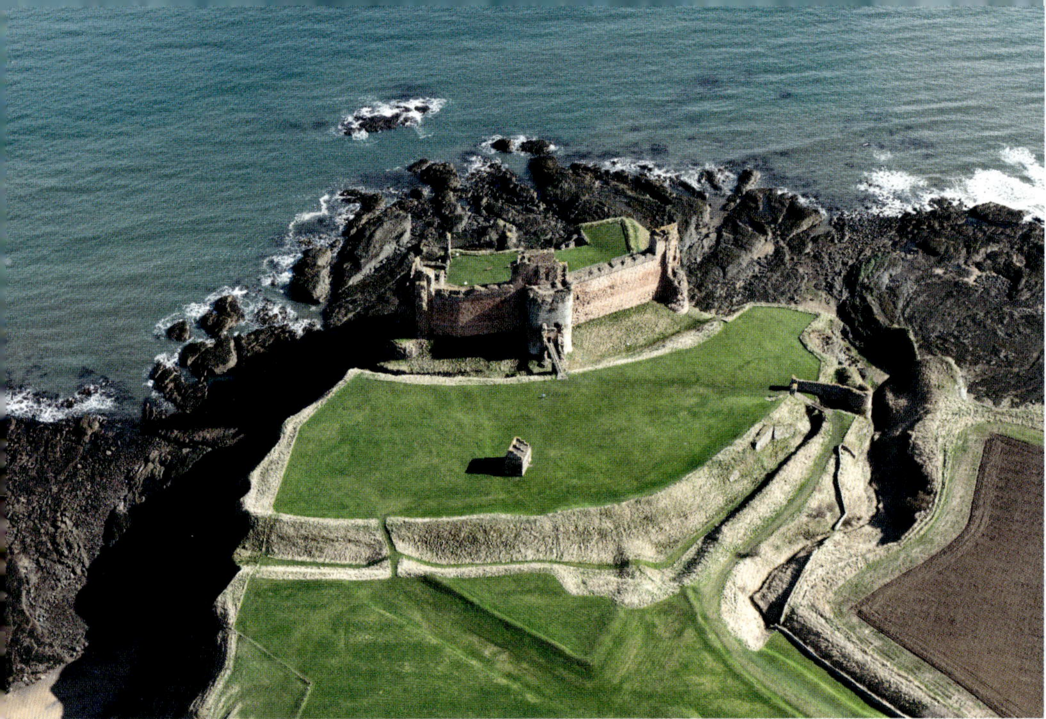

Tantallon Castle, East Lothian

The last great castle to be built in Scotland, Tantallon was the seat of one of the most powerful baronial families, the Red Douglases. Built in the 1350s, Tantallon remained a stronghold for 300 years, enduring sieges in 1491 and 1528. Attacked again in 1651 by Oliver Cromwell, the castle was devastated by gun-powdered artillery and abandoned.

DP228379, DP228377

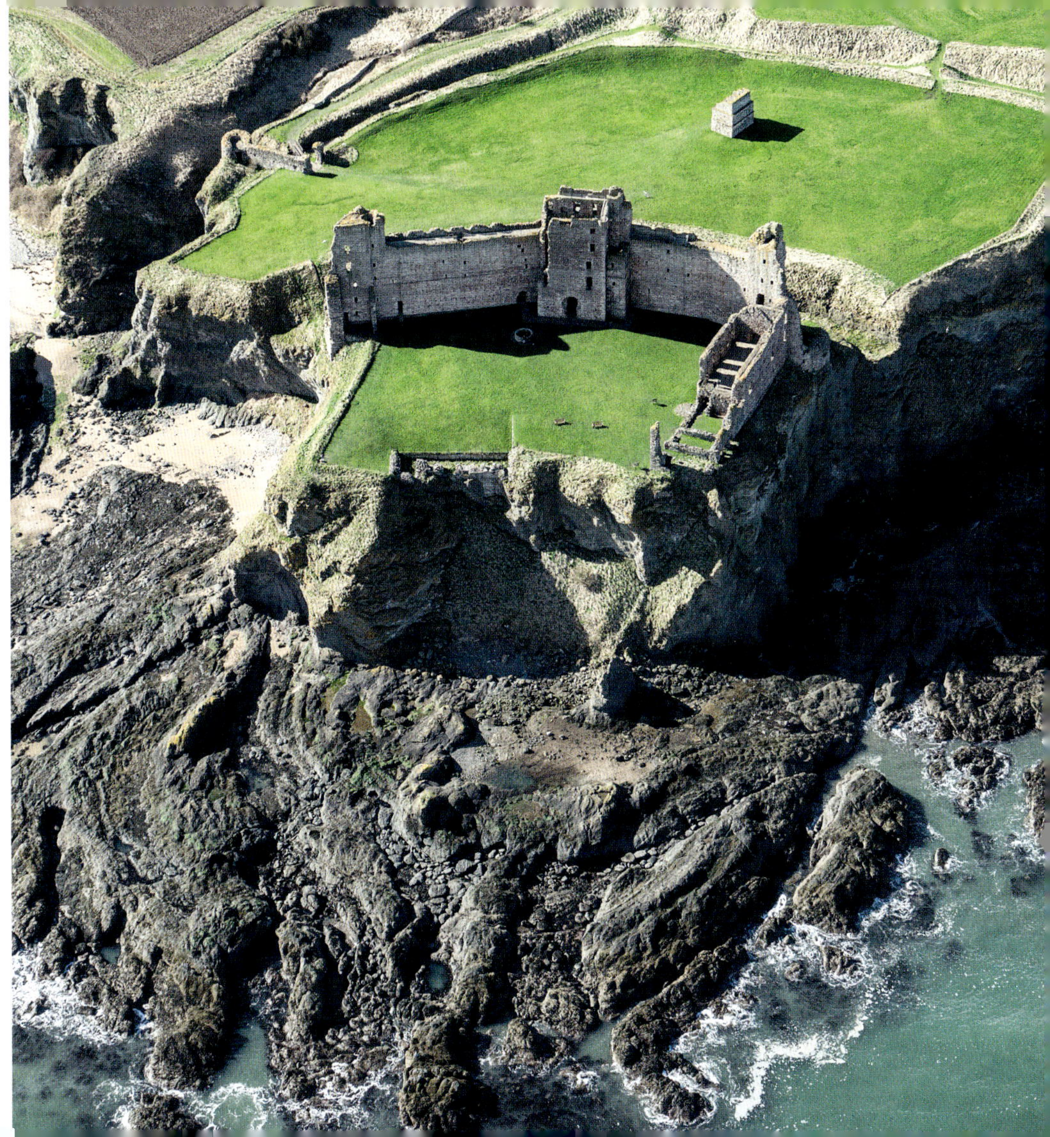

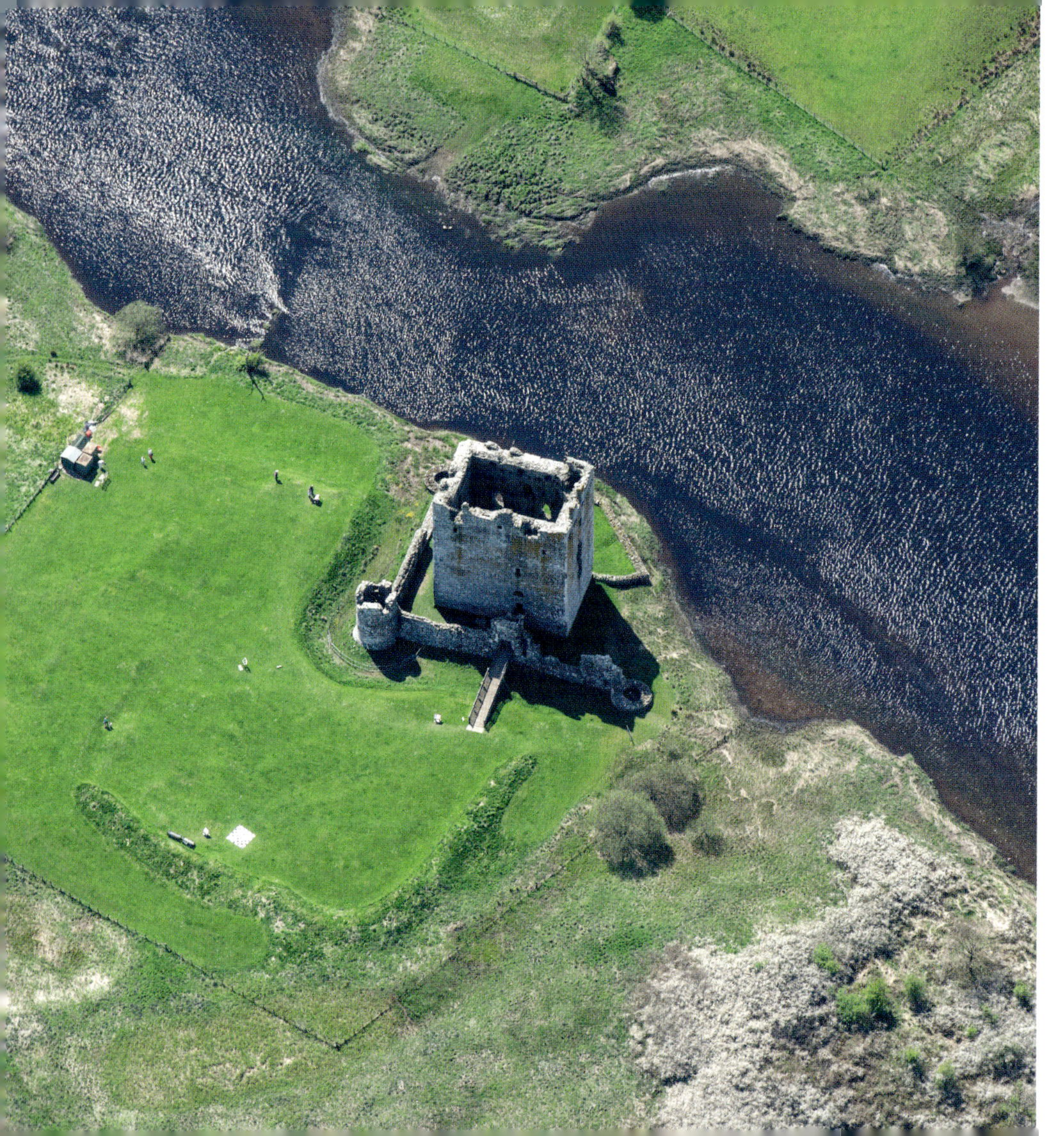

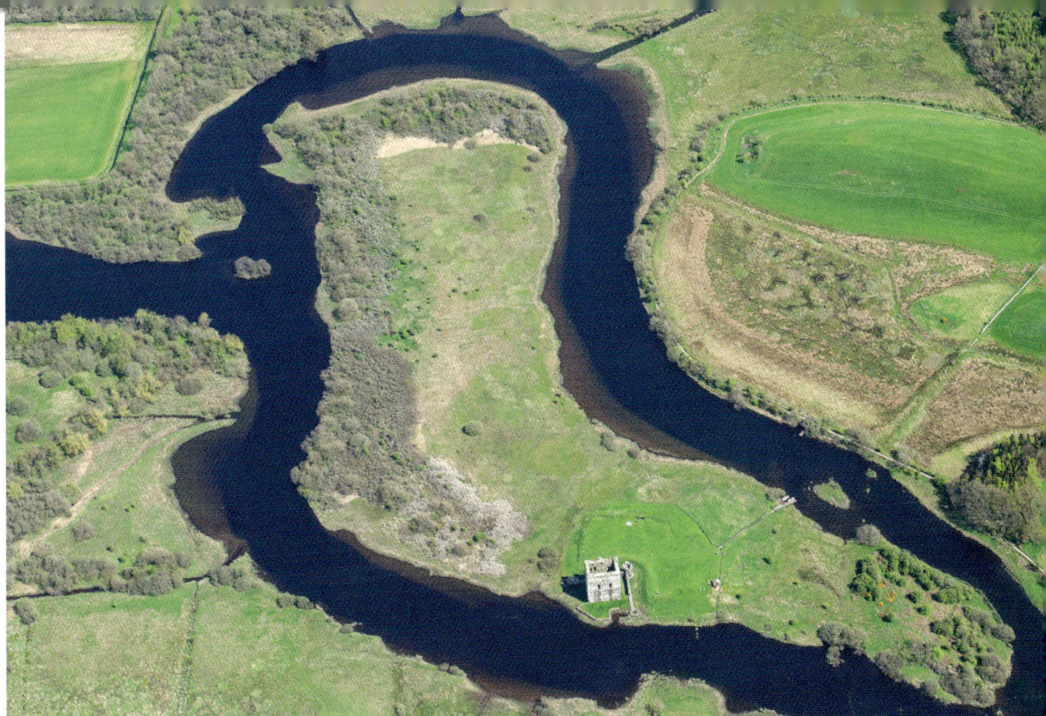

Threave Castle, Dumfries and Galloway

Sir Archibald Douglas, known as Archibald the Grim, built Threave Castle when he became Lord of Galloway in 1369. The downfall of his powerful noble family, the Black Douglases, occurred less than a century later in the wake of defeat in battle by King James II in 1455, whose forces besieged and took control of Threave Castle that same year. The imposing tower house, 30m in height, still looms over the surrounding River Dee.

DP276136, DP276130

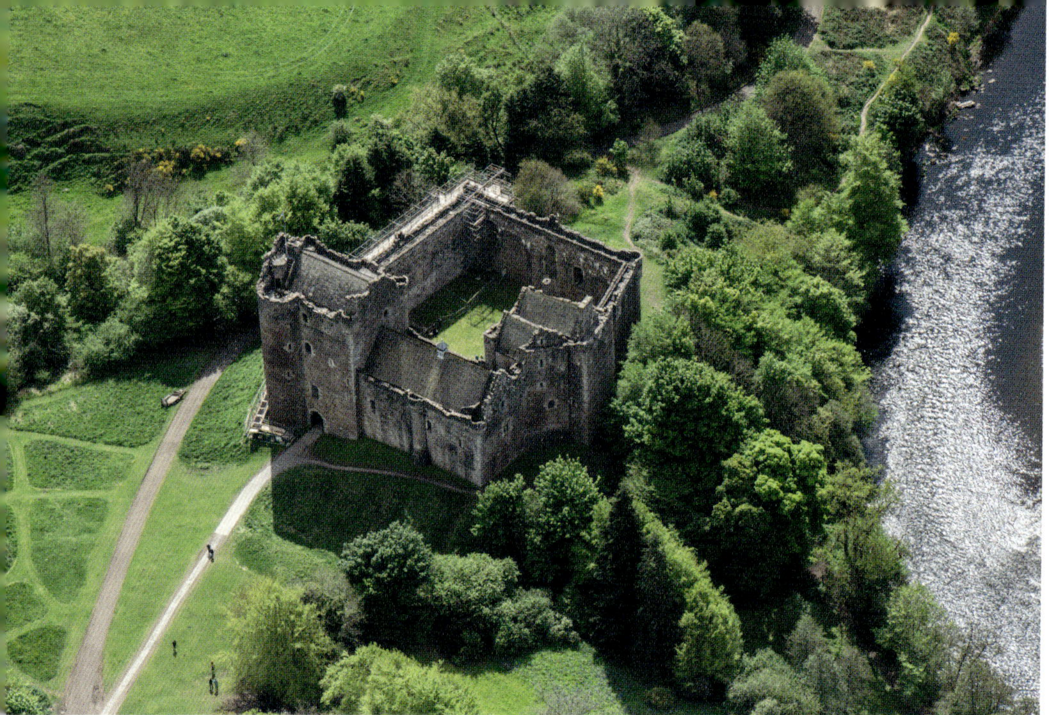

Doune Castle, Stirling

This castle became the stronghold of Robert Stewart, 1st Duke
of Albany, in 1361. He was effectively the ruler of the kingdom
during the reign of his older brother, Robert III, and gained the title
'Scotland's uncrowned king'. But after Albany's death in 1420 –
followed four years later by the execution of his son by Robert III's
heir James I – Doune became part of the royal estate.
DP258903

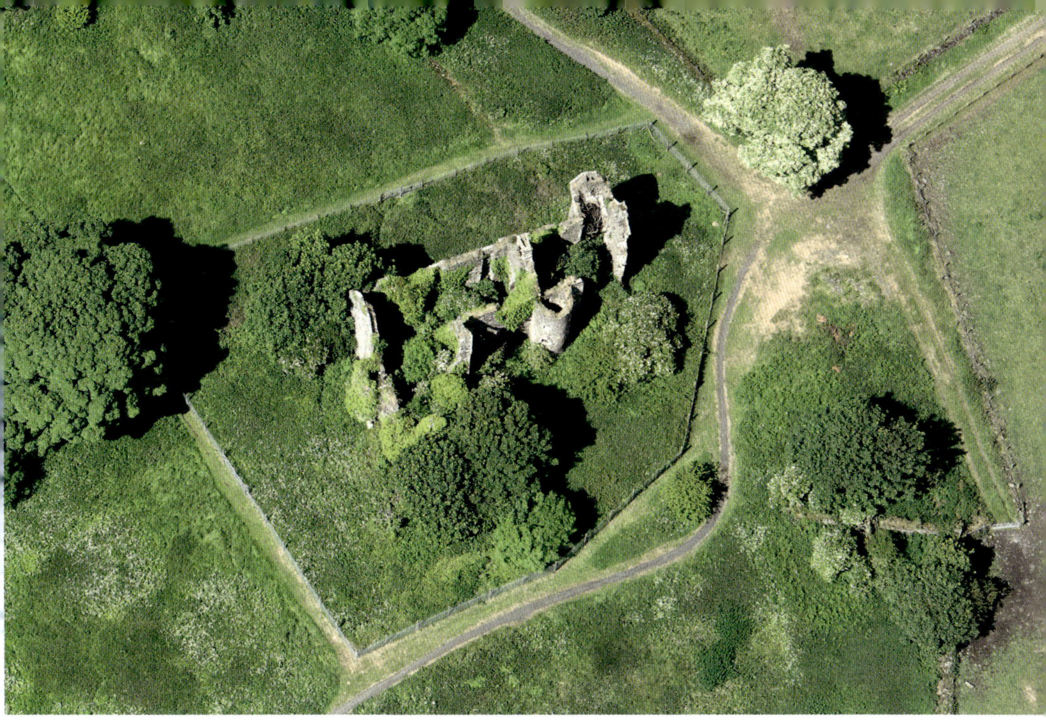

Auchans Castle, Ayrshire

A castle converted to a country house, Auchans fell into ruin
after its last occupant, Susannah, Countess of Eglinton, died in
1780. A roof still stood on the building in the early 1920s, but
collapsed soon after, allowing the surrounding trees and bushes
to take up residence.

DP071739

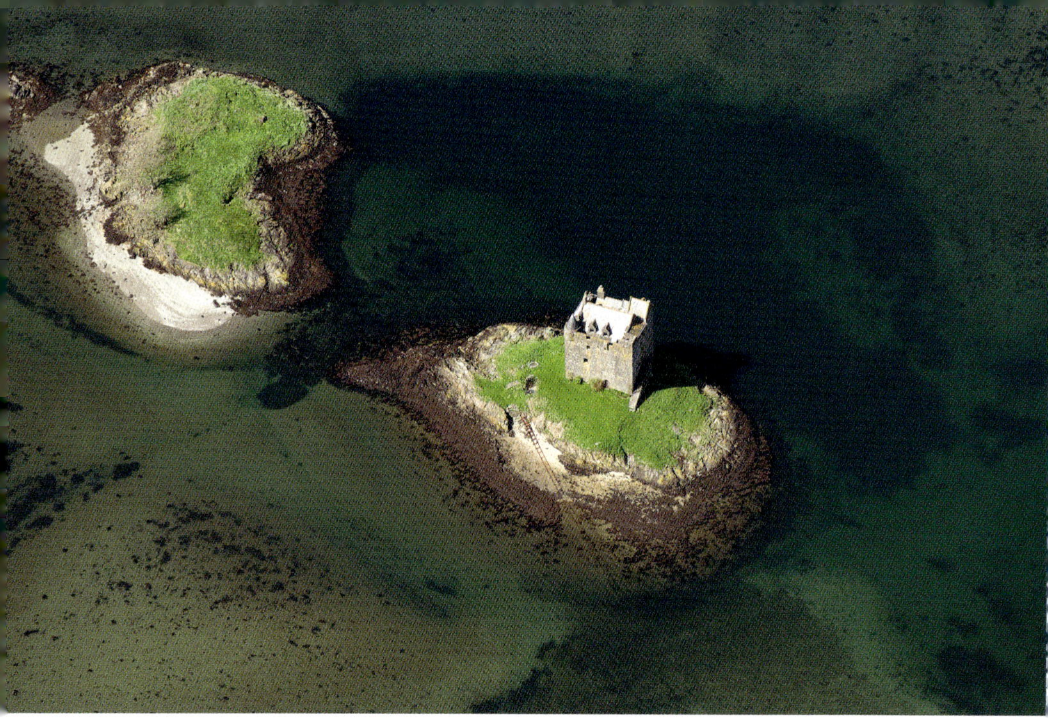

Castle Stalker, Argyll and Bute

Set against spectacular Highland scenery, Castle Stalker still retains much of its original character as it guards the mouth of Loch Laich. Built c1540 its rocky islet location underlines the importance of controlling the western seaways in medieval Scotland.

DP026789

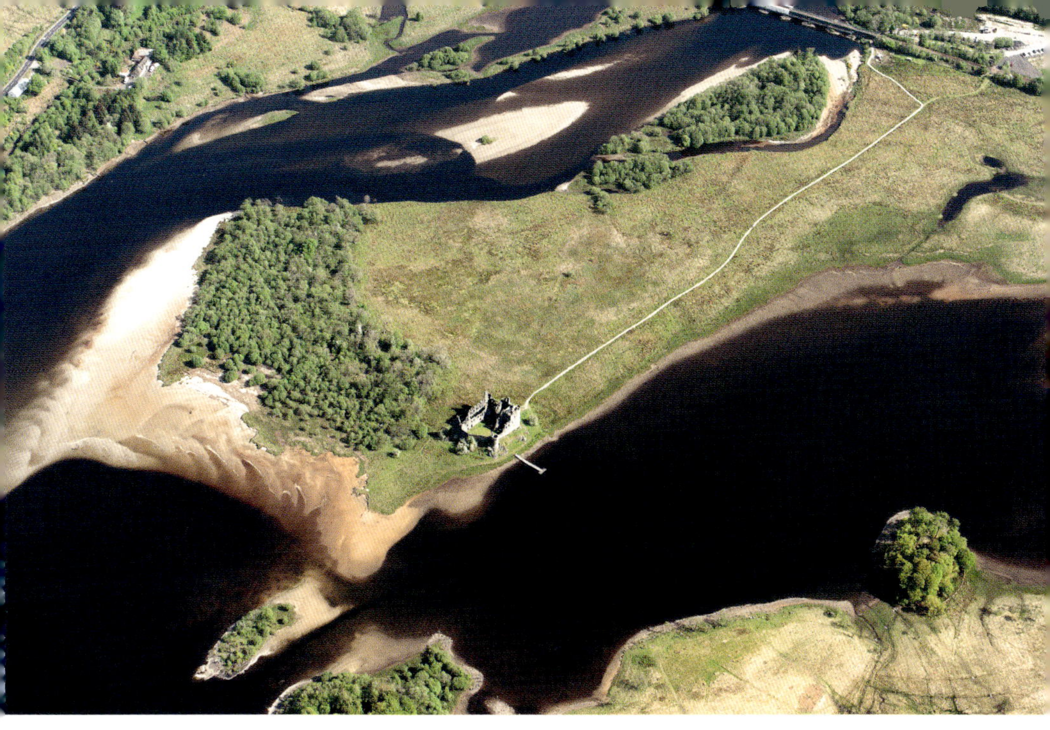

Kilchurn Castle, Argyll and Bute

The ruined form of Kilchurn Castle can be seen on the banks of Loch Awe, which was once a crucial waterway. There were two major stages of construction, in the mid 1400s and then the late 1600s. But after a lightning strike in 1760, the castle was not repaired and eventually became the shell that remains today.

DP297319

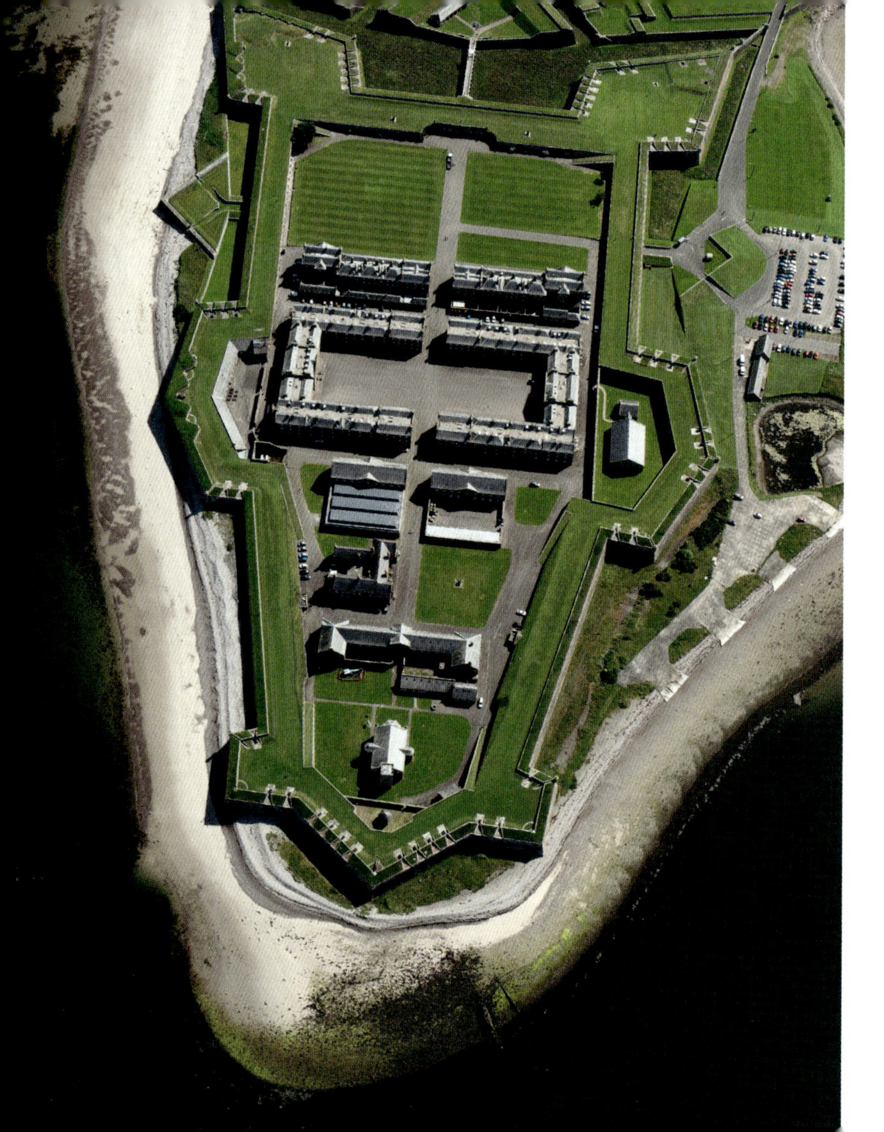

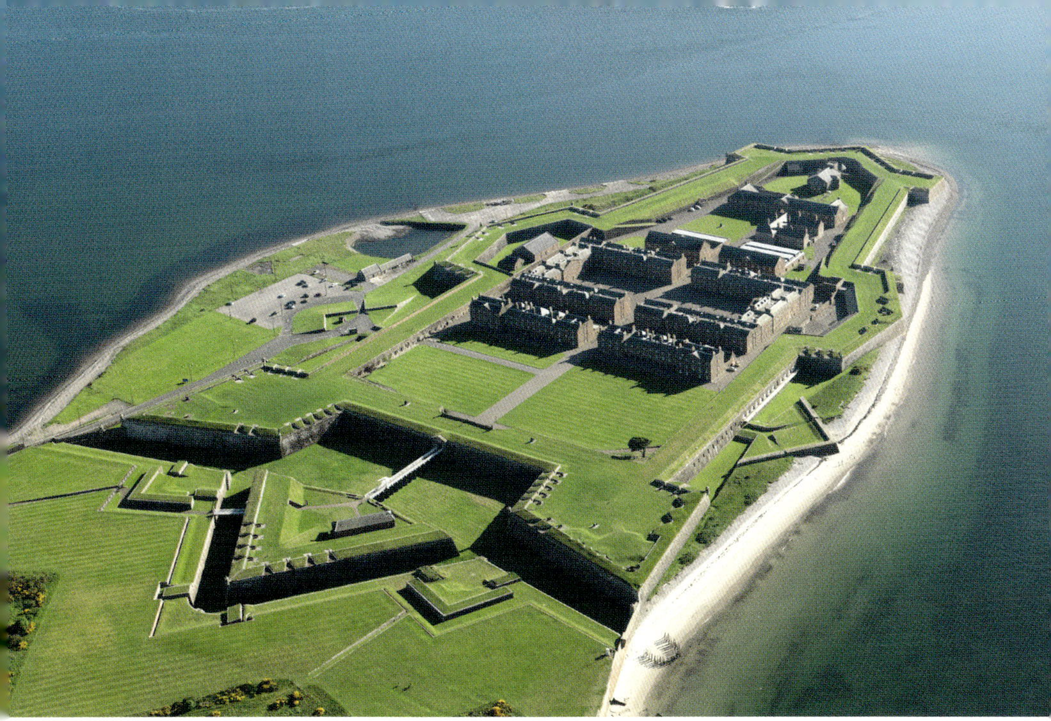

Fort George, Highlands

On a peninsula jutting into the Moray Firth, Fort George was built in the aftermath of the Battle of Culloden in 1746. Completed more than two decades later, this was a stamp of Hanoverian military authority in the Highlands – yet, by the time it was completed, the Jacobite threat had faded. It instead became a base for training young Highland recruits who were sent across the world to fight for the British Empire.

DP191417, DP080090

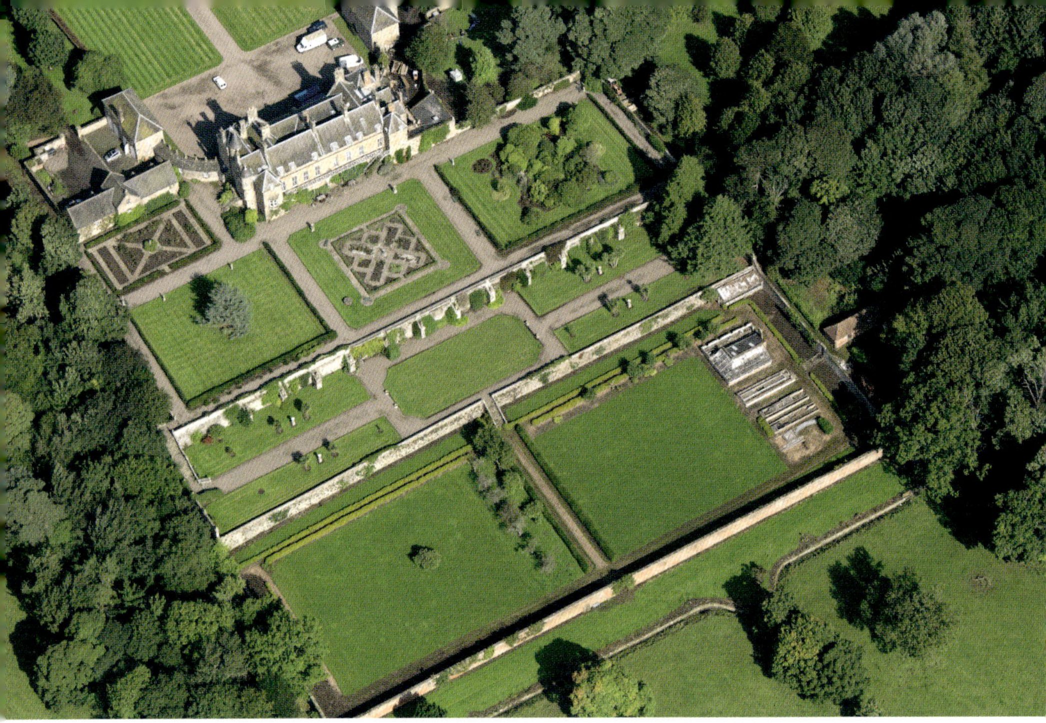

Balcaskie House, Fife

One of the most visible trends of the 1600s were the designed landscapes that took root next to castles and stately homes. At Balcaskie House, the notable architect Sir William Bruce laid out terraced gardens with a central axis focused on the Bass Rock out in the Firth of Forth.

DP050894

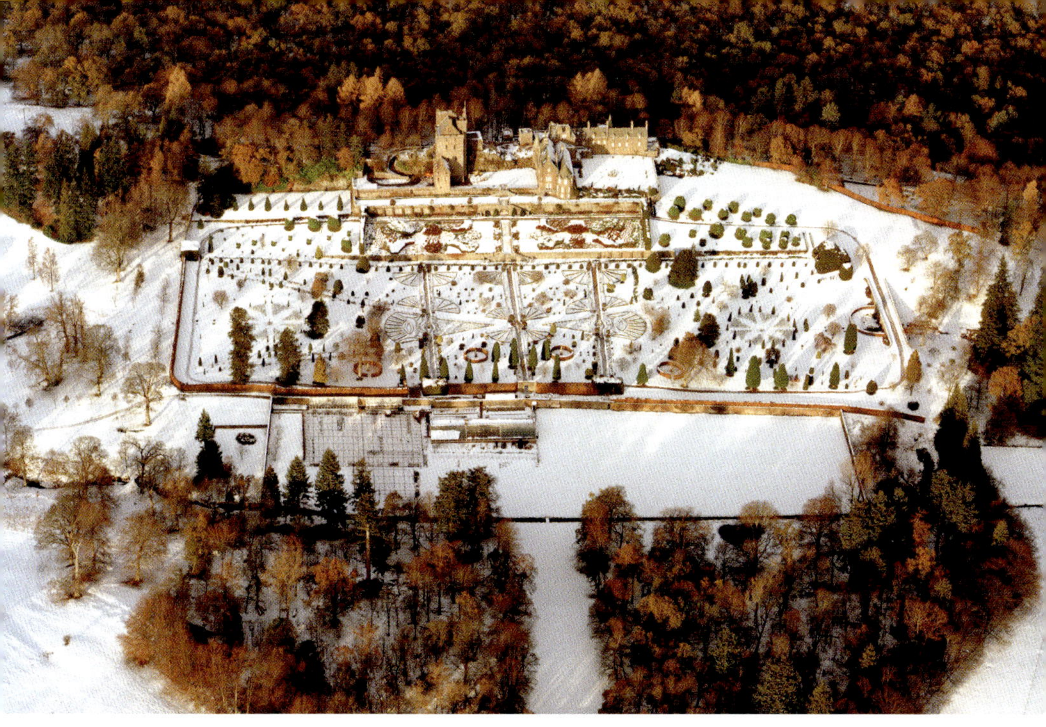

Drummond Castle, Perthshire

The grounds of Drummond Castle, seen here outlined in snow, showcase the best example of a formal terraced garden in Scotland. Begun in 1630, this spectacular piece of decorative landscaping remains the focal point for the wide expanse of surrounding parkland.

SC949575

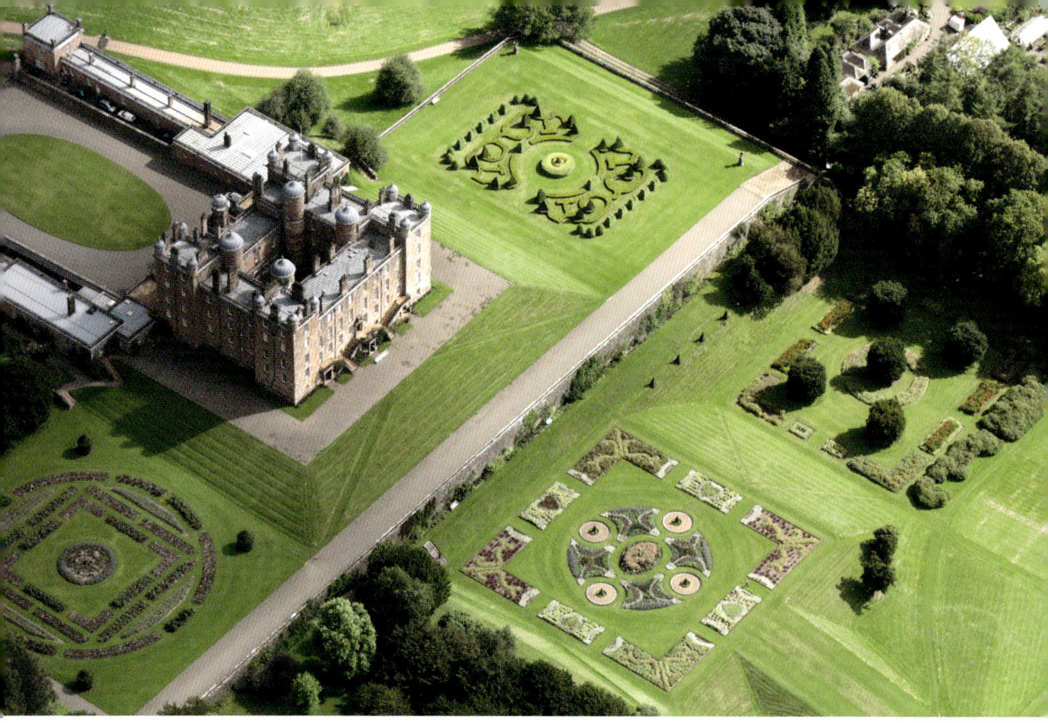

Drumlanrig Castle, Dumfries and Galloway

The Duke of Queensberry's castle at Drumlanrig, completed
in 1691, sits amid an extensive garden, with local rivers and
streams even diverted to create a waterfall. Early visitors,
including John Macky and Daniel Defoe, admired the results but
disliked the wild mountains that formed the backdrop. As tastes
changed, later visitors often preferred the natural surroundings
to the formality of the gardens.

DP104033

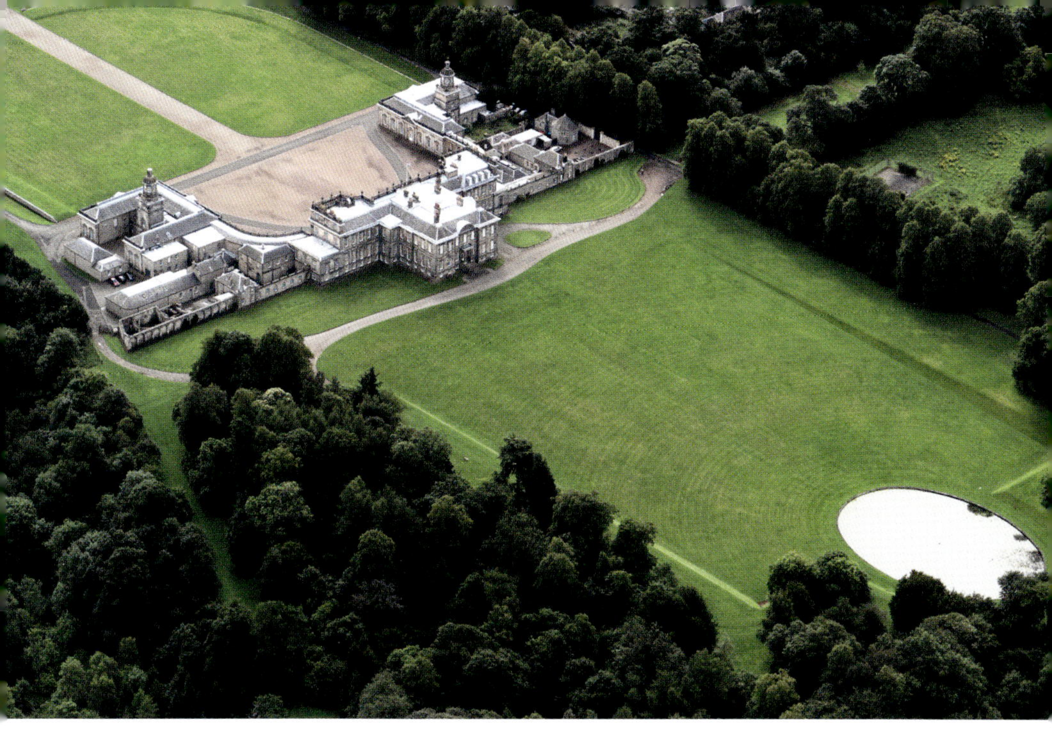

Hopetoun House, West Lothian

Begun in 1699, Hopetoun House was magnificently expanded from the 1720s by the famous Scottish architect William Adam and his sons, John and Robert. What followed was the transformation of a traditional country seat with an extensive designed landscape into an elegant estate which was dubbed the Scottish Versailles.

DP107101

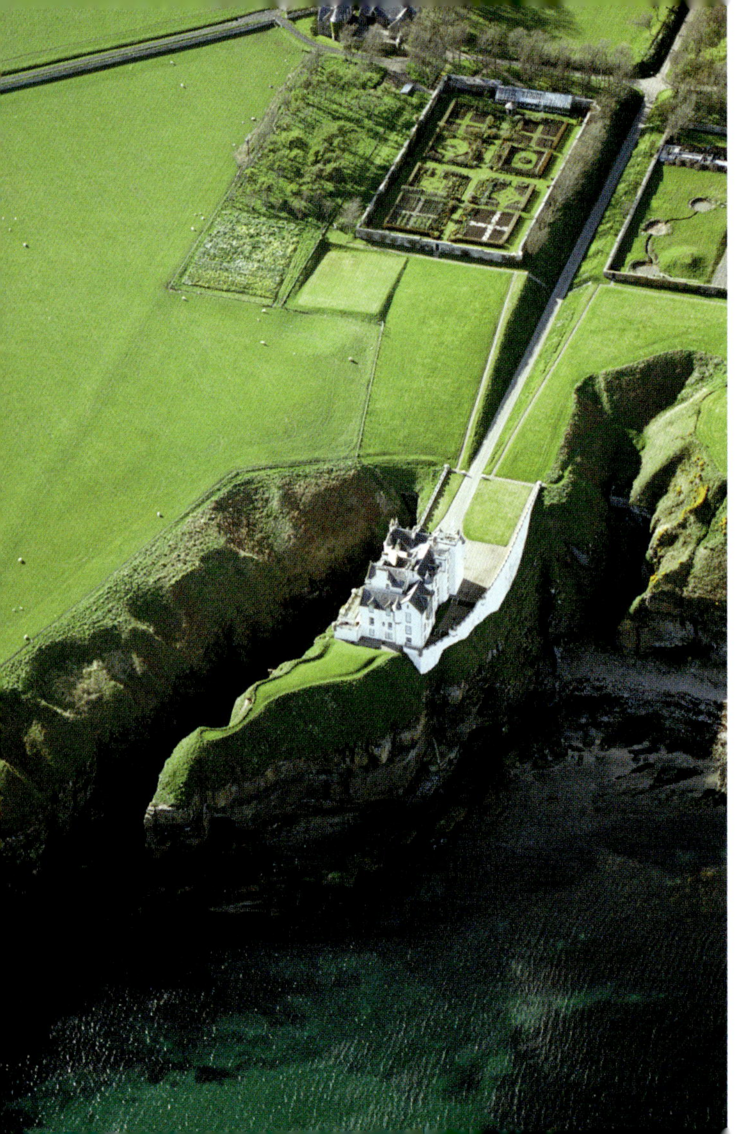

Dunbeath Castle, Highlands
Perched on the rocky Caithness coast, Dunbeath Castle's spectacular natural setting provided the stage for landscape theatre. Modelled in the mid 1800s, the long drive presents a glimpse of the castle, its full, cliff-side splendour only gradually revealed on the approach along the narrow, tree-lined avenue.
SC973870, SC973873

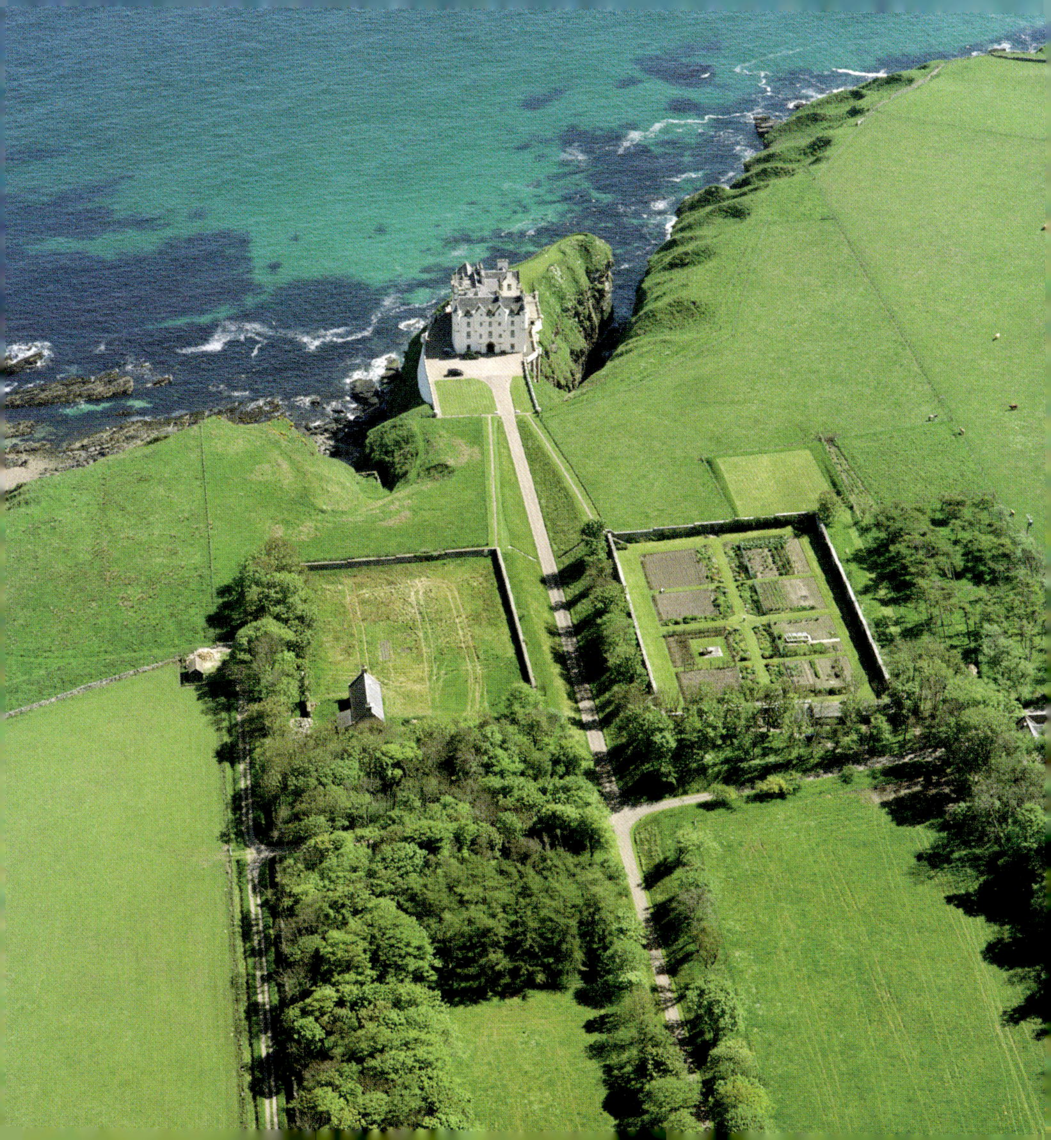

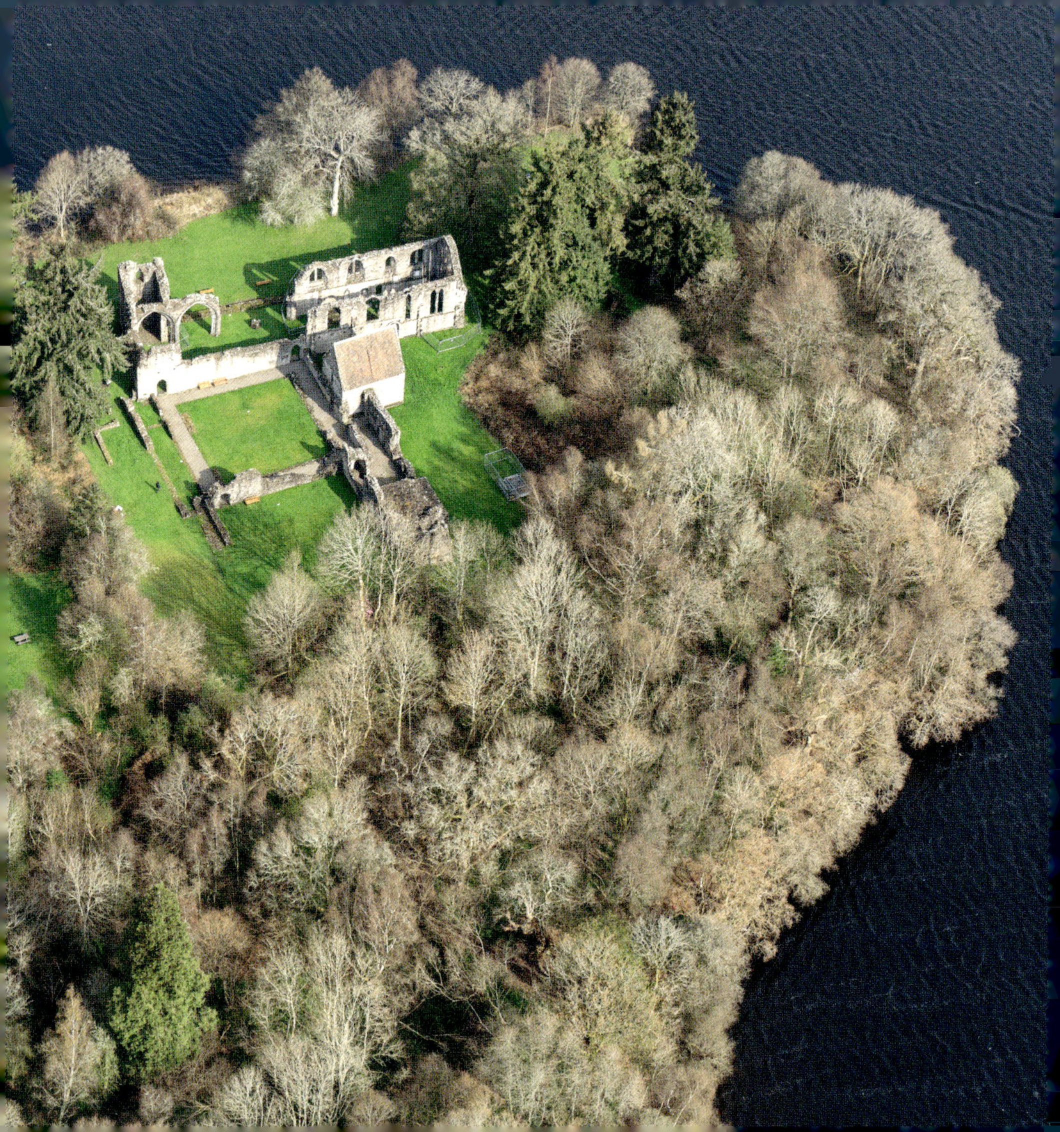

In ancient times, ceremony and ritual left an imprint on the landscape. As the years passed, this grand demonstration of faith continued, but as part of Christian beliefs.

The origins of Christianity in Scotland can be traced back to St Columba's arrival in Iona during the sixth century, and the island remains a place of pilgrimage. As Christianity spread, usurping pagan beliefs, abbeys and cathedrals were constructed across the country; great religious centres of wealth, power and learning. By the 1100s, the town of St Andrews had emerged as the centre of the Scottish Church, with the relics of Scotland's patron saint, St Andrew, housed in the awe-inspiring cathedral. The Protestant Reformation in the 1500s brought dramatic change, and many religious buildings were abandoned or neglected, becoming austere ruins. However, as the need for churches remained, some older churches and cathedrals were adapted for Protestant thinking, and new buildings were also constructed. As a result of this religious tradition, churches and places of prayer remain local landmarks throughout the country.

Inchmahome Priory, Stirling
On an island in the Lake of Menteith, Inchmahome Priory was founded as an Augustinian order by the powerful Comyn family in 1238. The island sanctuary remained in use for over 300 years. Although the ruins on the wooded island now look quite restrained, before the Reformation — as with other religious buildings — the priory church would have been richly and colourfully decorated.
DP292499

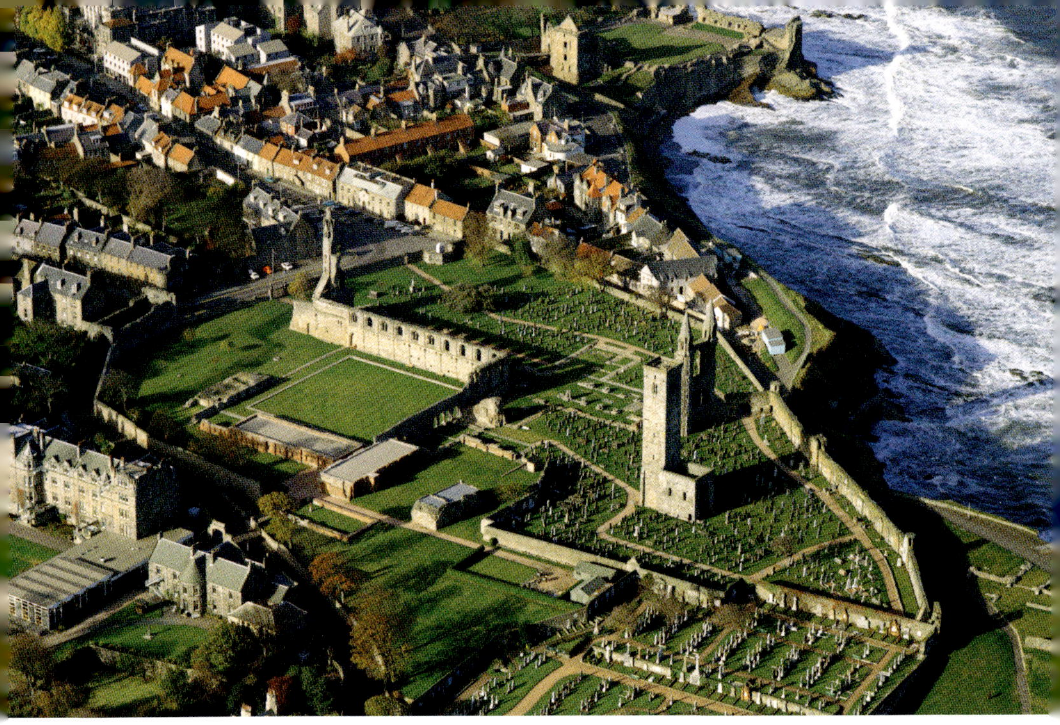

St Andrews Cathedral, Fife

The extensive ruins of St Andrews Cathedral provide a vivid
reminder of the power of religion and belief to change landscapes
forever. Built in 1318 and home to the relics of St Andrew, Scotland's
patron saint, it was the imposing headquarters for the medieval
church. But the rapid and sweeping changes of the Reformation saw
the cathedral abandoned in 1560 to be replaced by the parish church
as the focus for worship in the town.
SC369407

Elgin Cathedral, Moray

The power and influence of the Bishops of Moray is evident at Elgin Cathedral, an outstanding testament to medieval architecture and craftmanship. Known as the 'Lantern of the North' this cathedral, founded c1224, would have been finely decorated and embellished with carvings and stained glass.
SC1112803

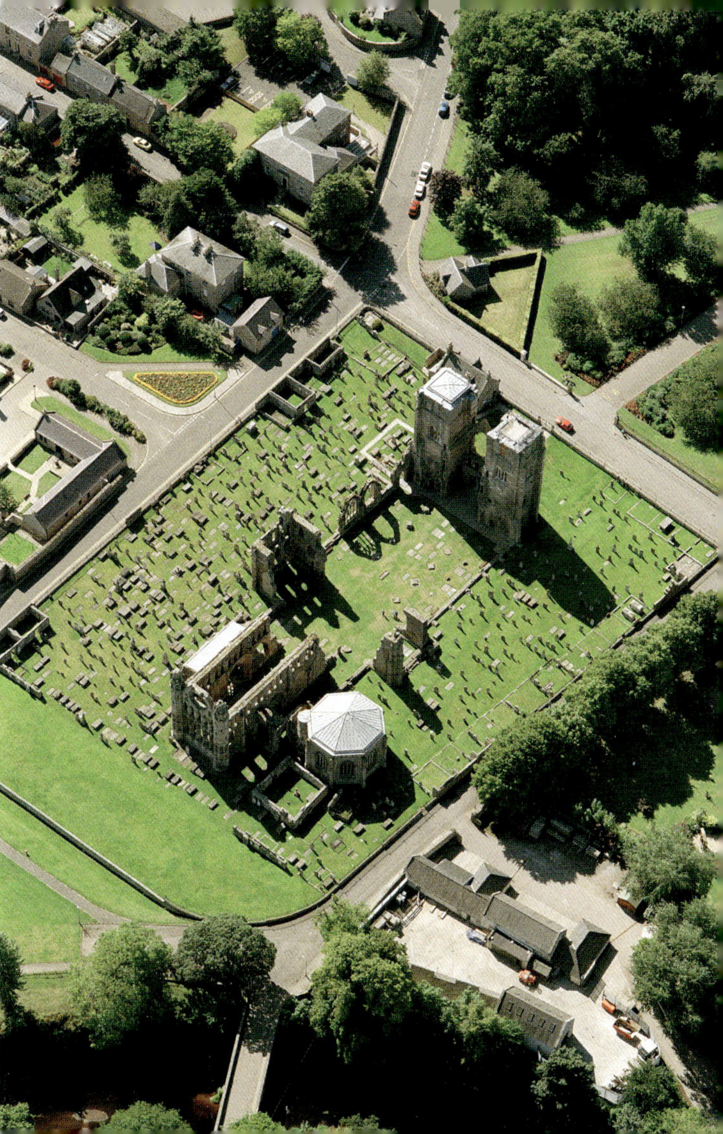

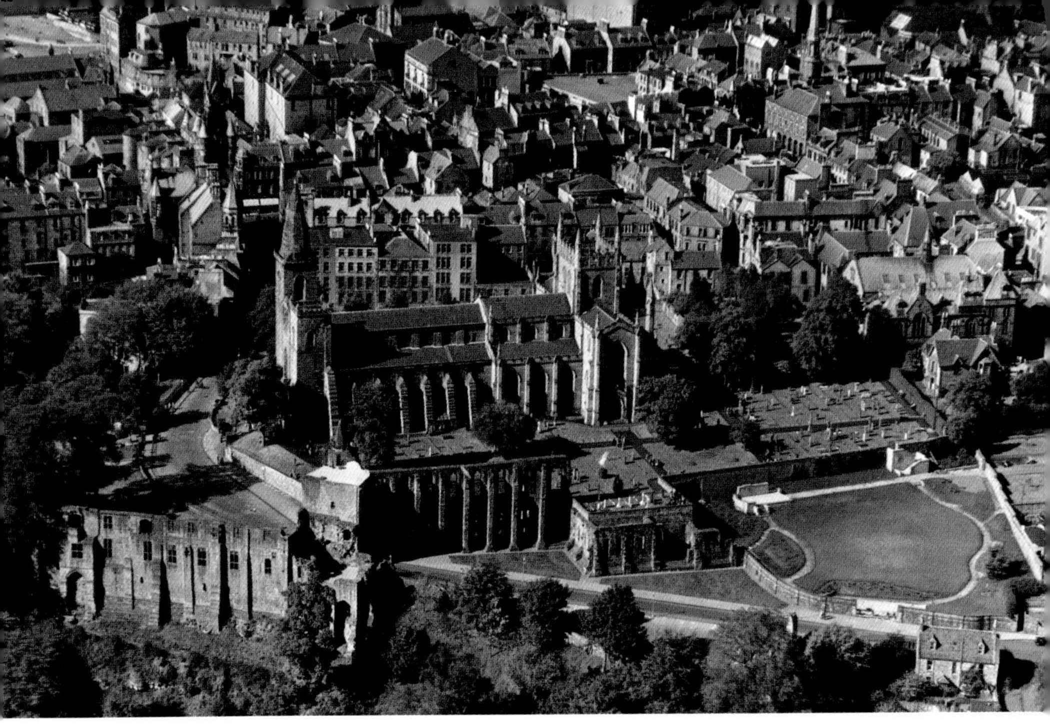

Dunfermline Abbey, Fife

A bank of houses looks out at the grand structure of Dunfermline Abbey set within its spacious grounds. After the collapse of the abbey's main tower in 1818, the remains of Robert the Bruce were found beneath the building, creating huge national interest. The former king was reburied and a new tower was built in commemoration. Robert the Bruce's heart, however, is not at Dunfermline – it is believed to be buried separately at Melrose Abbey.

SC1437958 (1952)

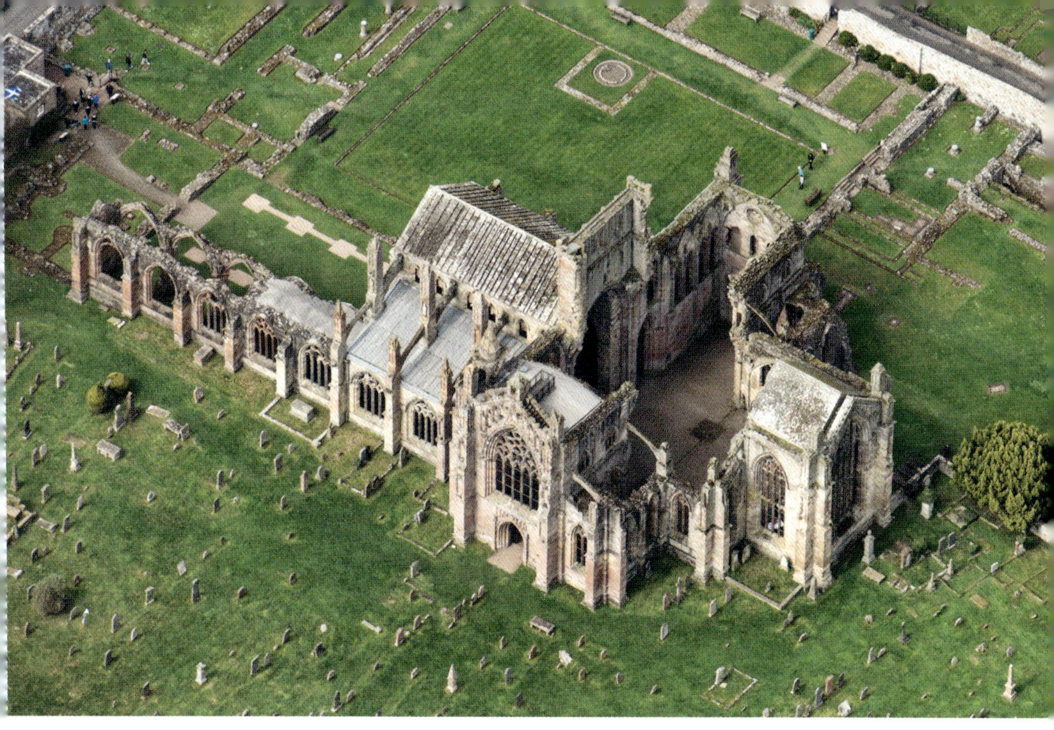

Melrose Abbey, the Scottish Borders

Founded in 1136 by David I as the first Cistercian monastery in
Scotland, Melrose Abbey was rebuilt in the 1380s and is one of the
finest examples of church architecture in Britain from this period.
Melrose Abbey was a centre of monastic life until the Protestant
Reformation of 1560, after which a parish church was established
inside the abbey church.

DP253566

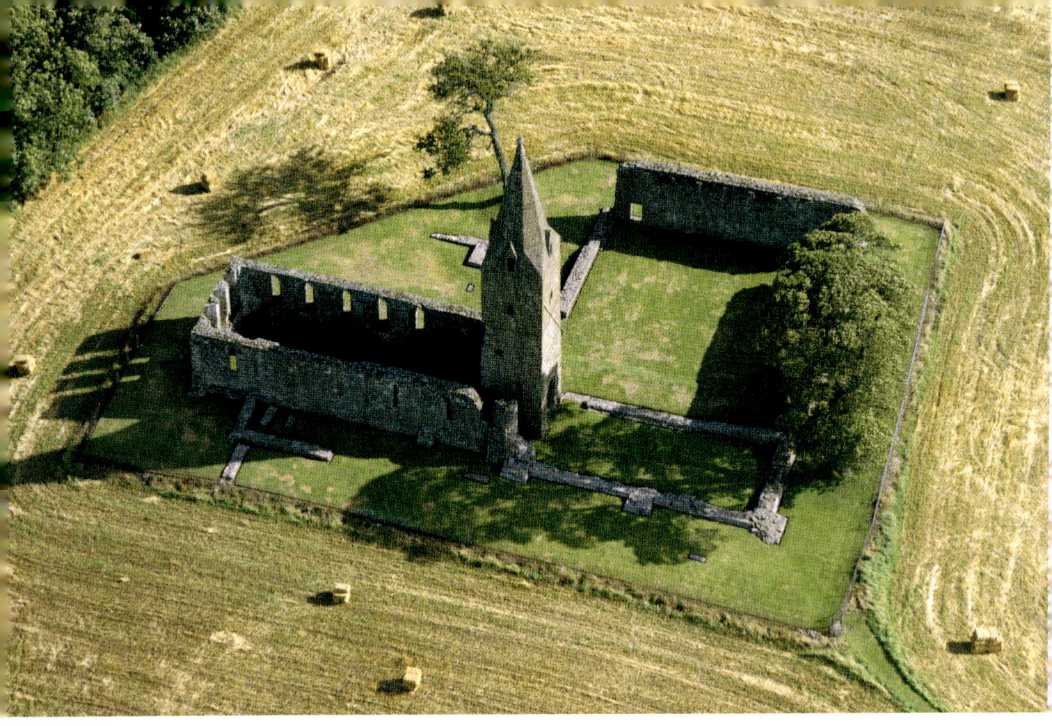

Restenneth Priory, Angus

A peaceful ruin surrounded by golden fields, Restenneth Priory near Forfar was favoured by early Scottish kings, including David I and Malcolm IV. The priory grew wealthy on its extensive land holdings and privileges, but gradually faded into obscurity after being damaged and burned during the Wars of Independence with England.

SC773014

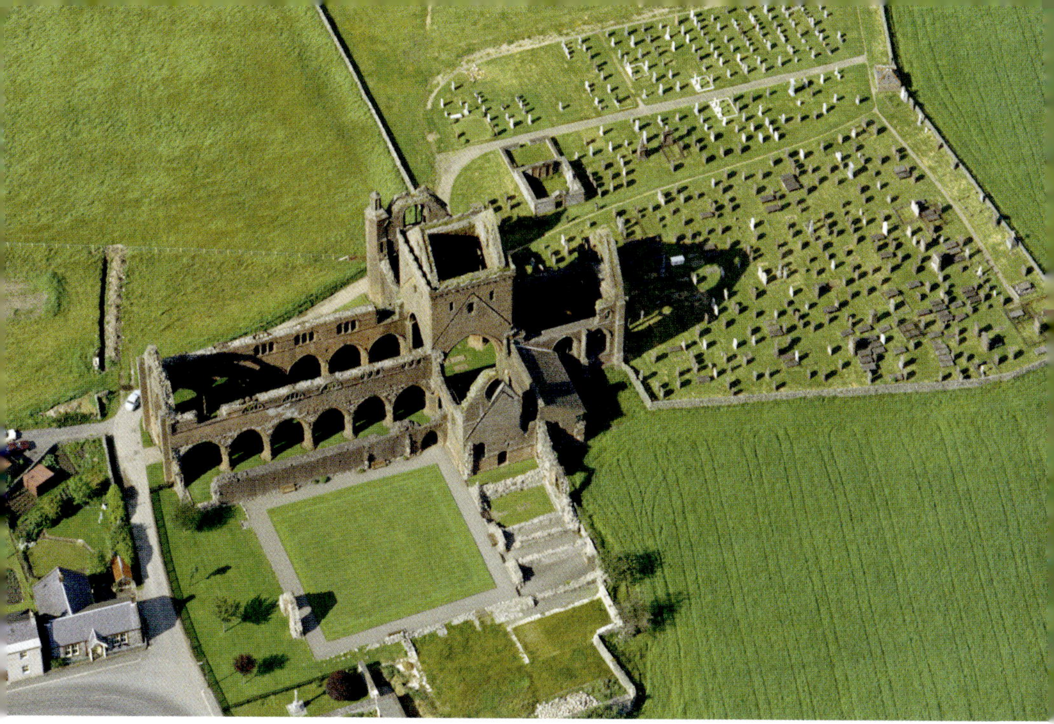

Sweetheart Abbey, Dumfries and Galloway

A monument to divine and human love, Sweetheart Abbey was
founded in 1273 by Lady Devorguilla of Galloway in memory of her
husband John Balliol. On her death, Lady Devorguilla was buried
in front of the abbey church's high altar, along with an ivory casket
which held the embalmed heart of her husband.
SC800175

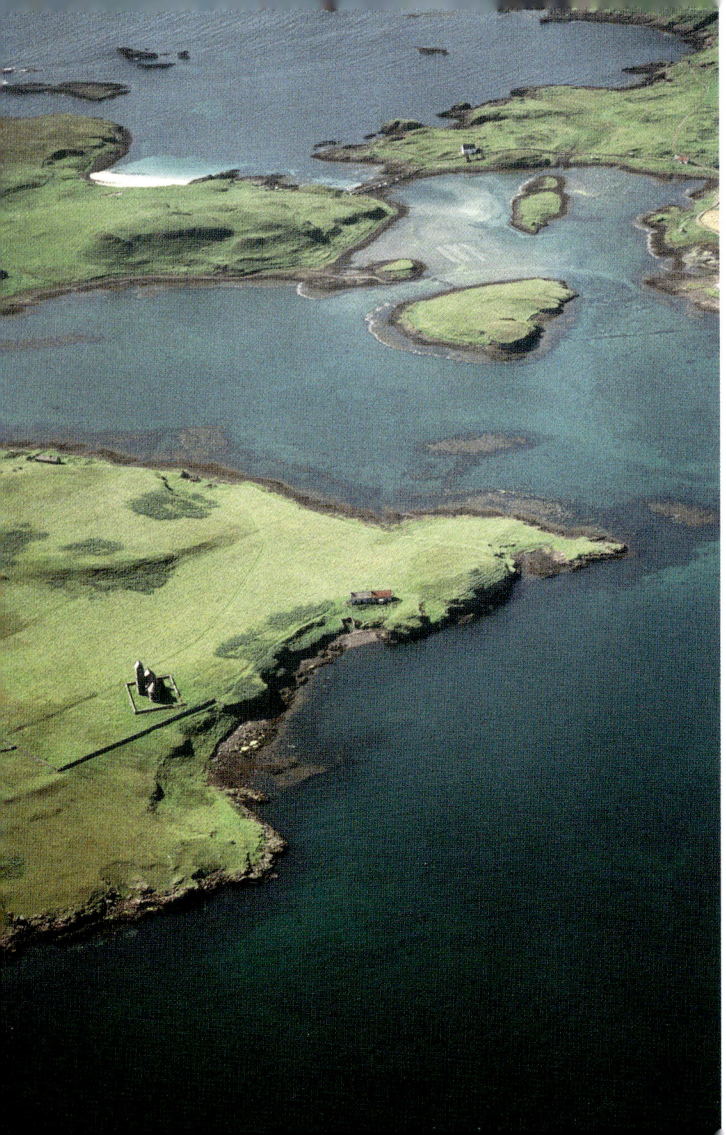

Roman Catholic Church of Edward the Confessor, Sanday, Highlands

The disused Roman Catholic Church of St Edward the Confessor in the Small Isles is still a notable landmark in the bay. Built between 1886 and 1890, it was closed in 1963, no longer required by a declining population.

SC794156

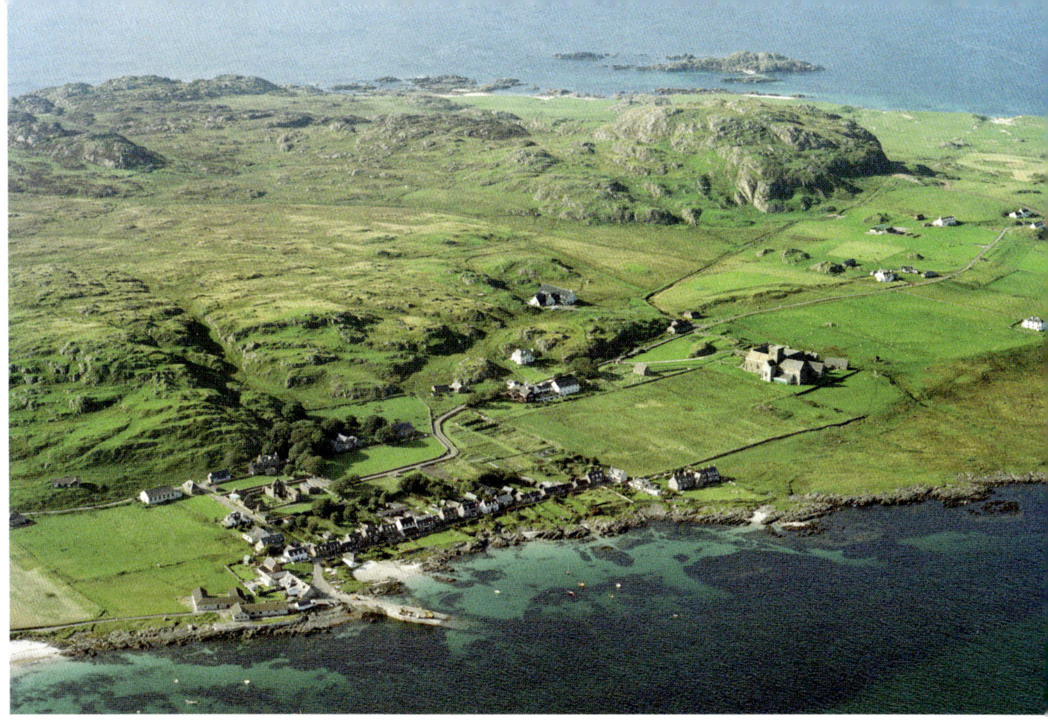

Iona Abbey, Argyll and Bute

The origins of Christianity in Scotland can be traced back to the island of Iona and a monastery founded by St Columba in the middle of the sixth century. This site, which would become one of the most important religious centres in Europe, was a seat of learning and the epicentre for the spread of the gospel throughout the country.
SC455539

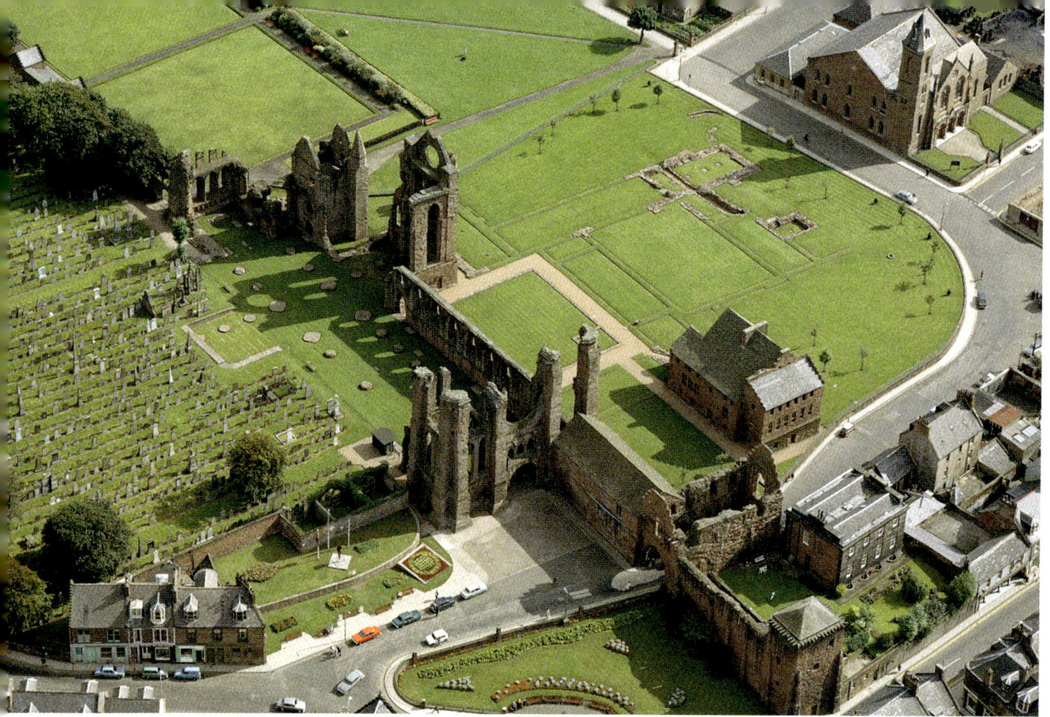

Arbroath Abbey, Angus

'It is in truth not for glory, nor riches, nor honours that we are fighting, but for freedom.' Drafted in the scriptorium of Arbroath Abbey in 1320, the Declaration of Arbroath, the most famous document in Scotland's history, saw the nation's nobles swear their independence from England. The abbey remains a powerful icon for Scottish nationalism. In 1951, in a highly symbolic act, the Stone of Destiny – which was taken as spoils of war by Edward I of England in 1296 – was removed from Westminster Abbey and later found within the remains of Arbroath Abbey.

SC798201

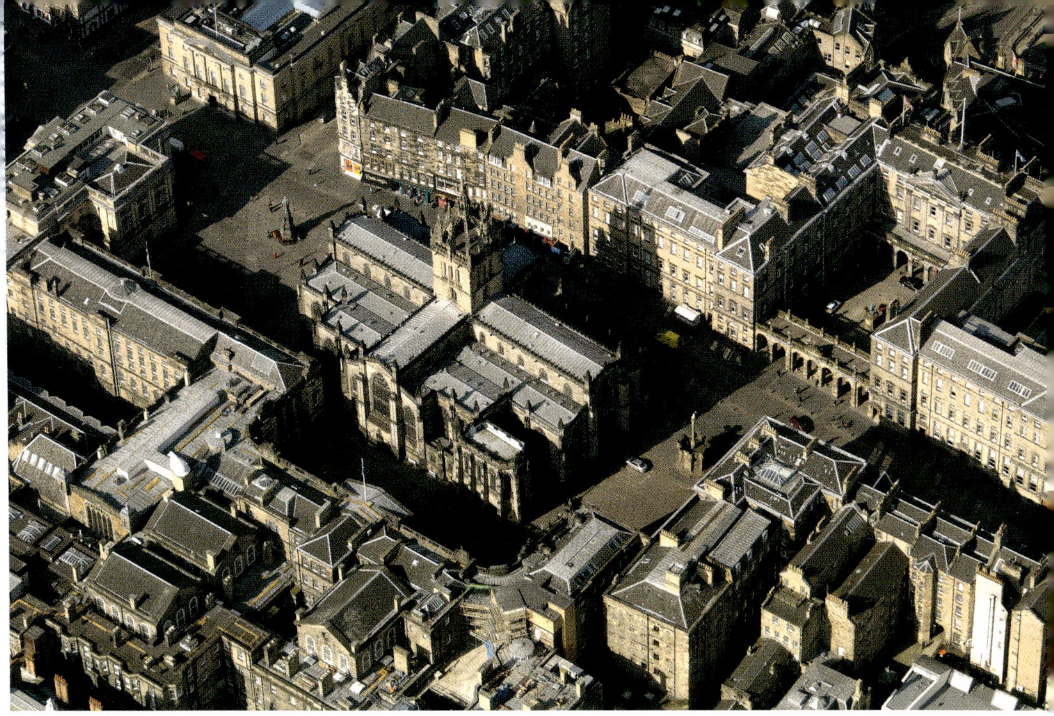

St Giles' Cathedral, Edinburgh

For almost a thousand years St Giles' High Kirk has been at the physical
and spiritual heart of Edinburgh. Founded in the 1100s, the building that
remains today has been shaped, moulded and rebuilt by history. Severely
damaged by fire during an English raid in 1385, its reconstruction saw the
creation of the distinctive Crown Spire. In the mid 1500s, the preaching
of John Knox put the church at the epicentre of the Reformation, but
over the following centuries it endured a period of disrepair. In 1829 the
exterior was refaced and remodelled and, between 1871 and 1883, the
interior was restored to its original single space.

DP075931

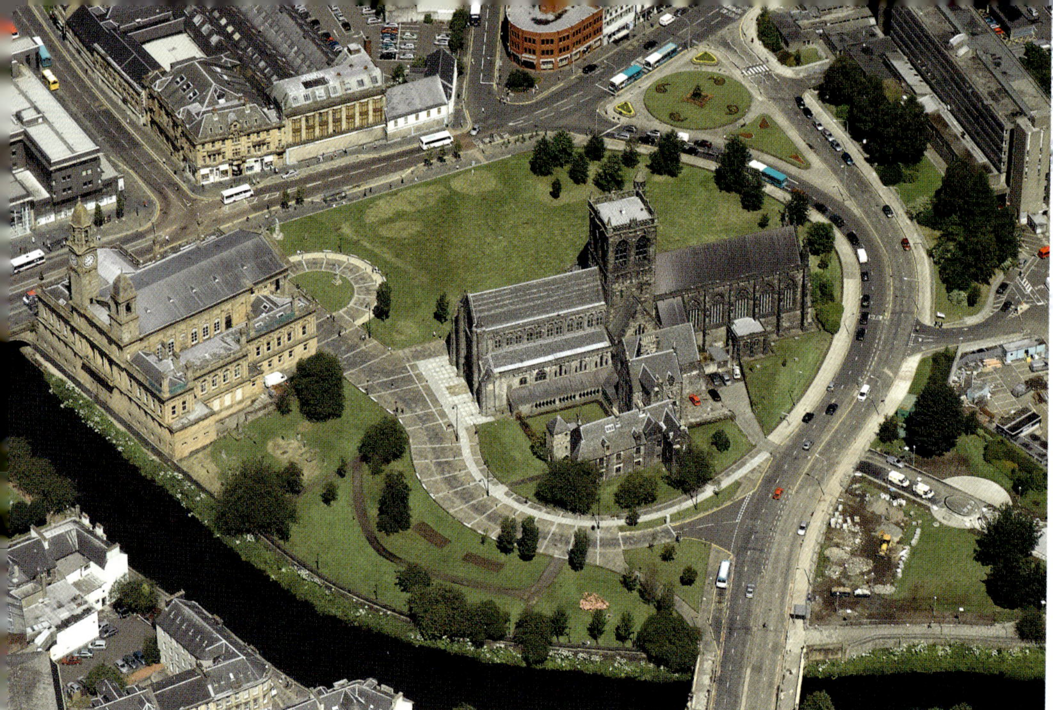

Paisley Abbey, Renfrewshire

Hemmed in by tarmac and concrete, Paisley Abbey remains awe-inspiring 900 years after its foundation. Initially founded as a Cluniac priory, it gained abbey status in 1245. By the late 1800s much of the abbey church lay in ruins but following extensive restoration work it is in use by the congregation today.

DP032408

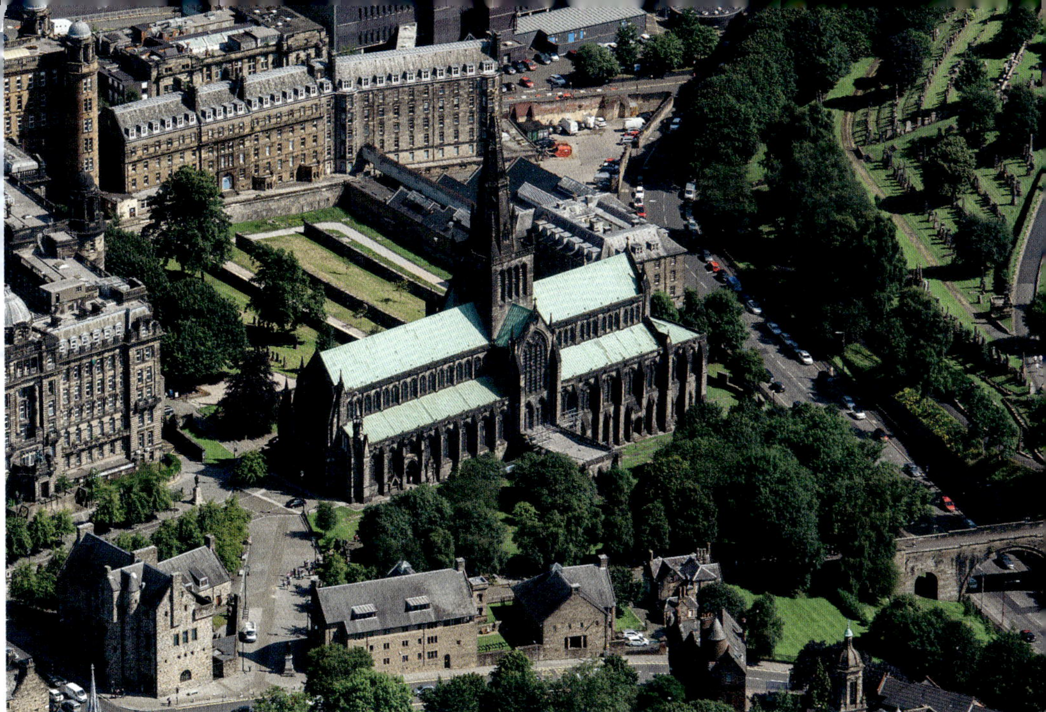

Glasgow Cathedral

A rare monument from the past, St Mungo's in Glasgow is the only medieval cathedral to have survived the Reformation largely intact. Most of the structure dates from the 1200s and, although the Reformation saw the removal of many decorative features, it remains as a grand medieval building lying at the heart of Scotland's largest city. The cathedral was integral to the creation of Glasgow: the city developed from the community that sprang up around it.
DP263232

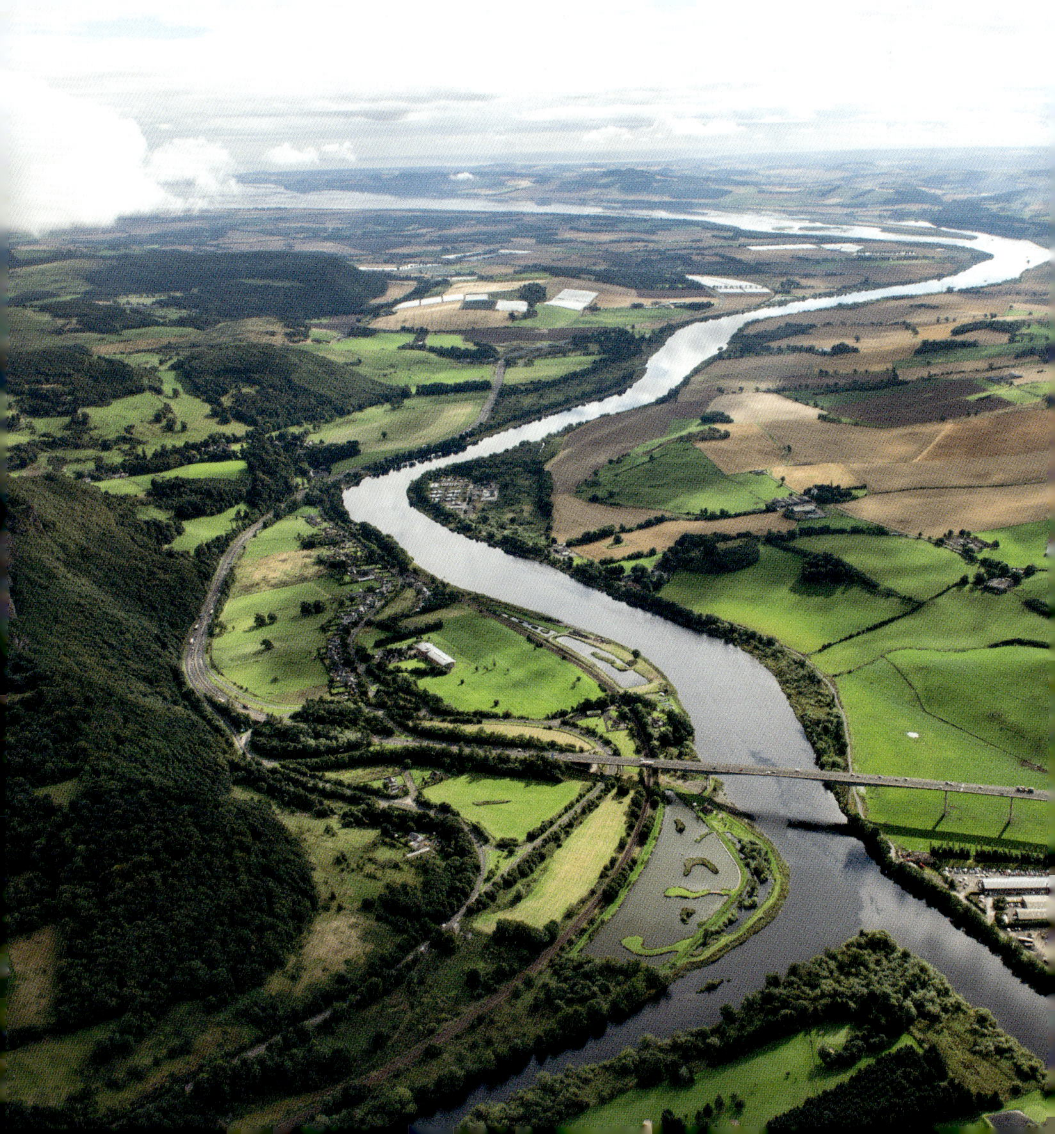

The impact of cultivation cannot be overstated – very little of Scotland's land has been left untouched by agriculture. The earliest farmers in Scotland began on a small scale, with compact areas of ground being cleared and worked. As communities increasingly invested in the ongoing demands of cultivation and livestock, they became tied to specific places. Over generations, this connection to the land spread across the country, largely unchanged. For many of our ancestors, the farming day and the seasons of the year would have been fundamental.

Modern farms cover vast expanses in comparison to the smallholdings of the past, with technology playing a significant role. But farming is not the only obvious way the land is worked. Railways, roads and canals criss-cross the country, robust bridges span rivers, forestry plantations cover hillsides. The need for energy has left its mark too, whether it is the traces of coal, shale or peat extraction, or towering wind farms and hydroelectric dams. The ways in which the land has been used is bound to the needs of the times.

Friarton Bridge over the Tay, Perthshire
The River Tay presents a major impediment to traffic. While Perth boasts four bridges, traffic wishing to bypass it can, since 1978, enjoy the views from the Friarton Bridge.
DP220515

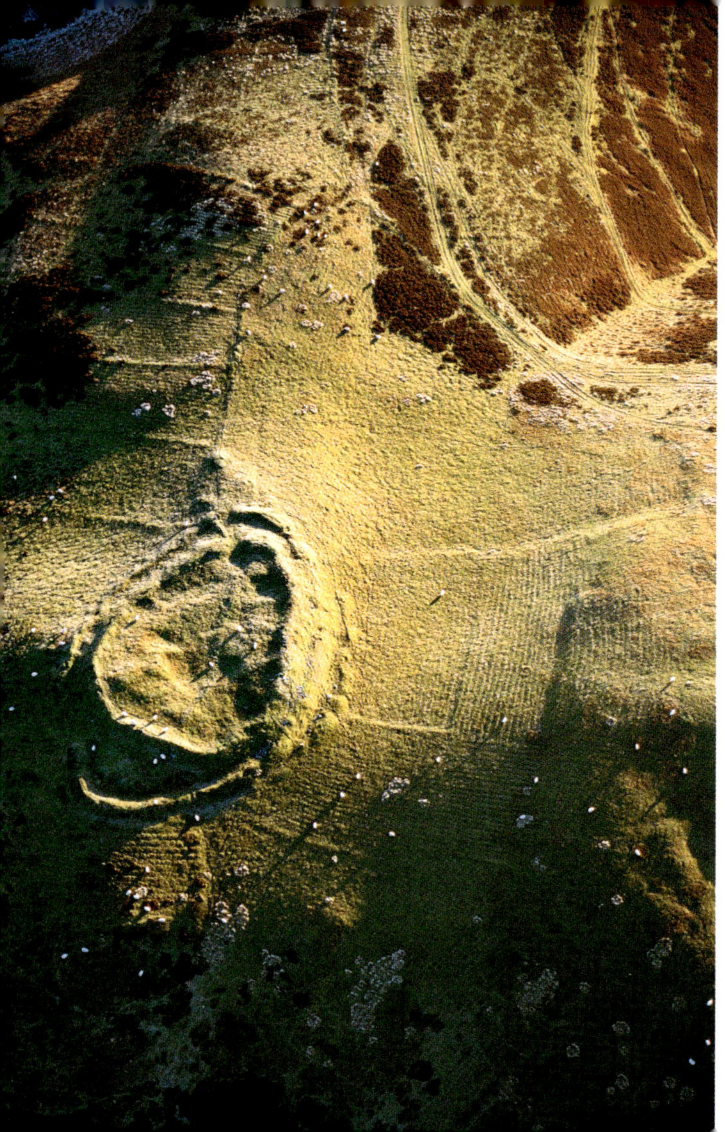

Iron Age fields at Hut Knowe, the Scottish Borders
The small fields and cord rig of prehistoric agriculture are rarely visible in the Scottish landscape because of modern land-use. These fields survive on a high ridge of the Cheviot Hills, beyond the reach of the modern plough.
DP249911

Arthur's Seat, Edinburgh

It is not just rural landscapes that hold on to the traces of ancient farming. Here, in the centre of Edinburgh, low light picks out the remnants of cultivation terraces on the slopes of Arthur's Seat in Holyrood Park.
DP049947

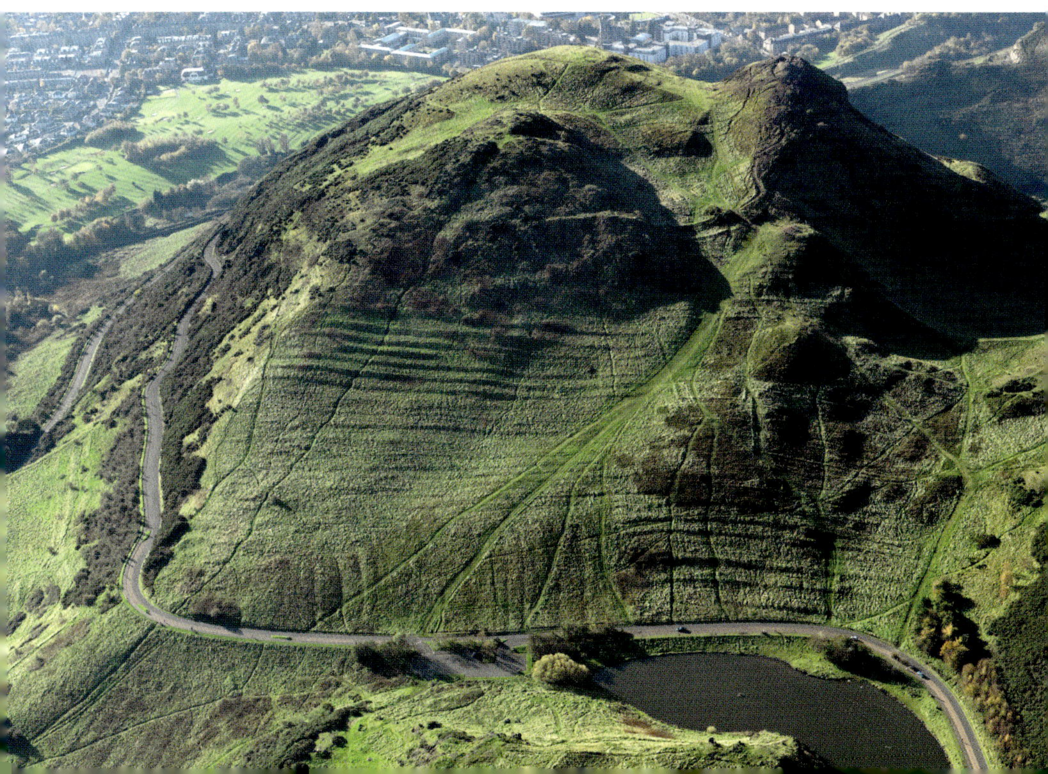

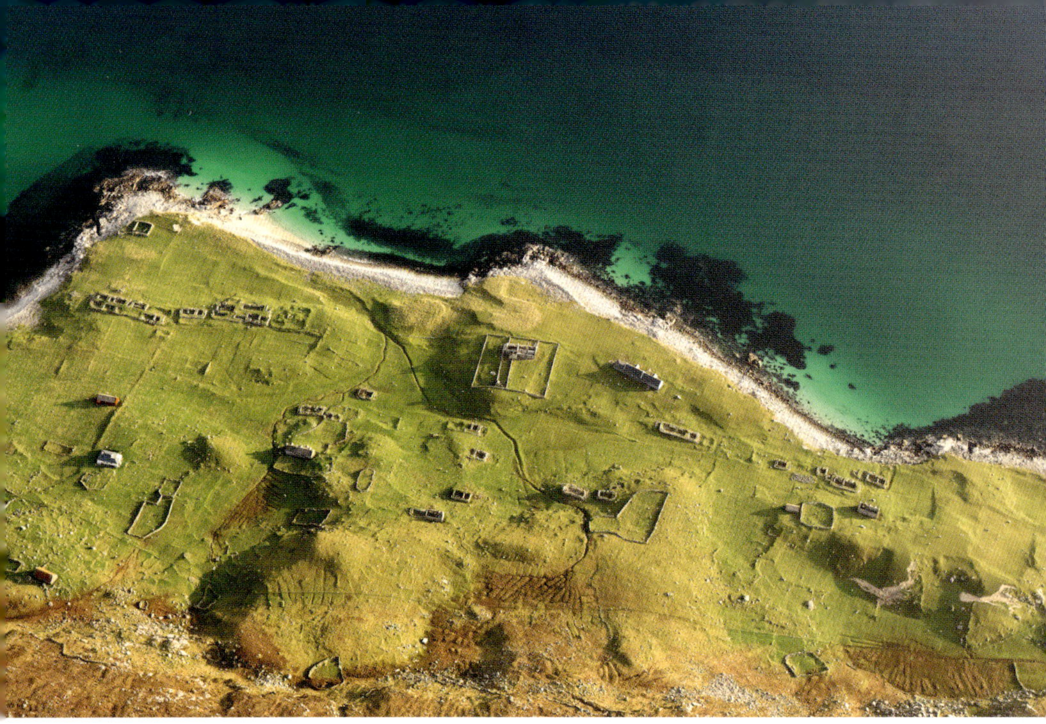

Scarp, Na h-Eileanan Siar

The uninhabited island of Scarp lies off the coast of Harris. It once had a population of around 200 people, but the last of them left in 1970. This image clearly shows the remains of the crofting township from the 1800s. Across the north and west, these remains are a testimony to the scale of depopulation over the last two centuries.

DP110773

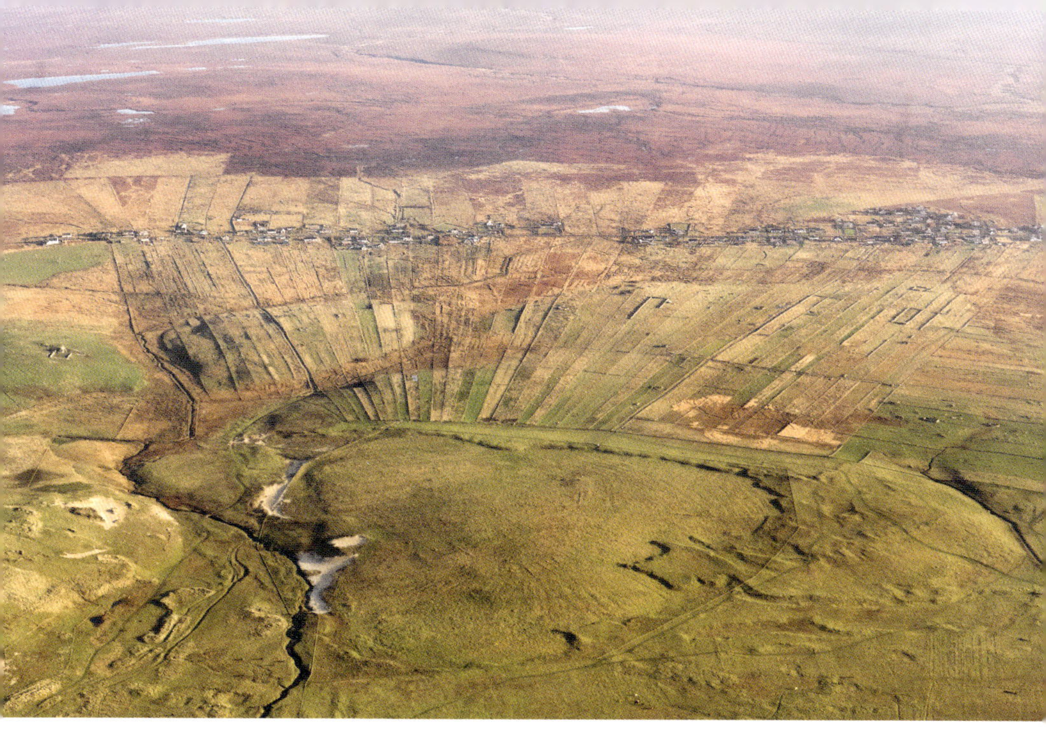

Upper and Lower Barabhas, Lewis, Na h-Eileanan Siar
The landscape surrounding the modern Barabhas townships reveals
a complex history of settlement and land-use, including pre-
Improvement settlement and crofts with long thin field patterns.
DP111150

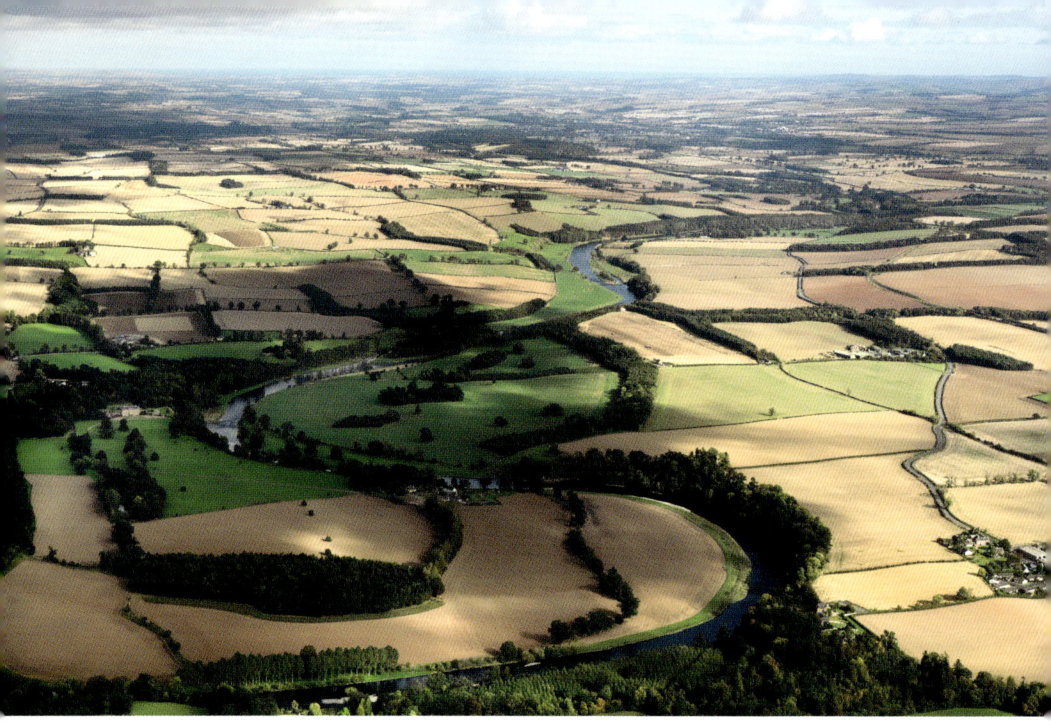

Farmland at Mertoun House, the Scottish Borders
The River Tweed meanders through the modern, intensively farmed
landscape that was created in the 1700s around Mertoun House: a
classic example of a lowland country estate and improved rectilinear
fields and farms.
DP082552

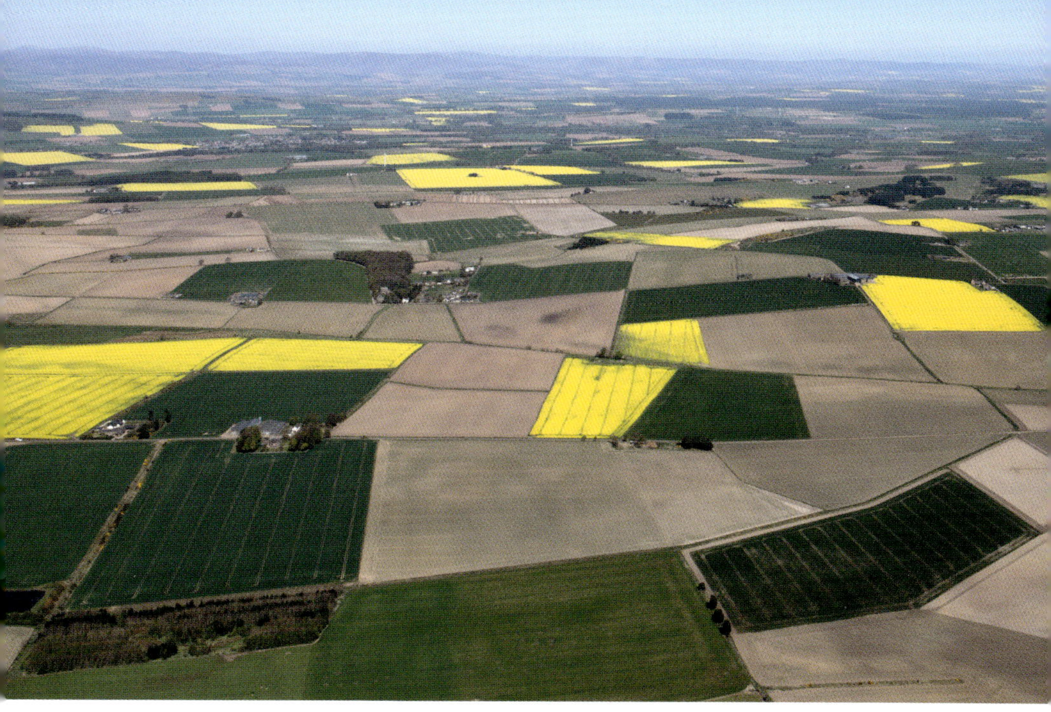

Farmland, Greystone, Angus

In the aftermath of the Second World War, UK agriculture focused on producing substantial quantities of cheap food. Large machinery aided the task, prompting the creation of even bigger fields to accommodate them. This in turn led to the amalgamation of more farms and the creation of the modern prairie-like farming. The village of Greystone in the centre left of the image is a rare relic of a settlement of medieval origin in a modern patchwork of fields.

DP255362

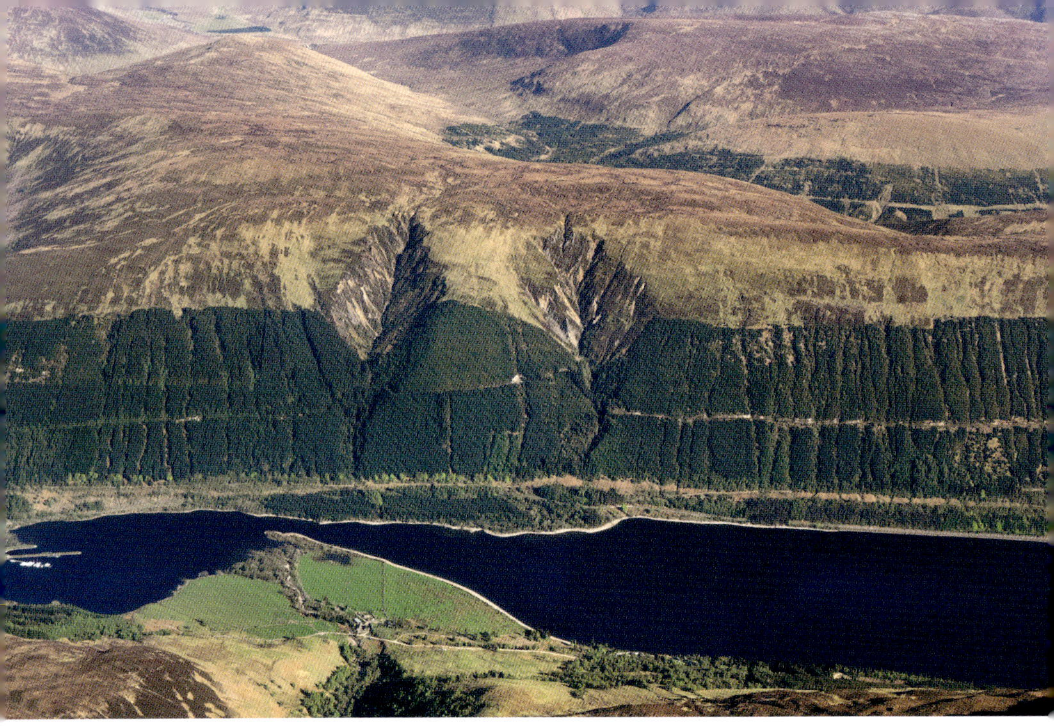

Forestry at Loch Lochy, Highlands

Straight lines of trees, such as here in the Great Glen, were
typical of plantations for much of the twentieth century. More
recent forestry, however, has a stronger focus on planting
native species and encouraging biodiversity.

DP111929

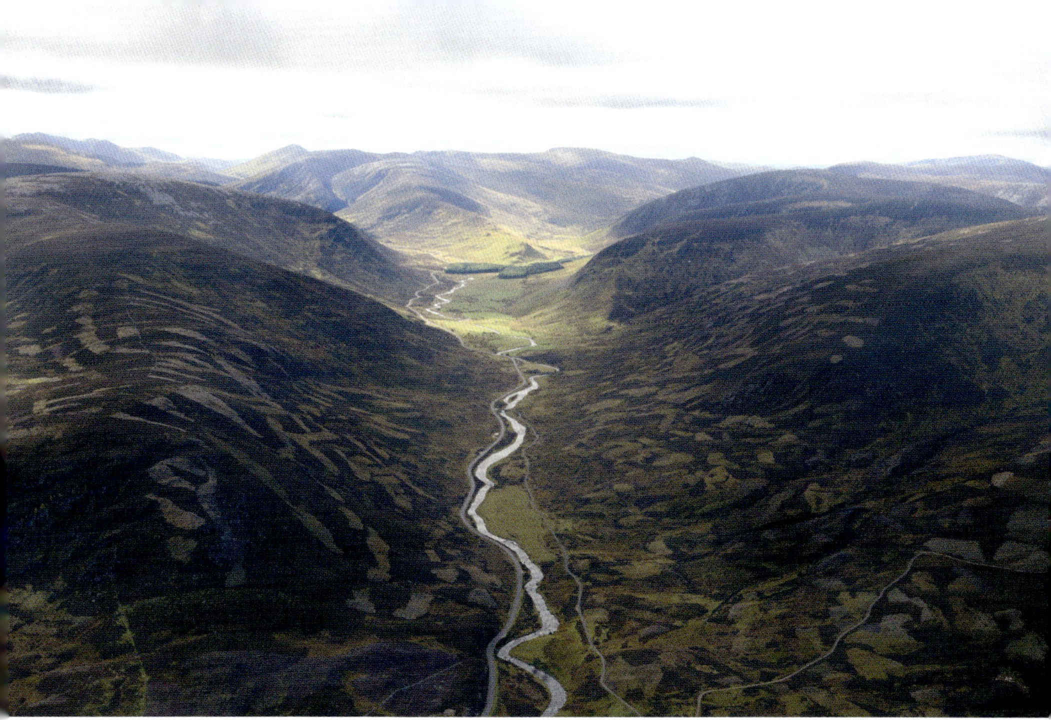

General Wade's Road at Glen Clunie, Perthshire

Built under the direction of Major Caulfeild between 1748 and 1757, the Military Road (on the right bank of the river) through Glen Clunie provides a route from the Lowlands to the centre of the Highlands, linking Coupar Angus to Braemar and Fort George near Inverness

DP144757

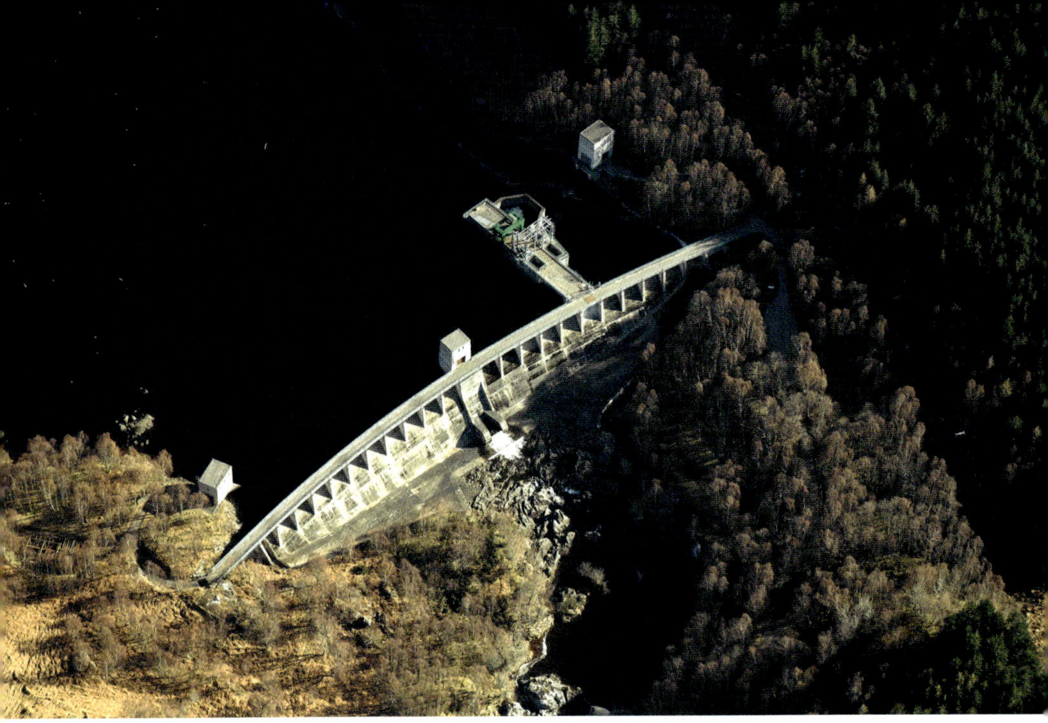

Loch Meig Dam, Highlands

This dam holds back water from the River Meig catchment,
which is then piped to Loch Luichart and on to the Loch Luichart
Power Station. The topography and weather of locations such
as this means that, of 145 hydro schemes in Scotland, more than
half are in the Highlands and Islands.
DP024943

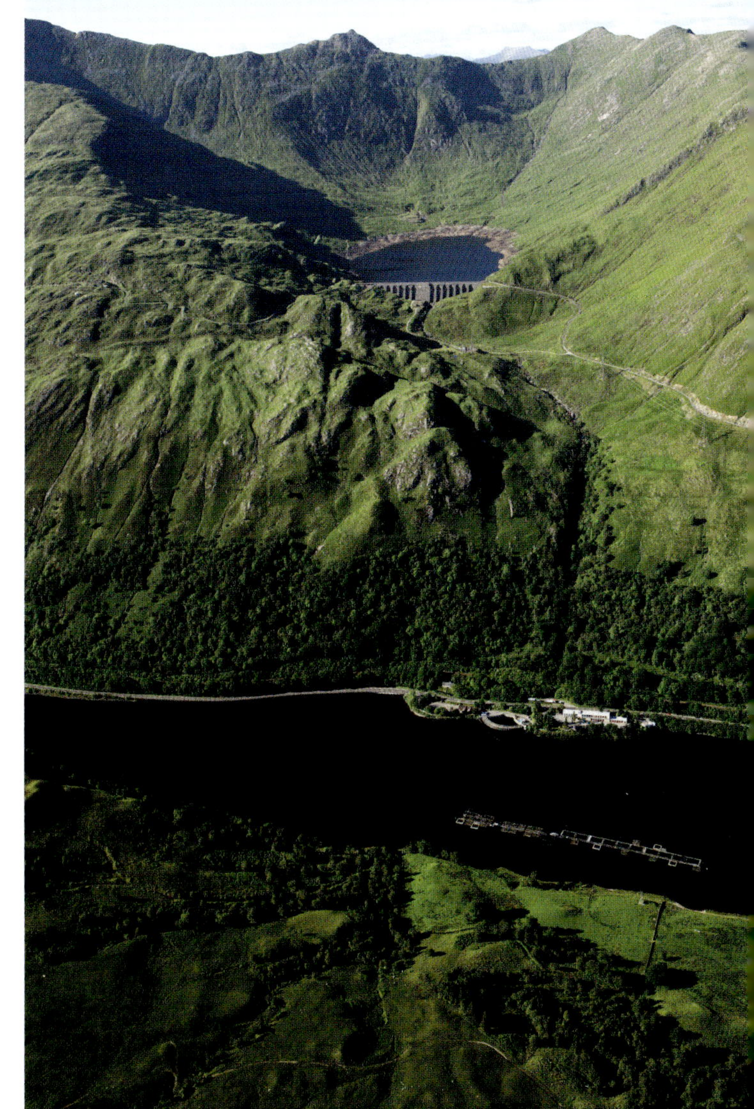

Cruachan Dam,
Argyll and Bute

Huge, solid and imposing,
Cruachan Dam – constructed
between 1959 and 1965 – rises
up out of the rocks above Loch
Awe as if it has always been a
part of the landscape.
DP017797

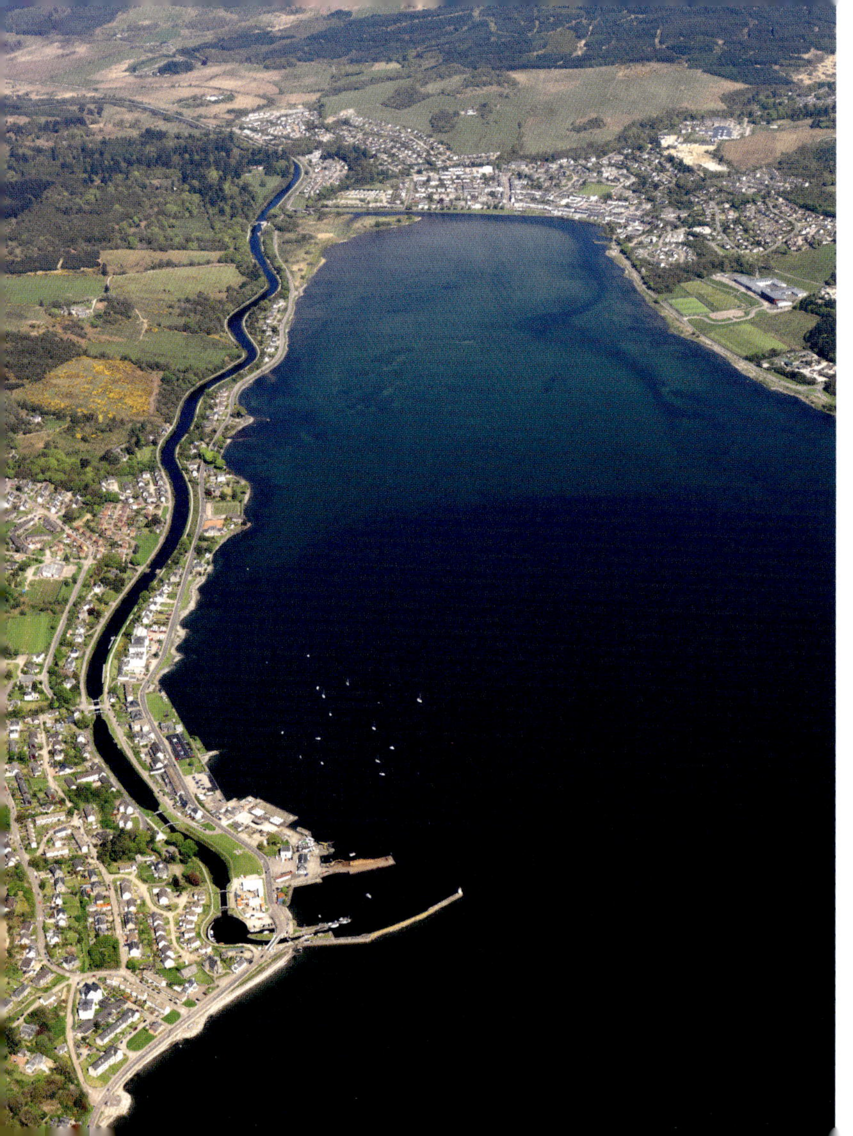

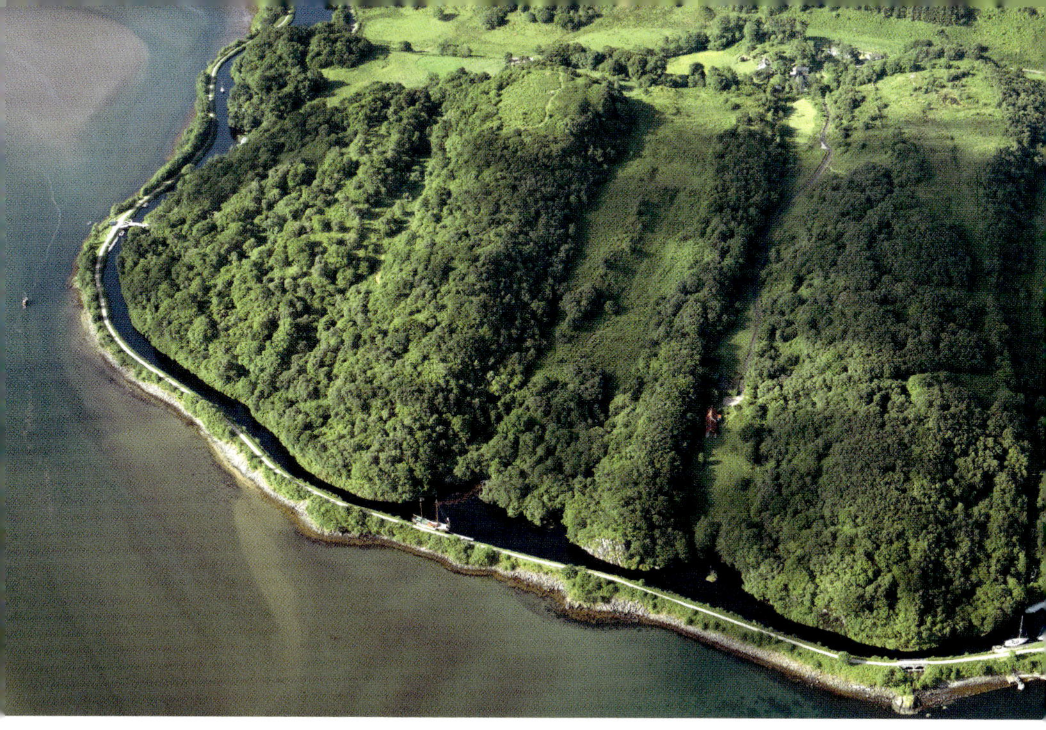

Crinan Canal, Argyll and Bute

Scotland's canals were significant works of engineering, primarily constructed to allow for the movement of industrial products such as coal and iron ore, as well as agricultural and commercial goods. The Crinan Canal was begun in 1794, and, despite being only 9 miles in length, drastically improved transport by linking the Firth of Clyde with the Sound of Jura. Nevertheless, the prominence of canals was short lived, as they were pushed aside by the railways. Today, however, many canals are once again in frequent use, this time by local communities.
DP112115, DP017931

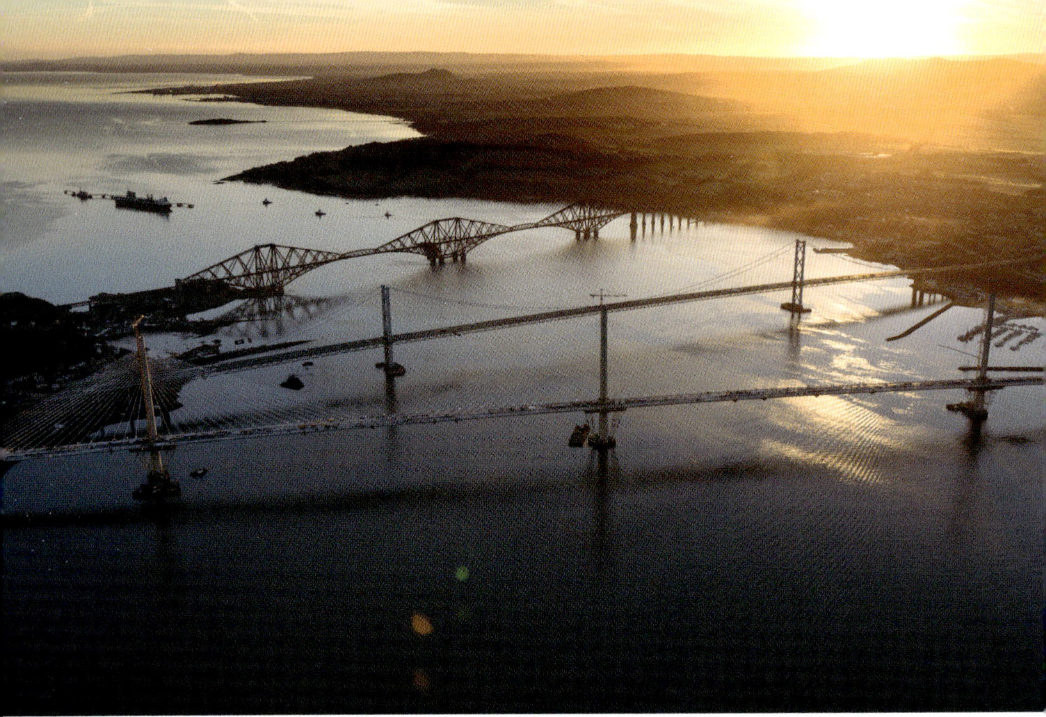

**Forth Railway Bridge, Queensferry Crossing and
Forth Road Bridge, Edinburgh**

Three bridges reach across the 2.5km expanse of the Firth of Forth
to connect North Queensferry with South Queensferry. The bridges
embody three centuries of engineering – the red railway bridge
being a wonder of nineteenth century design and construction,
the suspension bridge meeting the needs of traffic in the twentieth
century (and now accessible to pedestrians and cyclists) and the
cable-stayed Queensferry Crossing completing the trio when it
opened to traffic in the twenty-first century.

DP246367

Forth Railway Bridge, Edinburgh

The Luftwaffe made their first attack on Scotland – a raid on Royal Navy ships near the Forth Bridge – on 16 October 1939. This aerial reconnaissance photograph by the Luftwaffe dates from earlier in that month, and intelligence notes describe the rail bridge and anti-aircraft defences.

SC372380 (1939)

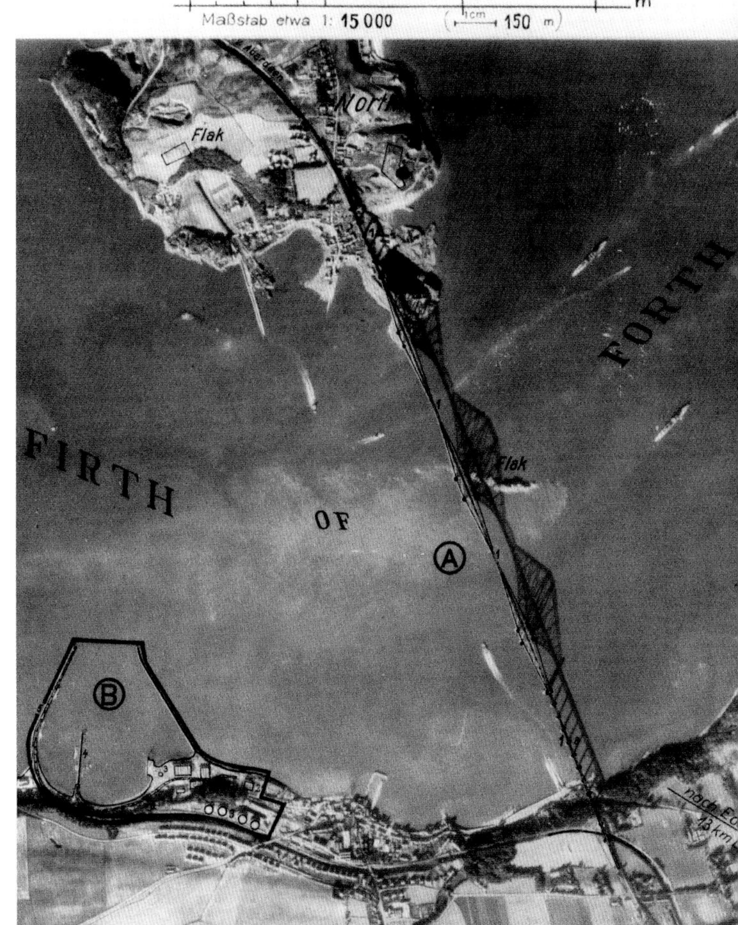

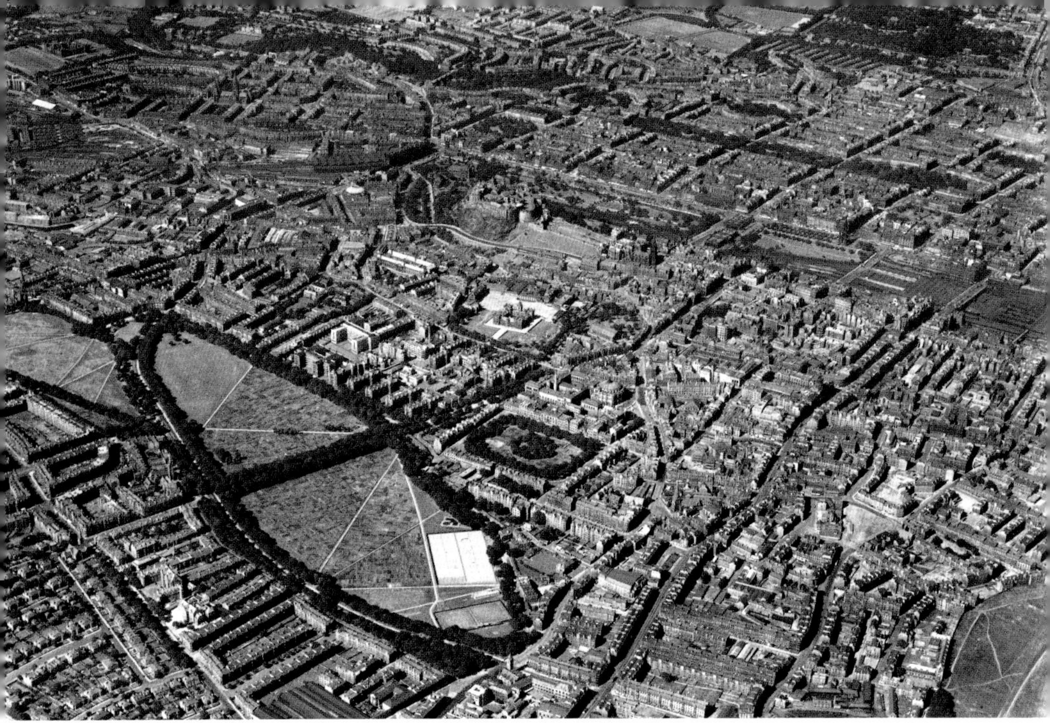

The Meadows, Edinburgh

Captured here in August 1947, the Meadows – a 63-acre public park found just to the south of Edinburgh's historic Old Town – has been transformed into a vast garden plot for some 500 allotments. This was the government's famous 'Dig for Victory' propaganda campaign in action.

SC1268680 (1947)

**Anti-tank barriers,
Longniddry Bents,
East Lothian**
During the Second World
War, the nation held its breath
in the expectation that enemy
craft would land somewhere
on the 11,000 mile coastline
of Britain. To combat this
eventuality, every possible
landing point, such as here in
East Lothian was protected
with anti-tank barriers.
DP054831

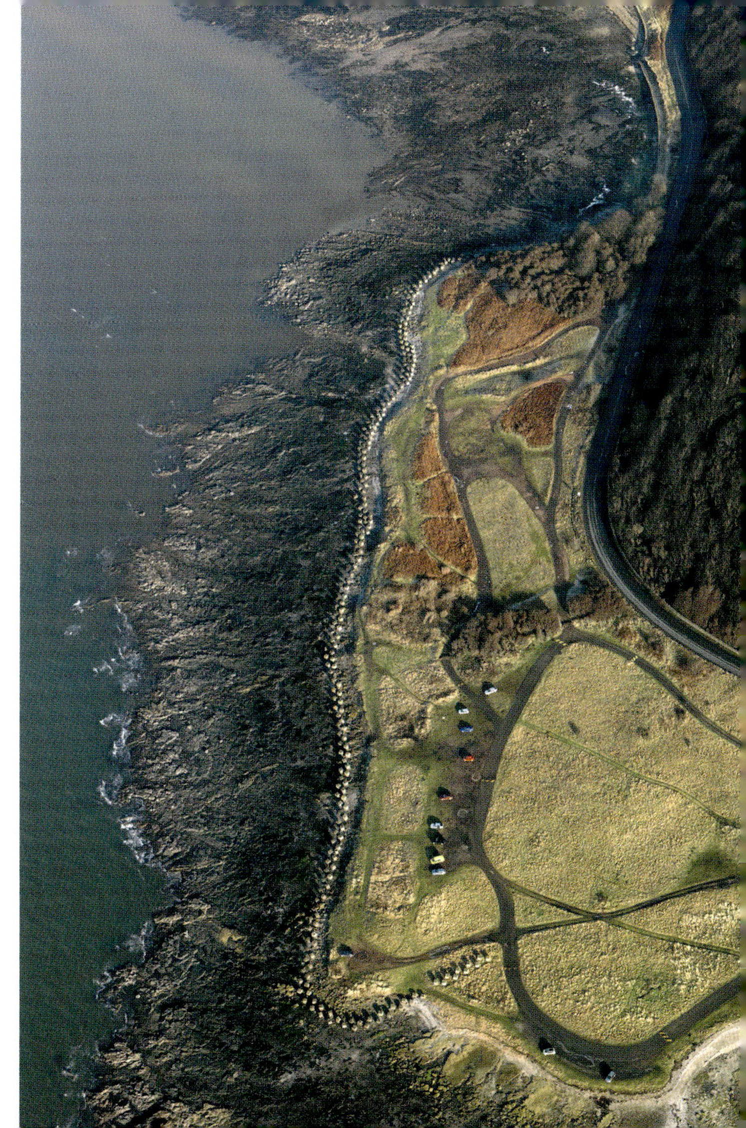

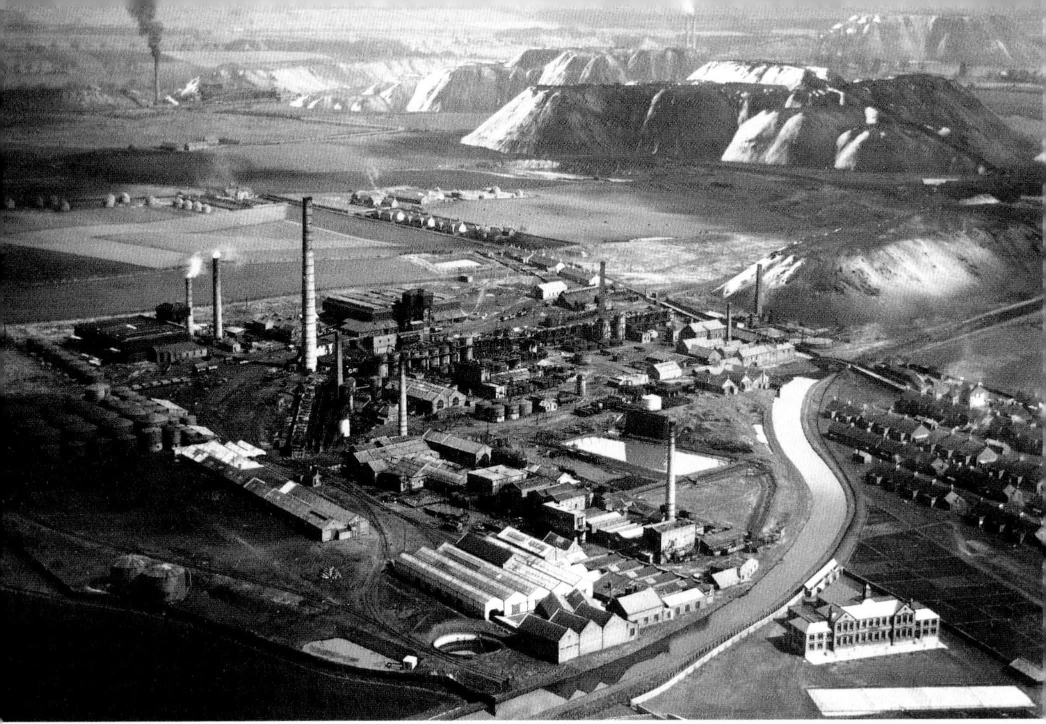

Broxburn Oil Works, West Lothian

From the mid 1800s, West Lothian lay at the heart of Scotland's shale oil industry, distilling shale rock to produce oil and other chemicals on an industrial scale. However, by 1927 the Broxburn Oil Works, shown here, had closed. Now only their great bings – sculpted from the masses of waste created by the shale oil process – survive as a familiar landscape feature.

SC1315377 (1927)

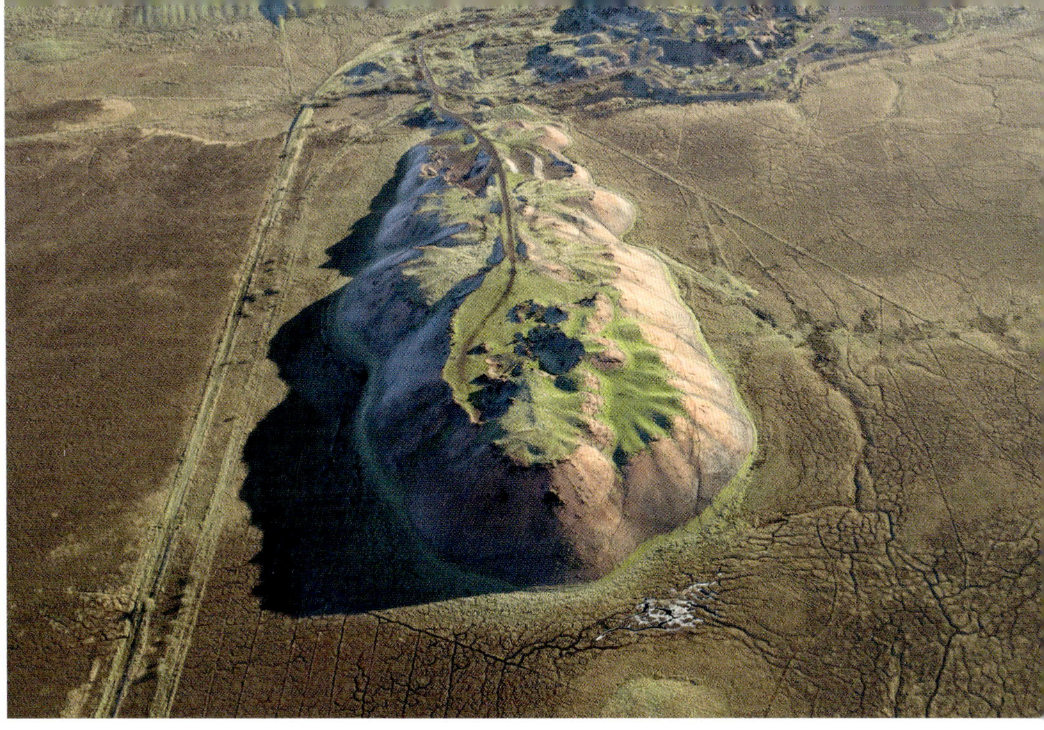

Tarbrax Oil Works, South Lanarkshire
As at Broxburn, the Tarbrax works were relatively short lived,
producing shale oll from 1864 to 1925. The bings remain as an
enduring landmark, outlasting the industry that created them.
DP012067

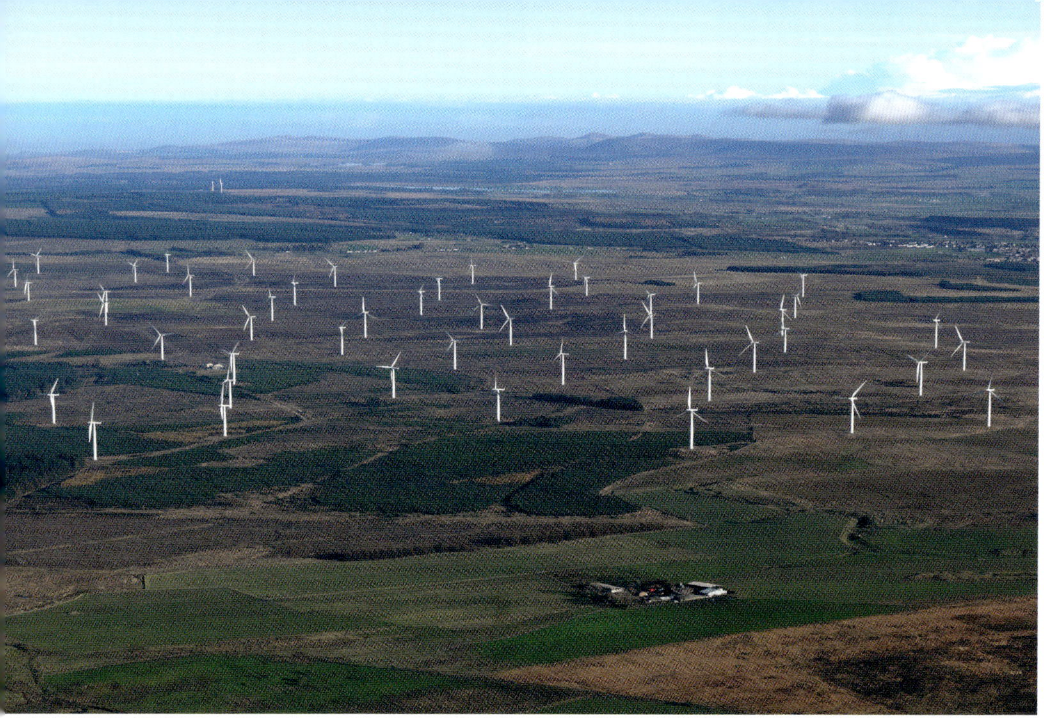

Black Law Wind Farm, South Lanarkshire

One of the most striking new features on Scotland's landscapes – both on- and offshore – are wind farms, where the Scottish weather can make a considerable contribution to producing renewable energy. Here, at Black Law Wind Farm, the turbines rotate against a backdrop of the Pentland Hills.

DP084498

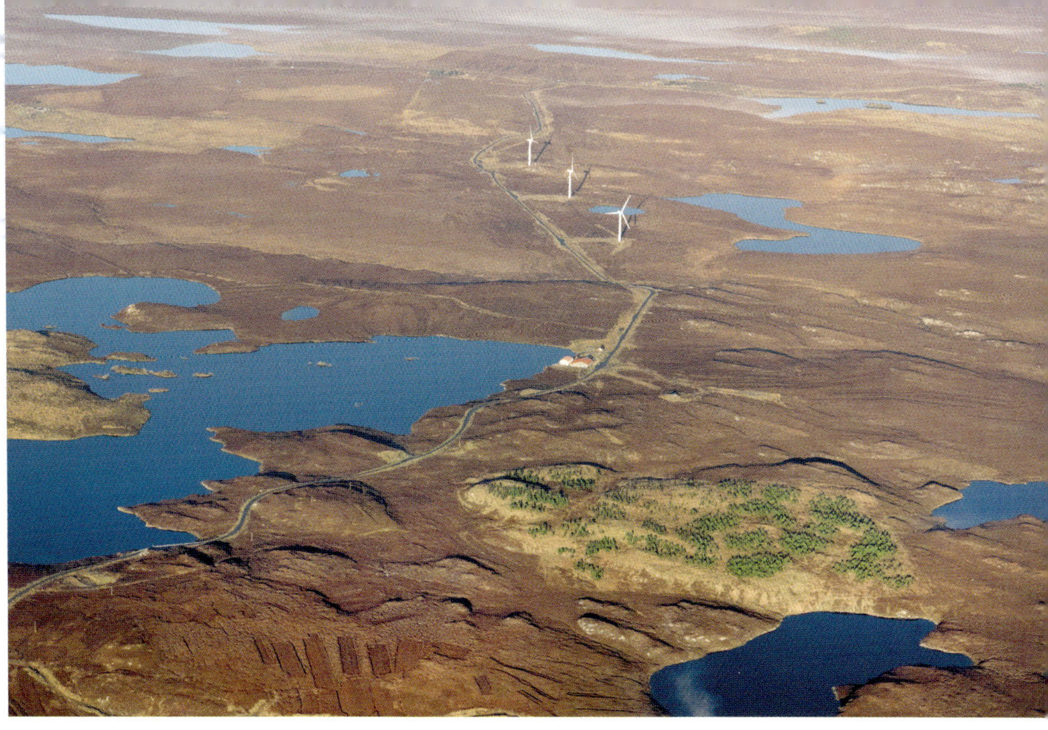

Lochs Wind Farm, Lewis, Na h-Eileanan Siar
The shadows of the wind turbines stretch across the island
landscape. Old and new ways of working the land sit together –
in the foreground are the remains of peat cutting, as well as one
of the few conifer plantations on Lewis.
DP111266

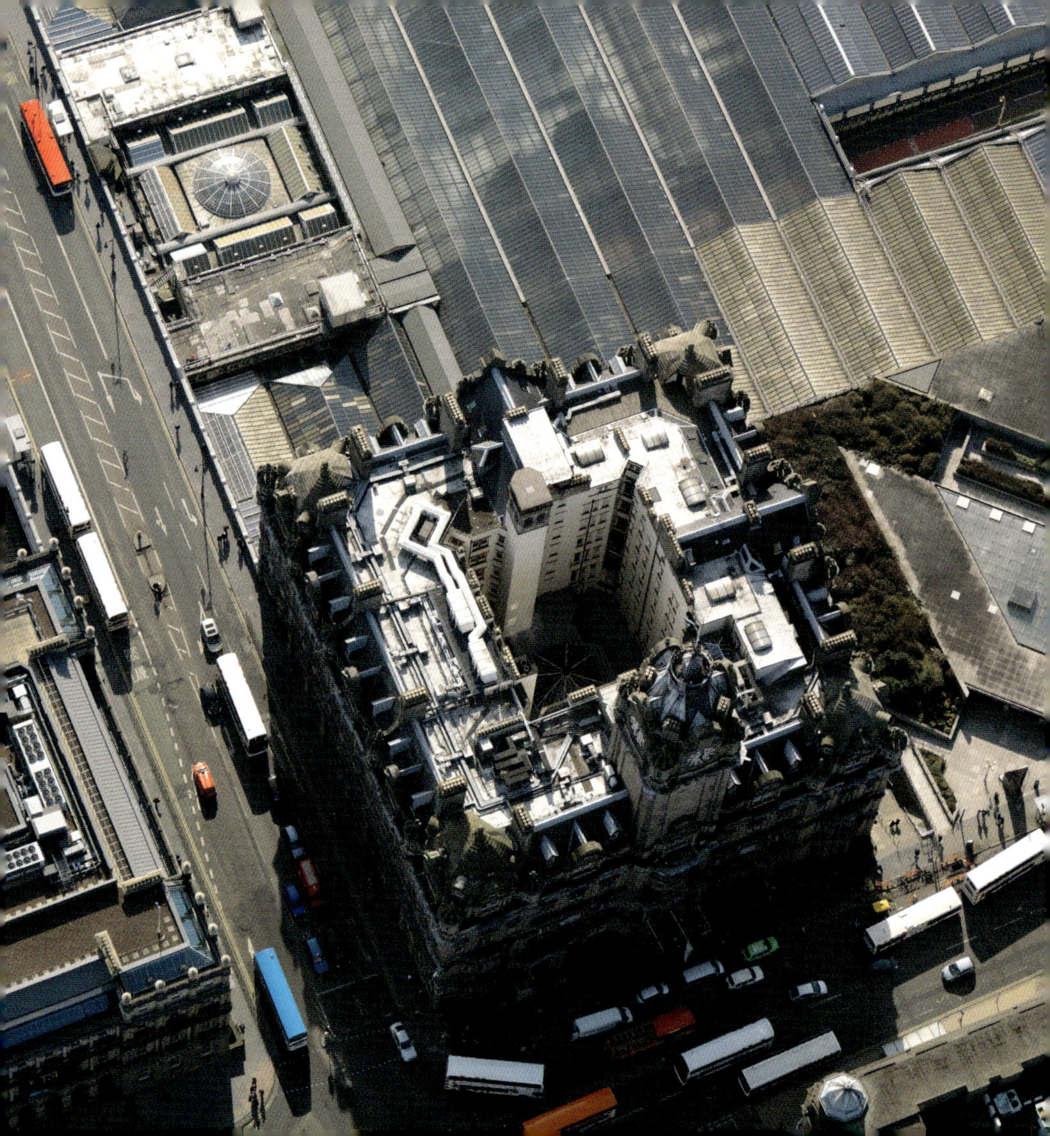

Towns and cities began to appear in the Scottish landscape around 1,000 years ago, and since then the balance of the country's population has been shifting from rural to urban. This change has often been a result of the pressures of population growth and changes in land-use – such as in the wake of the Highland clearances.

Scotland's cities – Edinburgh, Glasgow, Inverness, Perth, Stirling, Dundee, Aberdeen and Dunfermline (which became Scotland's newest city in 2022) – all have unique characteristics which can be interpreted most clearly from above. When walking down a teeming city-centre street, the history of the cityscapes can be hard to read. But aerial photography can reveal the natural features that have twisted a city into shape, or the wynds of medieval streets next to rows of Victorian tenements, or transport links fanning out from industrial and economic hubs to postwar housing estates.

Scotland's urban centres continue to attract a wide range of residents and visitors. They are never static – they are focal points for ideas and connections, just as they have been for hundreds of years.

Balmoral Hotel, Edinburgh
Next to Waverley Station, a procession of buses winds past the edifice of the Balmoral Hotel – this Edinburgh landmark originally opened in 1902 as the North British Hotel.
DP075889

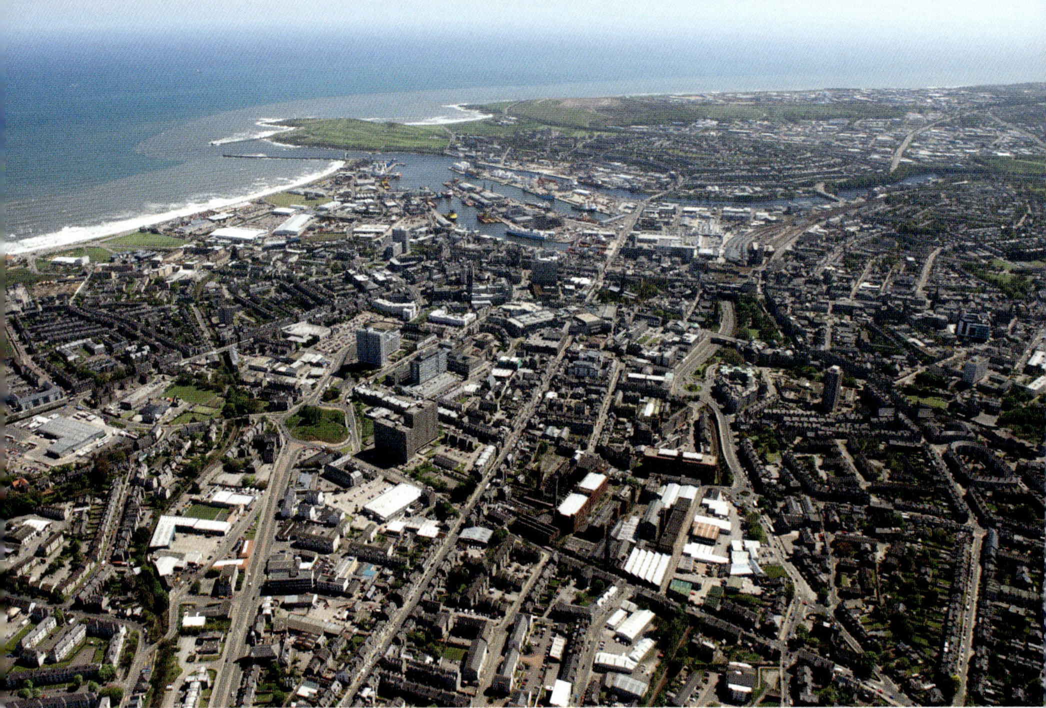

Aberdeen Harbour, Aberdeen

The granite city of Aberdeen expanded rapidly during the boom times of Queen Victoria and the Empire. Yet, unusually for a modern city, Aberdeen's ancient origin point – its harbour – remains its economic heart. From prehistory to the present day, the sheltered river mouth has sustained merchant traders, trawl-fishermen, tea clippers, granite exporters and, today, the massive infrastructure of the offshore oil and gas industries.

DP154684

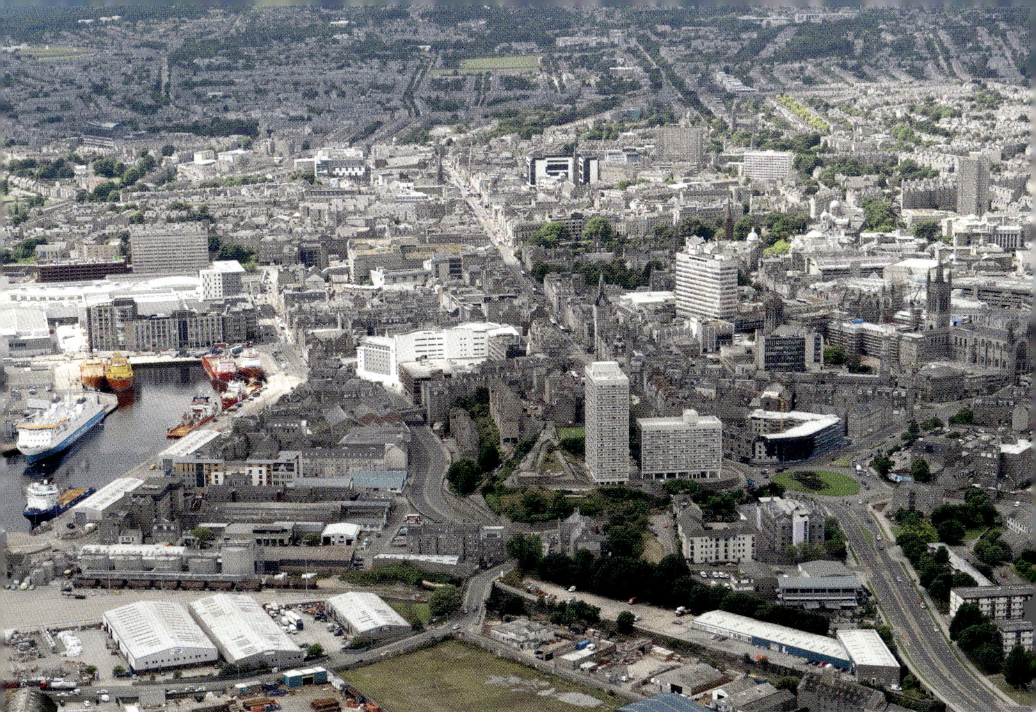

City Centre, Aberdeen

While granite provided the raw material for a phenomenal period of growth in Aberdeen, it was a combination of the expert masonry of local builders and the clean visions of the dominant architects of the day that created the mould for the modern city.

DP091646

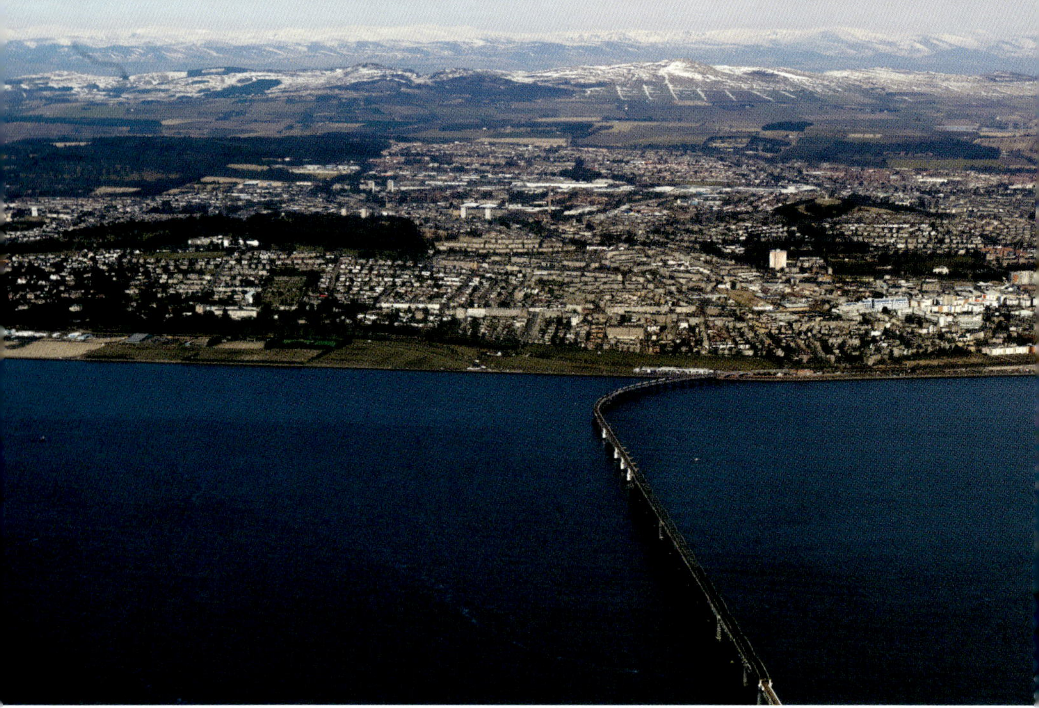

Tay Bridge, Dundee

A line of iron and steel, the Tay Rail Bridge crosses the Firth of Tay and arcs towards the Dundee harbour-front. Still surviving directly alongside this crossing are the stumps of the piers that once supported the preceding Tay Bridge – on the night of 28 December 1879, as the 5.27pm service from Burntisland crossed the structure during a fierce storm, the bridge's central span and high girders collapsed, sending 72 passengers and rail staff to their deaths in the icy waters. The North British Railway Company commissioned this second bridge – which opened in 1886 – as a muscular, over-engineered crossing whose appearance of fortitude was just as important as its actual physical strength.

DP075810

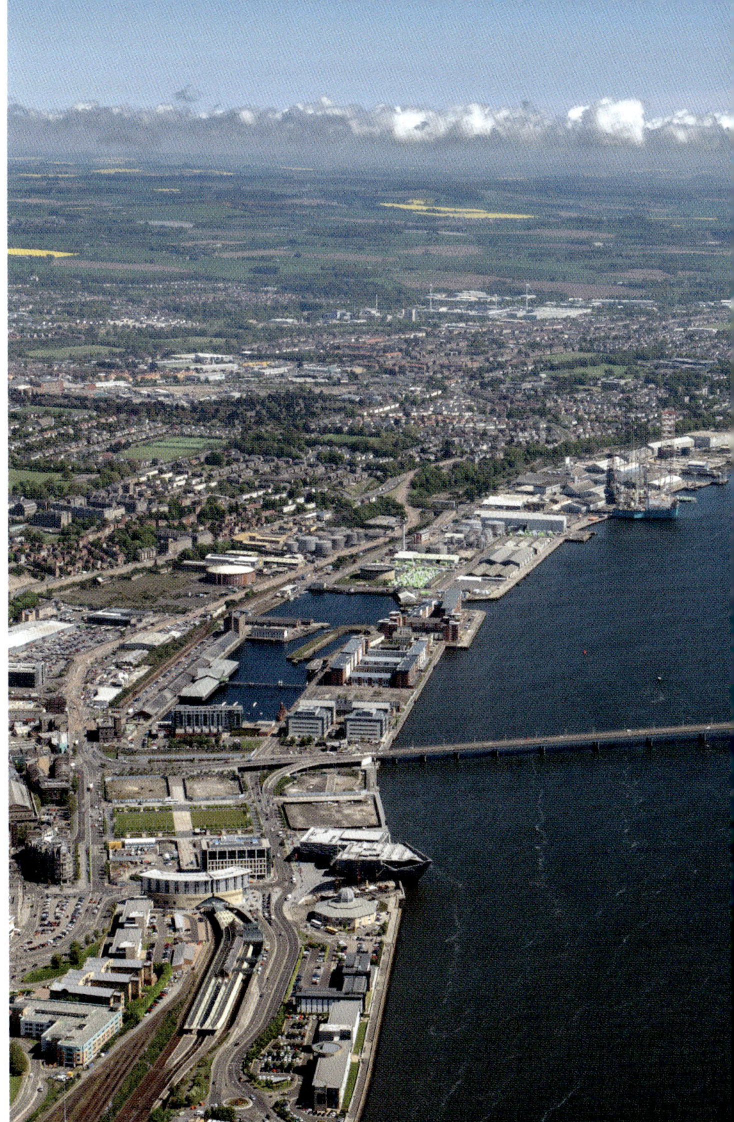

Waterfront, Dundee

Change is underway in Dundee. The waterfront is being developed, reflecting the shifting priorities of this historic city. The V&A Dundee is a centrepiece, sitting alongside the RRS *Discovery* – the old and the new together, all connecting the river and the city.

DP304569

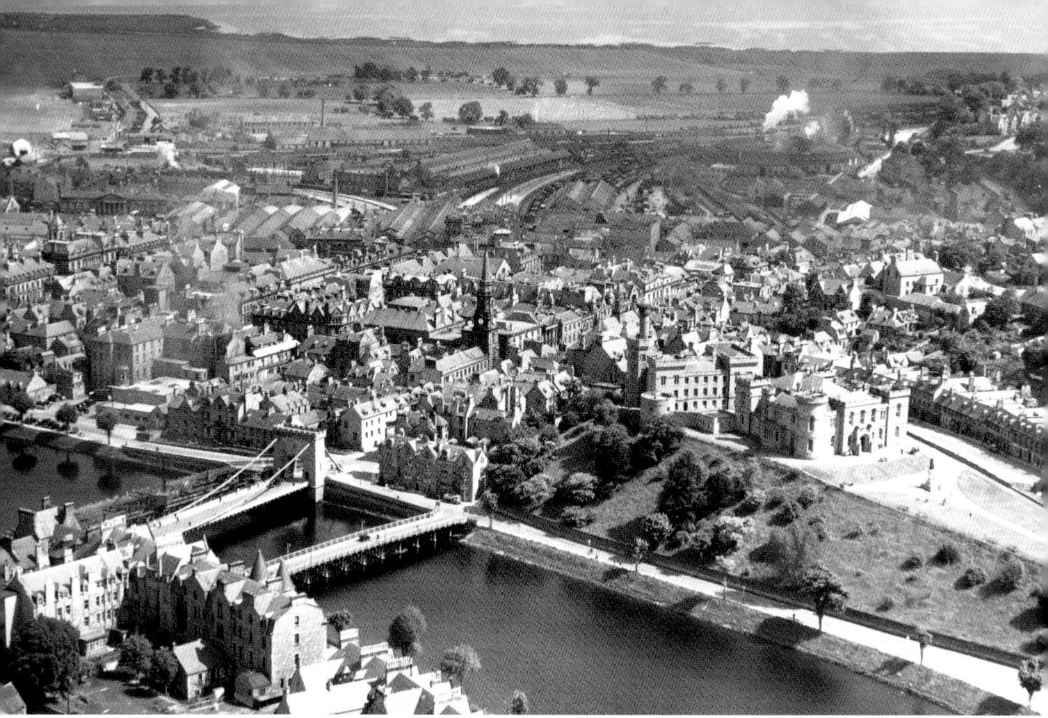

Ness Bridge, Inverness

Linking the ancient town centre to the west bank of the river, the Ness Bridge has existed in one incarnation or another since the eleventh century. The earliest structures were wooden-built and were regularly destroyed by flood or war, and it wasn't until 1685 that the first stone bridge appeared. The river claimed this bridge in 1849, and in 1855 a 'flood-proof' suspension bridge was built as a replacement. But, as the motorcar industry developed, planners were forced to re-imagine the crossing once again. Pictured here in 1947, a new bridge is under construction alongside the earlier span, while a temporary structure has been erected to allow the flow of traffic to continue. SC1268500 (1947)

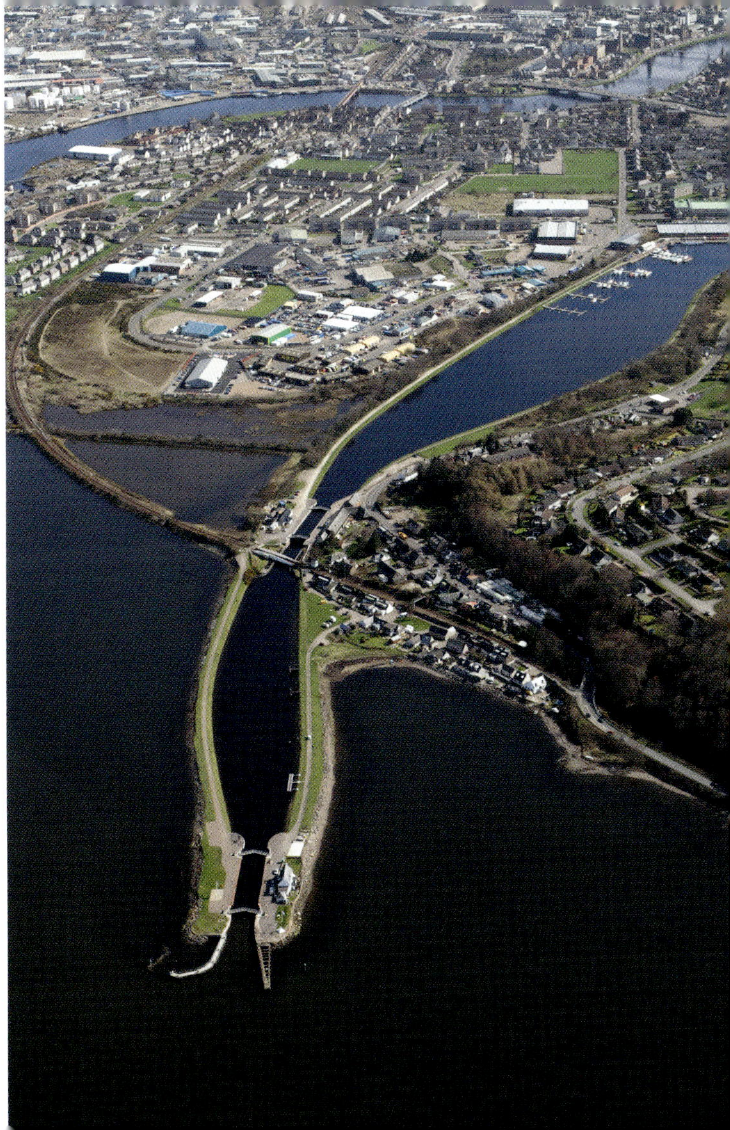

Caledonian Canal, Inverness

While the natural bend of the River Ness curves through the centre of the city, here at Clachnaharry the Caledonian Canal expands into the artificial bow of the Muirtown basin before exiting into the Firth through the twin spits of reclaimed land forming its most north-easterly lock.

DP024658

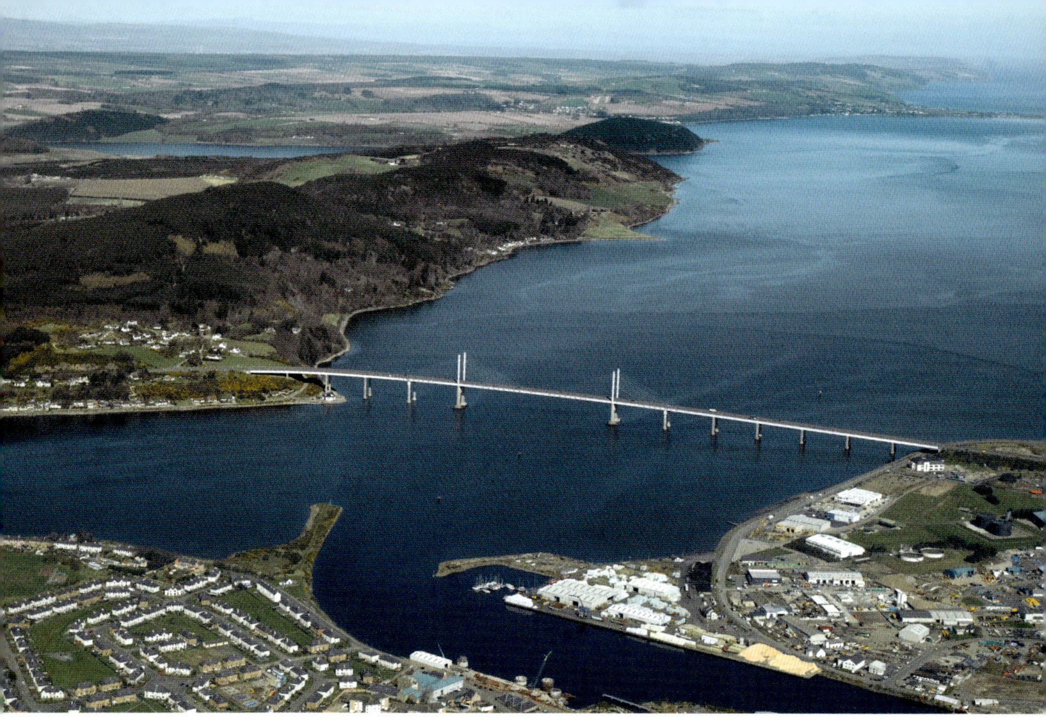

Kessock Bridge, Inverness

Stretching out across the wide mouth of the Moray Firth, from the air
the Kessock Bridge appears as a thin, delicate strip. Yet its 1,052m of
continuous steel superstructure have been one of the major factors
in the growth of Inverness over the past 30 years.
DP024672, DP024656

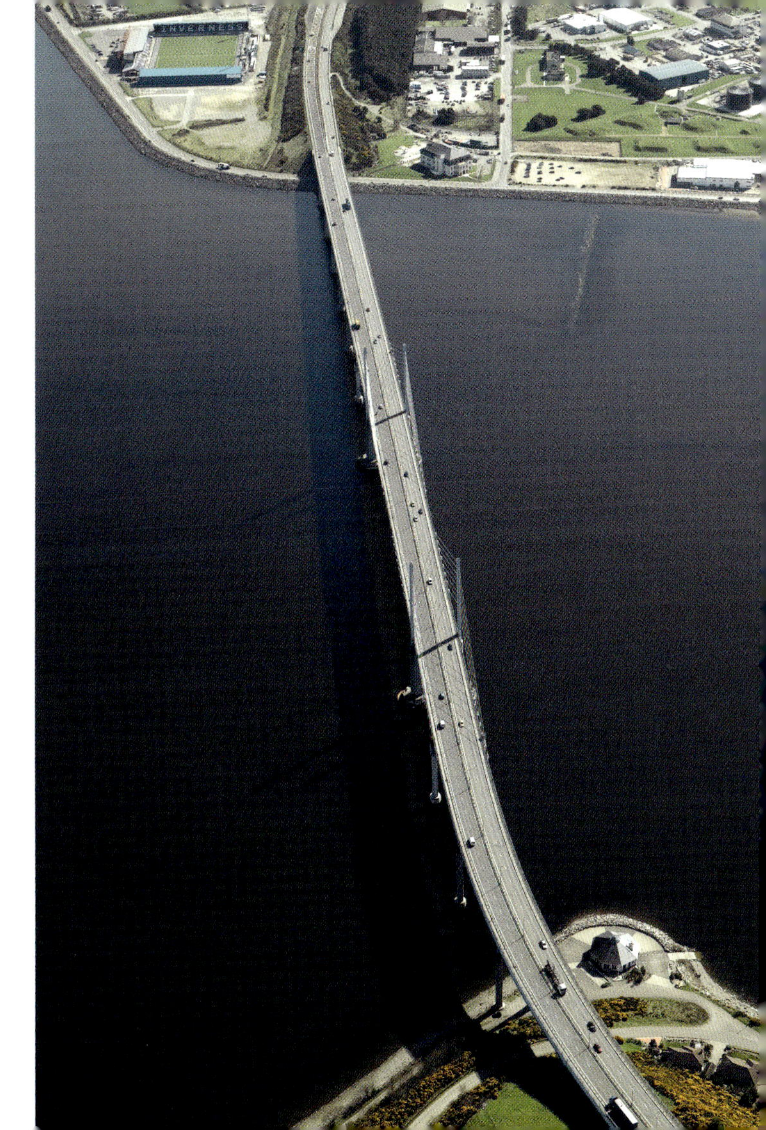
INVERNESS

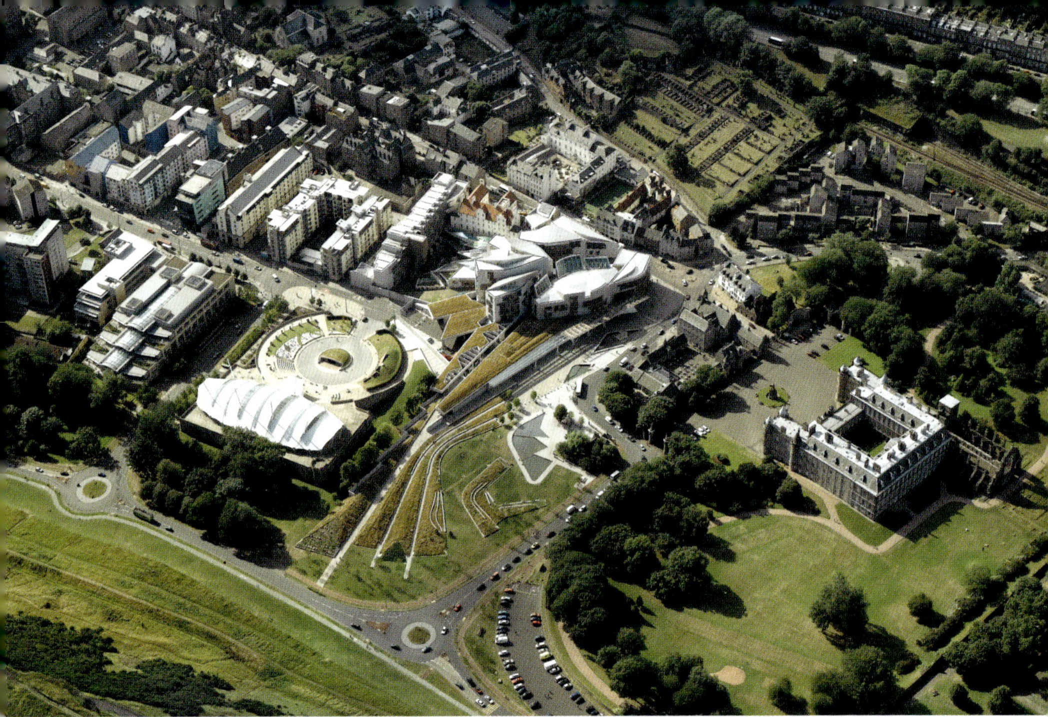

Holyrood Palace and the Scottish Parliament, Edinburgh

This site at the foot of the Old Town is a study in both preservation and change. The ruins of an abbey building dating back to the 1200s still cling to a royal residence from the 1500s. On the other side of Queen's Drive and Horse Wynd, however, the breweries, gasworks and tenements of the early twentieth century have been replaced by the Scottish Parliament, a grand post-modern statement in steel, oak and granite.

DP014137

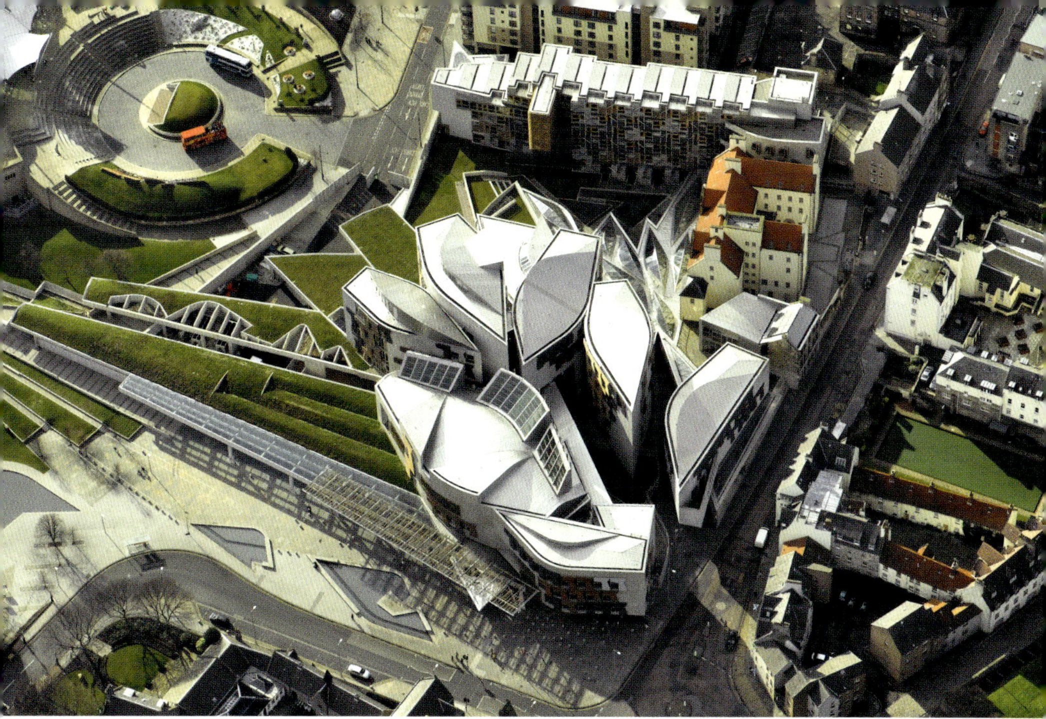

Scottish Parliament, Edinburgh

Catalan architect Enric Miralles' bold vision for the Scottish
Parliament appears as an elegant mesh of overlapping shapes and
forms. Symbolism played a major role in the location choice –
positioned at the foot of the medieval spine of the Royal Mile, and
opposite the Palace of Holyroodhouse, seat of royal power for
centuries, the parliament emerged from the brownfield site of a
former brewery, reinvigorating a post-industrial landscape that had
been in decline for decades.

DP025693

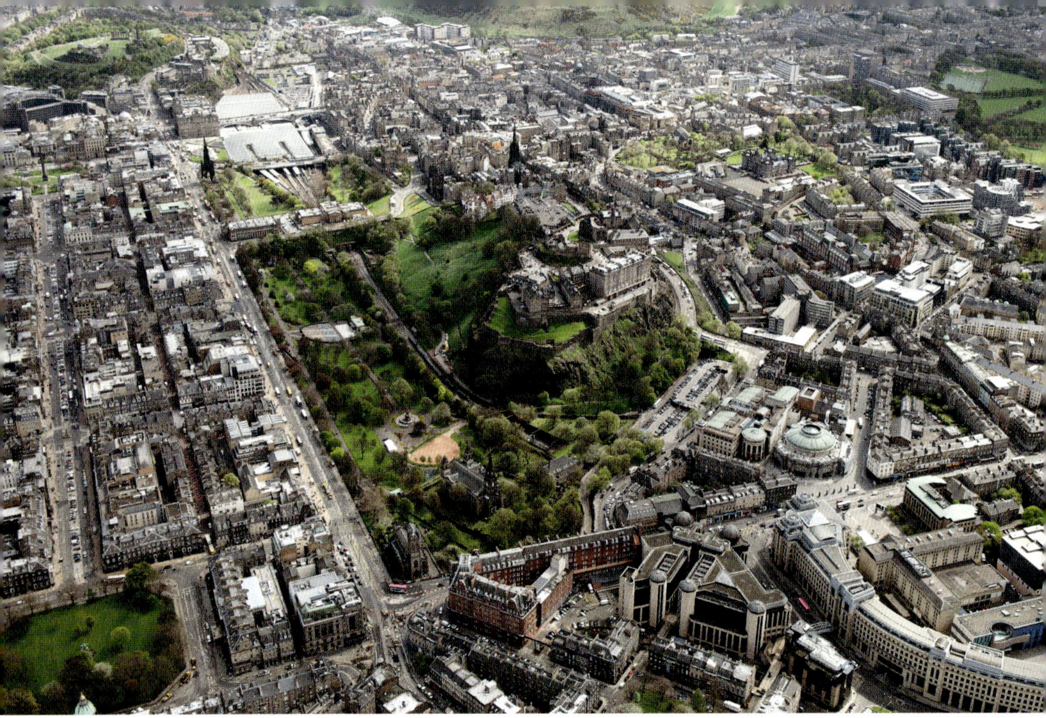

Old and New Towns, Edinburgh

Edinburgh's Old Town sprung up around the historic route of the
Royal Mile, but poor conditions led to the development of the elegant
Georgian New Town, a masterpiece of city planning built in stages from
1767. Emerging like a fault line between the Old Town and the New
Town, the railtracks of Waverley Station burst through an ancient glacial
hollow to cross the sculpted parkland of Princes Street.

DP154383

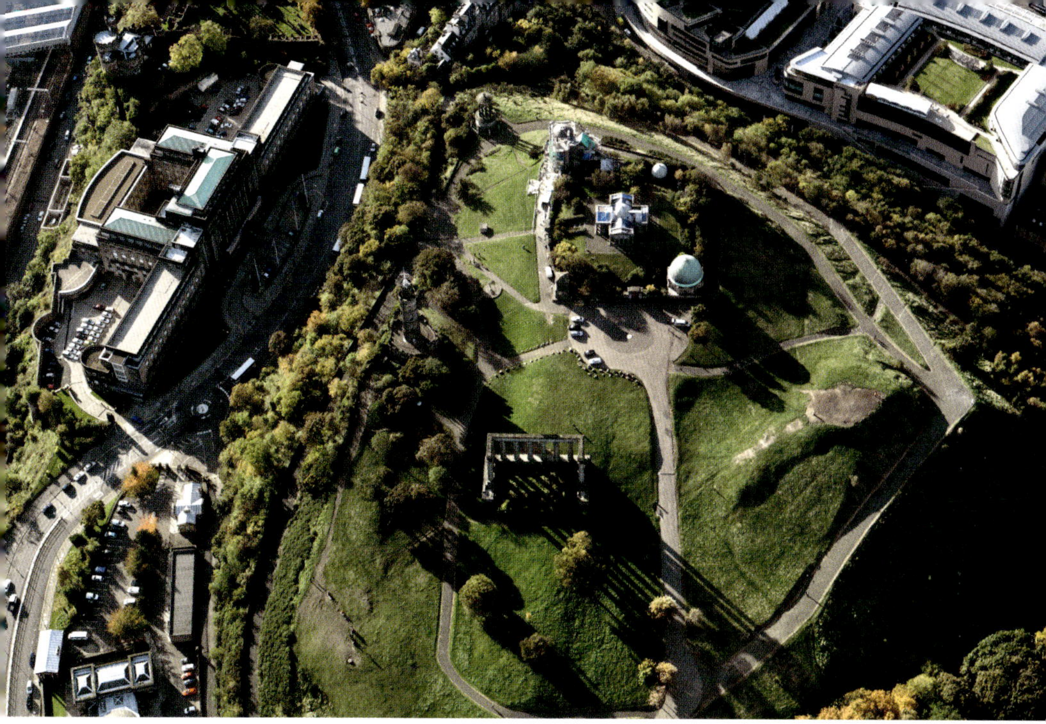

Calton Hill, Edinburgh

The rounded summit of Calton Hill became the canvas for a sequence of neoclassical monuments in pursuit of Enlightenment Edinburgh's dream of becoming a 'Modern Athens'. On the landscape below the hill another enduring Enlightenment project was being realised – the wide streets and graceful crescents of Edinburgh's New Town.

DP051311

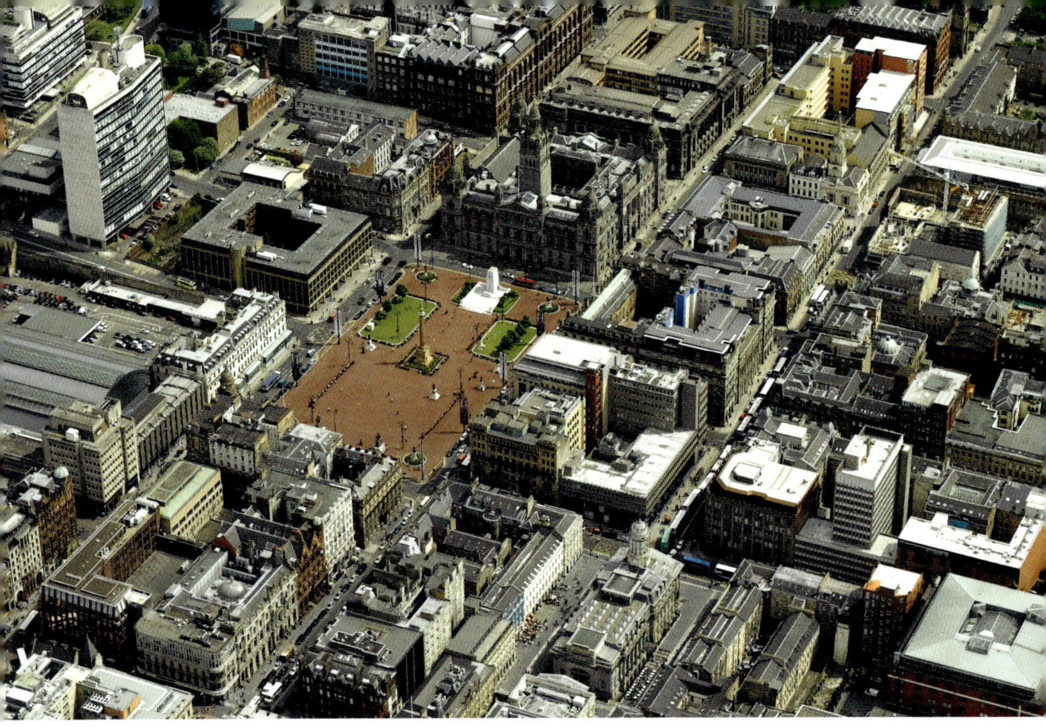

George Square, Glasgow

Construction of Glasgow's Merchant City began in the mid 1700s with regimented blocks of shops, warehouses and residential accommodation spreading across the open land to the west of the medieval High Street and to the north of the Trongate. Today, George Square, looked over by the imposing late Victorian bulk of the City Chambers, is still the civic and political centre of the city.

DP015615

City Centre, Glasgow

Pictured here in 1947, a jumbled wave of buildings, roads and warehouses meets the solid shore of Glasgow's regimented Georgian street grid. Just over 20 years after this photograph was taken, the wide concrete and tarmac of the M8 motorway would be laid directly through this inner-city landscape.

SC802946 (1947)

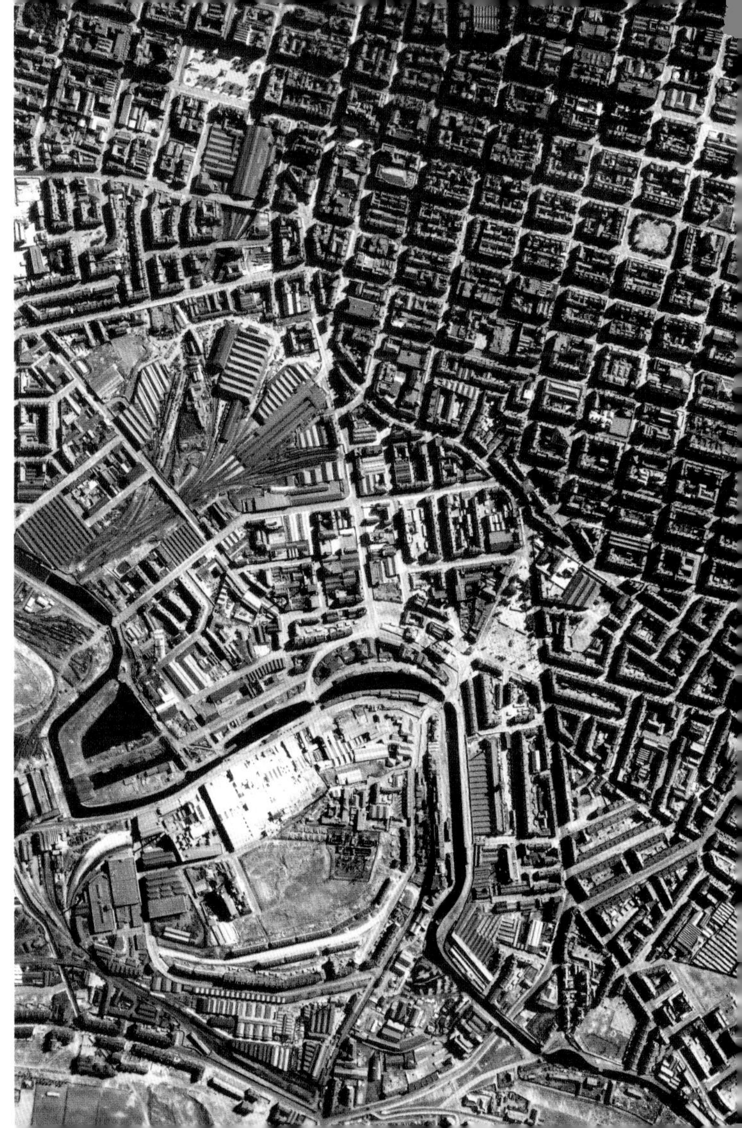

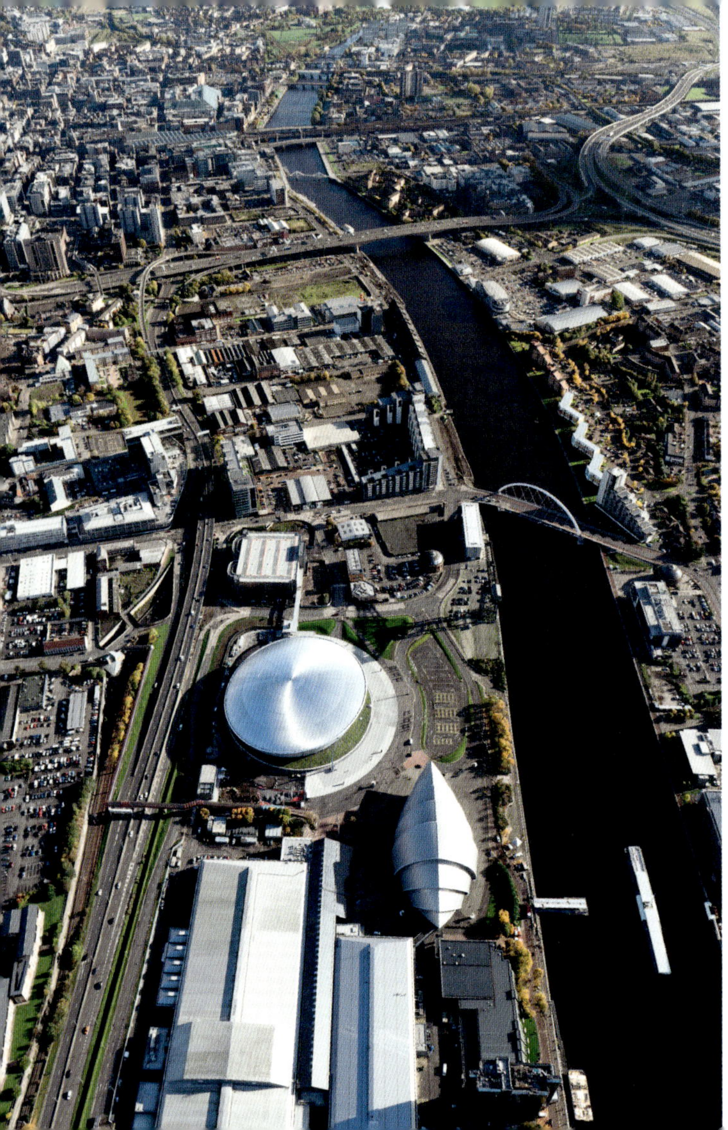

The Hydro, Glasgow
The long shadow of the Finnieston Crane reaches out to touch the 1,400-tonne latticed-steel dome of the Hydro, a recent addition to the banks of the River Clyde. Now in its ninth decade, the Finnieston Crane has witnessed the incredible transformation of its surroundings – from mid twentieth century industrial powerhouse to 1970s and 80s dereliction, to design-led, cultural and architectural renewal.
DP164490

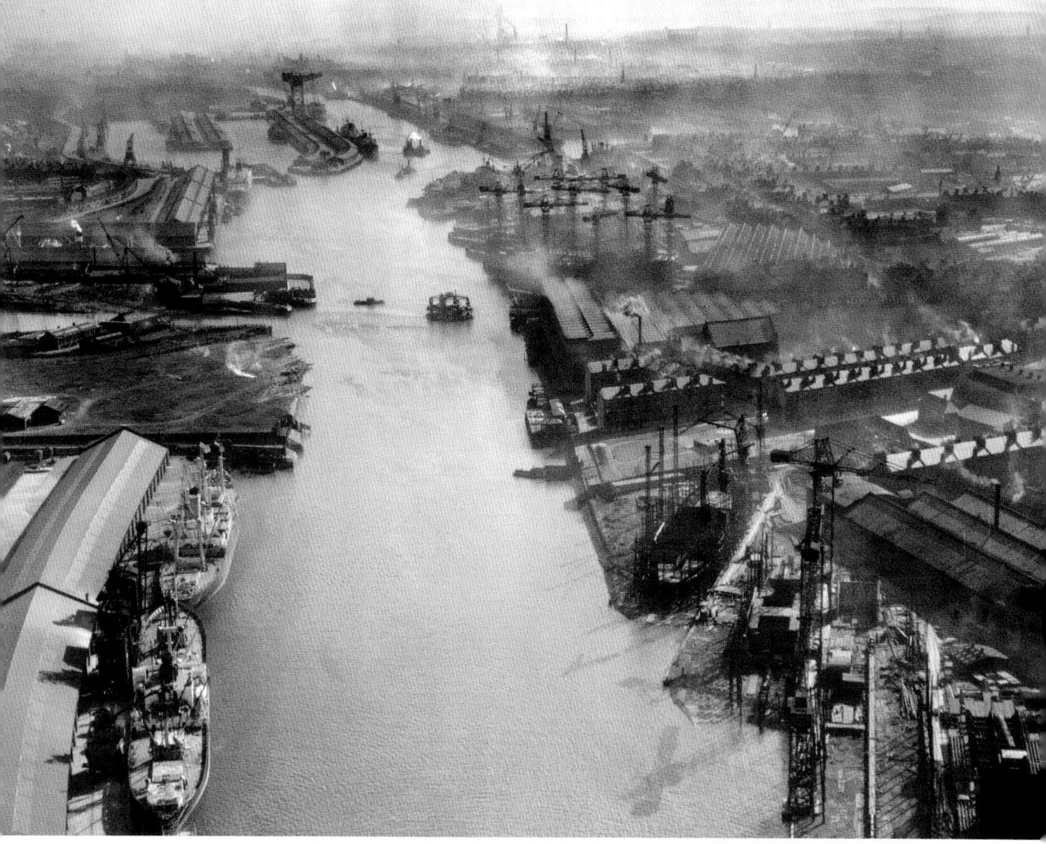

Queen's Docks and Prince's Docks, Glasgow

A forest of cranes rises up above the smog, while boats throng
the quaysides. These are bustling, muscular scenes of a city hard at
work. Almost nothing you can see here remains today. Only the
silhouette of the Finnieston Crane, first built in 1926, has remained
a fixture of the Glasgow skyline – a stalwart of vanished industry.
SC1096029 (1950)

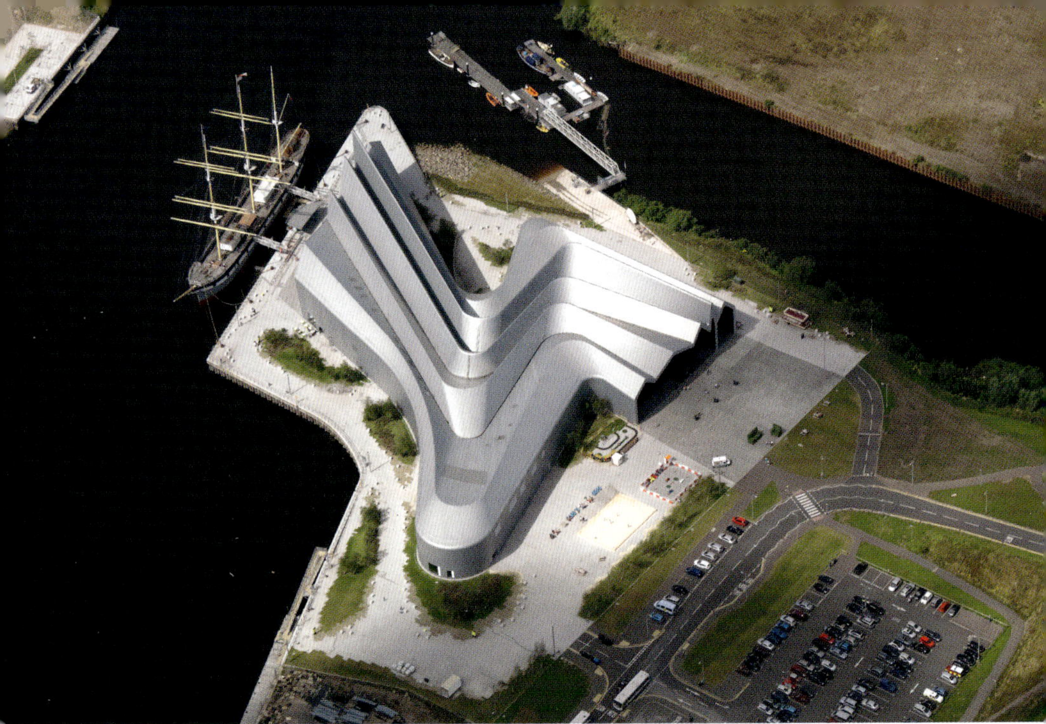

The Riverside Museum, Glasgow

Cities continually rewrite themselves – it is an unstoppable and inevitable process. Here, at the mouth of the River Kelvin, an architectural icon opened in 2011. Designed by the late Zaha Hadid, this futuristic building is now the home of Glasgow's Transport Museum – housed previously just a short stretch upriver in the Kelvin Hall.

DP139998

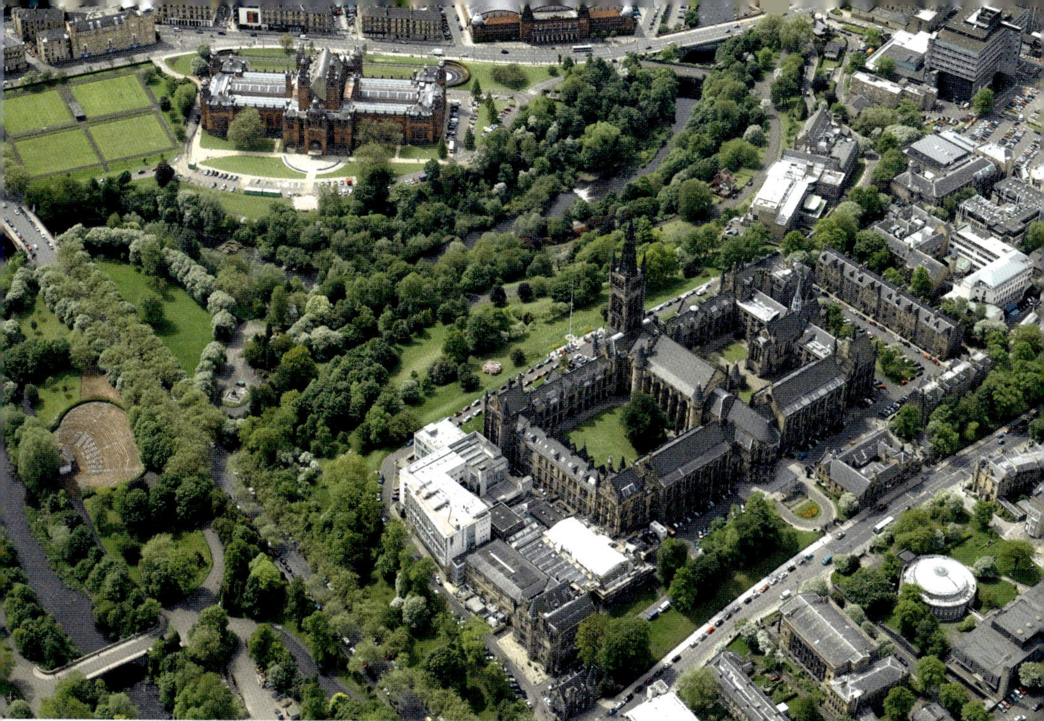

Glasgow University and Kelvingrove Art Gallery and Museum
Two Victorian icons face each other across the River Kelvin. Built
between 1866 and 1886, the colossal gothic edifice of Glasgow
University towers over Kelvingrove Art Gallery and Museum.
Kelvingrove emerged in 1901 as an enormous, carved baroque slab of
deep-red sandstone.
DP015695

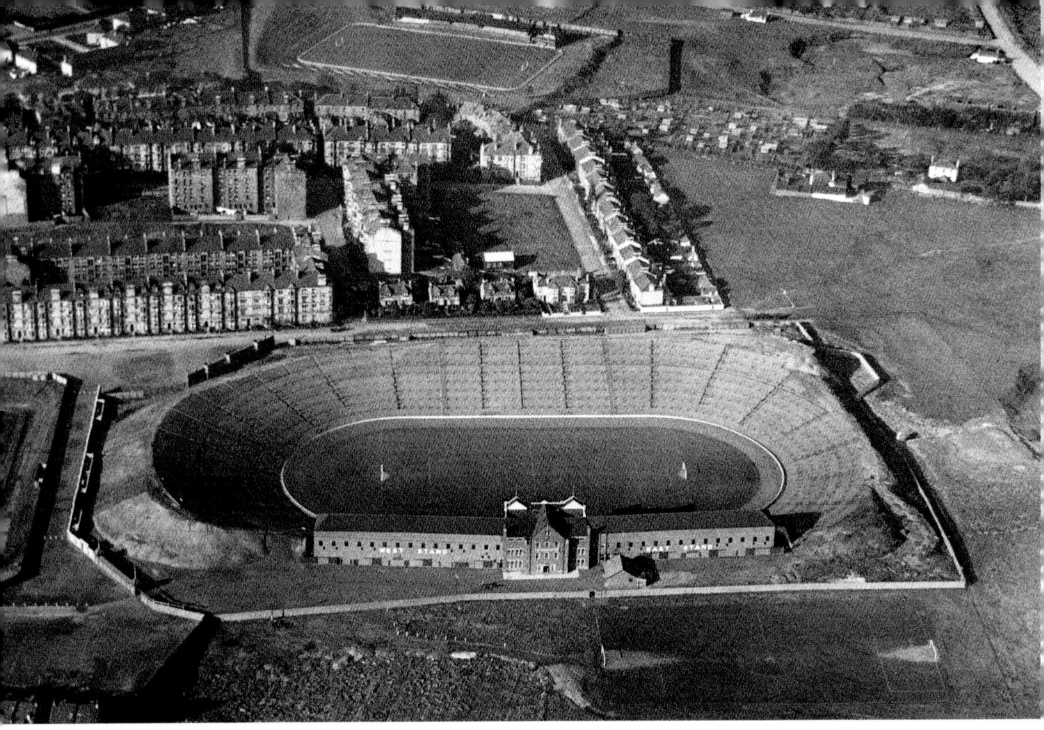

Hampden Park, Glasgow

Sitting proudly among the tenements and terraced housing of Mount Florida, Scotland's national football stadium of Hampden Park was once the largest in the world. It even still retains the European record for the highest attendance at a single game – a 149,415 turnout for Scotland against England in the 1937 British Home Championship. The wide, extensive terraces that allowed for such huge numbers have now disappeared. Safety requirements resulted in the reconstruction of Hampden, and, in 1999, it was reborn as a 52,000-capacity, all-seater stadium.

DP048143 (1927), DP009532

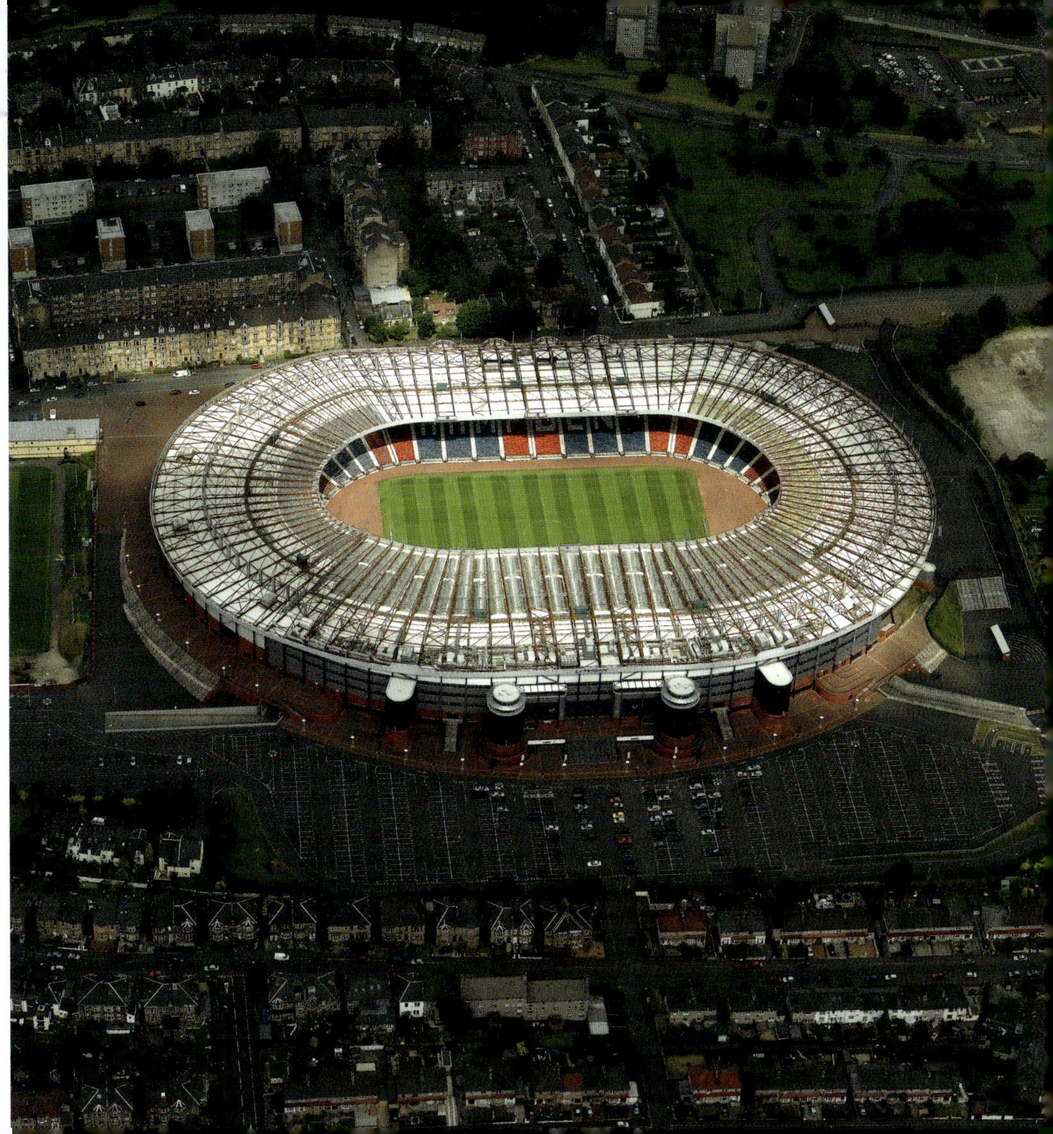

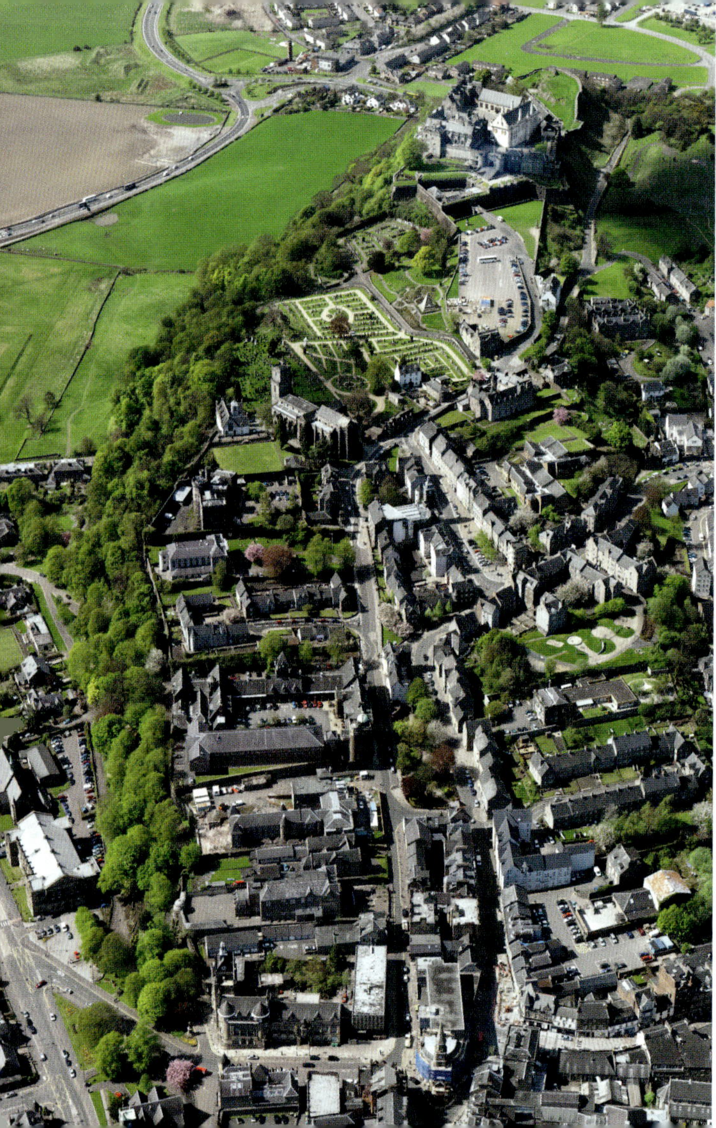

Stirling Castle

Besieged, sacked and rebuilt numerous times, Stirling Castle is a battle-scarred monument to a nation's history, a structure of fragmentary architecture ranging from Robert II's imposing North Gate – dating from 1381 – to the extensive Outer Defences, created in the 1700s to withstand the Jacobite Uprisings. The Town Wall – seen here as a thick line of trees – was strengthened considerably amid the turbulence of the late 1700s, 'for resisting our auld innimeis of Ingland' as the burgh fathers said in 1547. Built of giant whinstone boulders, the wall once continued its curve around the foot of the town, but over the centuries has been subsumed and replaced by modern growth.

DP079040

Wallace Monument, Stirling

The Wallace Monument was the dream of a Victorian society fascinated by the romantic exploits of ancient Scottish heroes, and eager to revive the architecture of gothic medievalism. The spot chosen for this monument was Abbey Craig, a volcanic mound rising above the Carse of Forth – and reputedly where William Wallace had camped to watch the English army gather in the floodplain before the Battle of Stirling Bridge in 1297.

DP078991

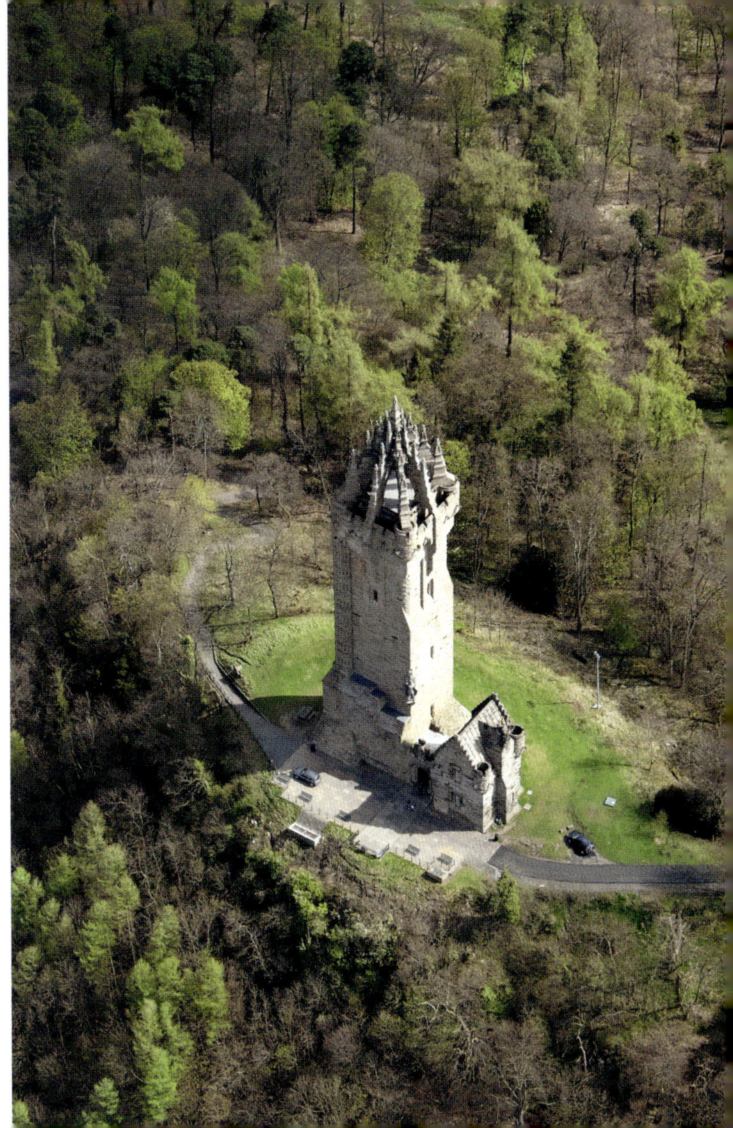

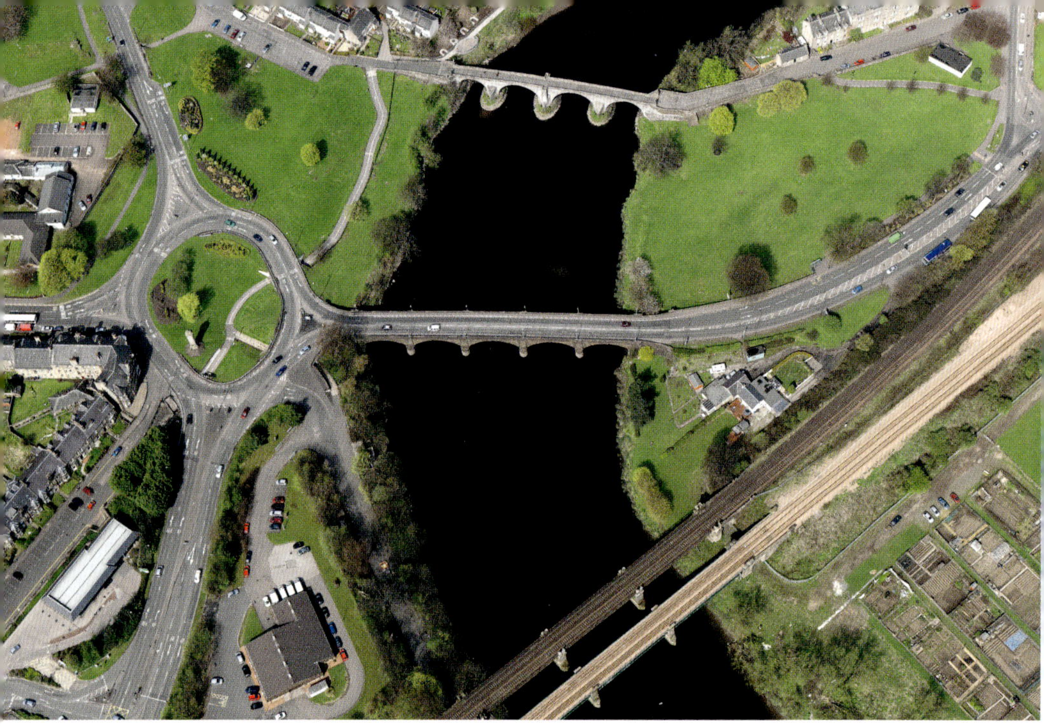

Old Bridge, New Bridge and Caledonian Railway Bridge, Stirling

Hundreds of years of history, progress and development are preserved in the bridges meeting at this meandering bend of the Forth. Although not the actual bridge on which William Wallace fought and defeated the English in 1297 – believed to have been a timber structure around a half-mile westwards at Kildean – the picturesque stone monument of Stirling's Old Bridge, dating to the 1400s, remains one of the nation's finest surviving medieval crossings. Stirling's New Bridge was completed in 1832 and, less than two decades later, came the transformative arrival of the railway.

DP079005

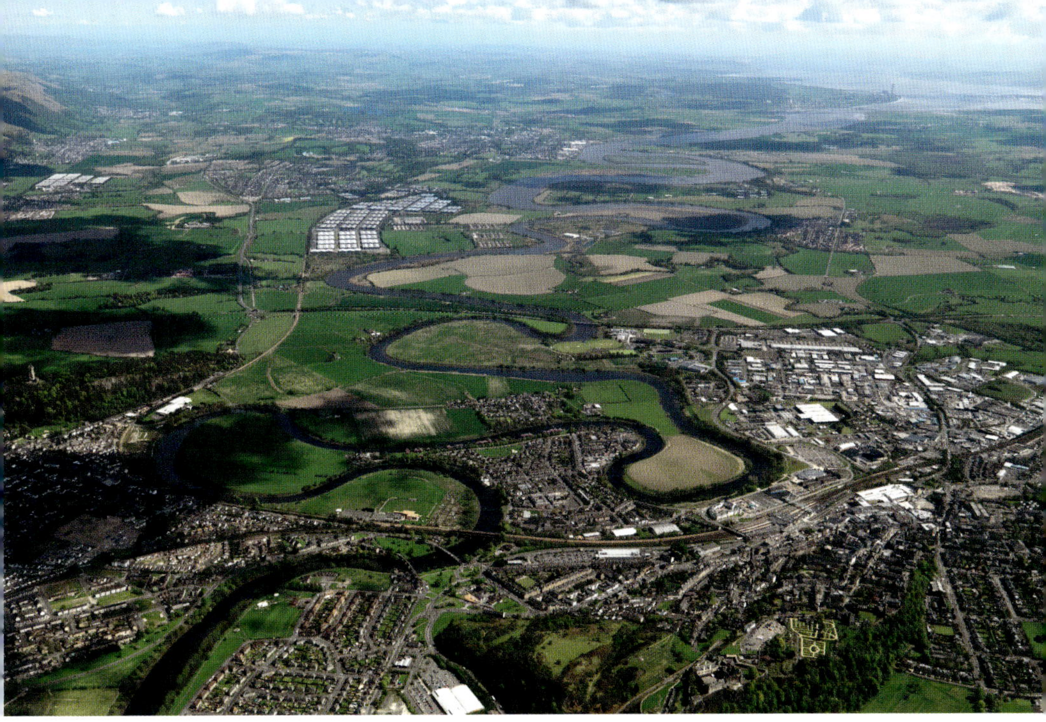

River Forth, Stirling

The carselands of the River Forth – the expanse of fertile land surrounding the river – are a remarkable landscape archive of environmental change and human activity. This whole area was inundated by the sea some 9,000 years ago. Around 7,000 years ago the waters receded, and the carse began to be covered in woodland and raised peat bog. From the mid 1700s, this floodplain was a focal point for the agricultural 'improvers', as the massive peat deposits were cleared to reach the fertile earth beneath. Today, the carse is one of the most productive agricultural landscapes in Scotland.

DP079016

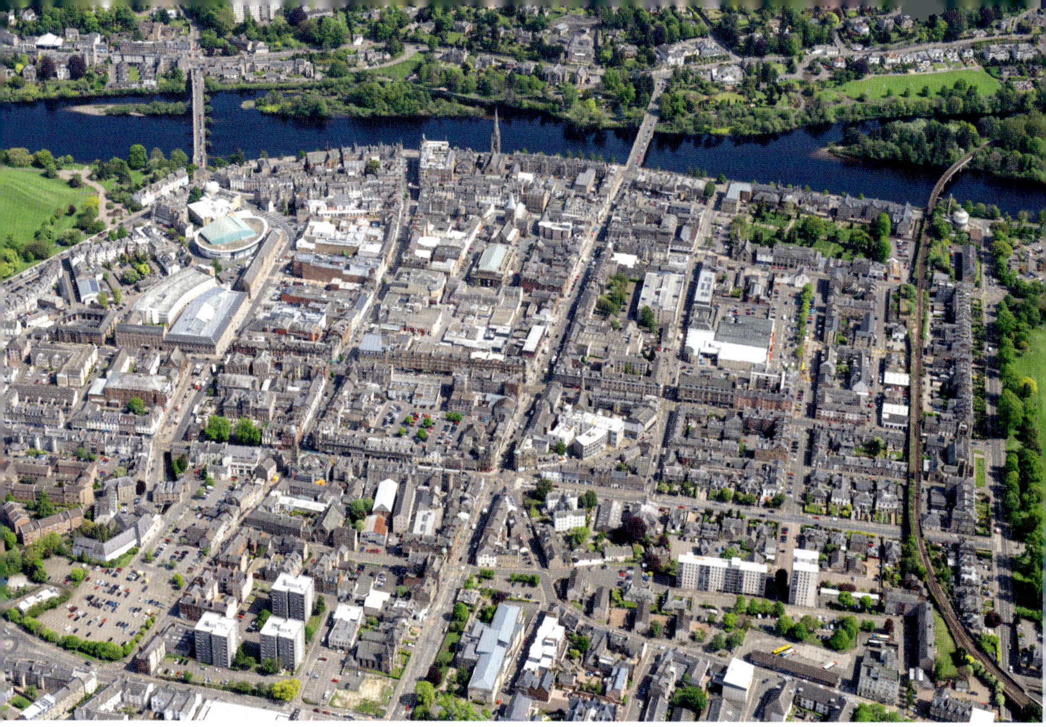

City Centre, Perth

Known as the 'Fair City', Perth is situated in the expansive Perthshire countryside on the banks of the River Tay. A former Royal Burgh, Perth has played a significant role throughout Scotland's history.

DP298726, DP228878

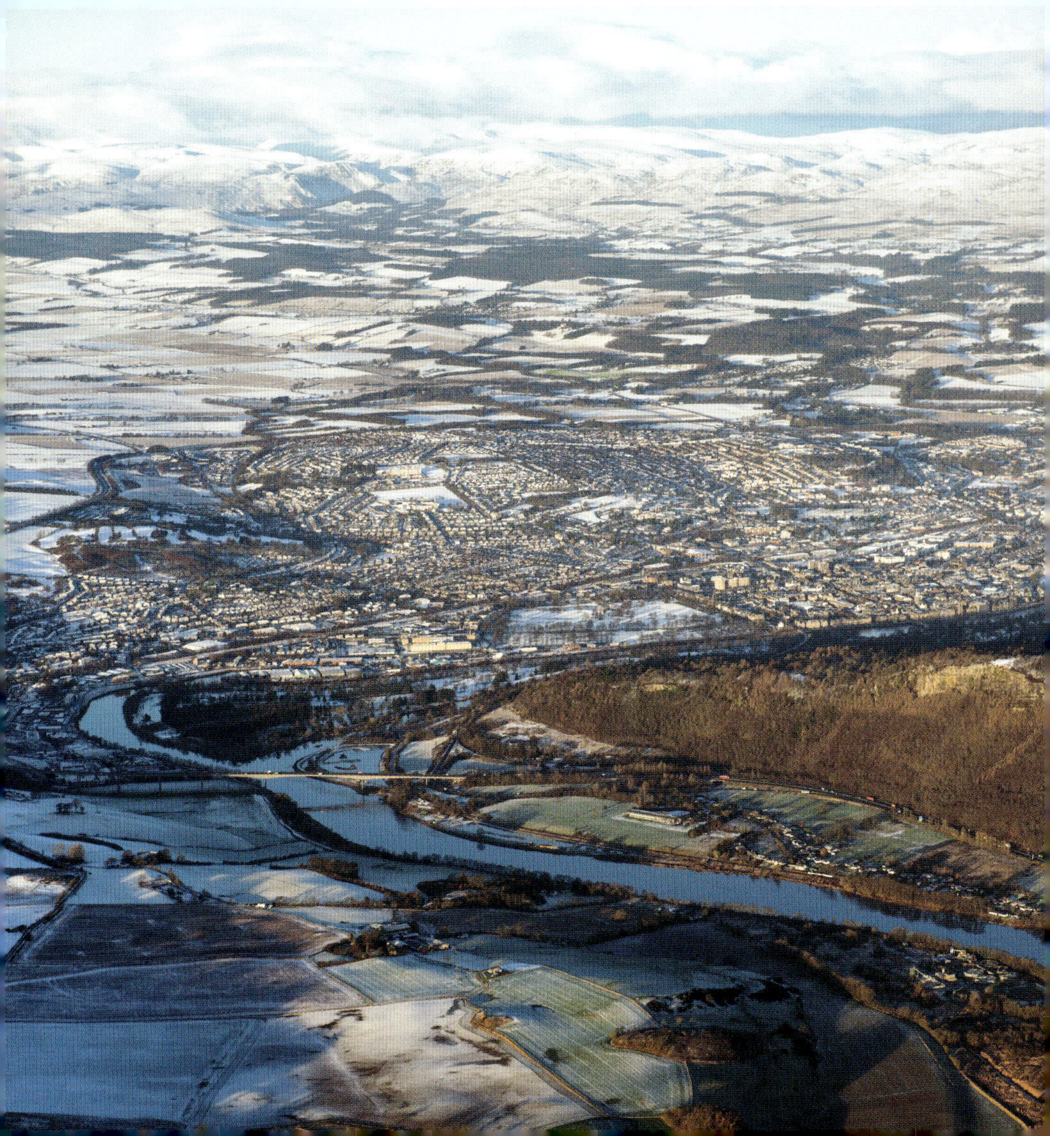

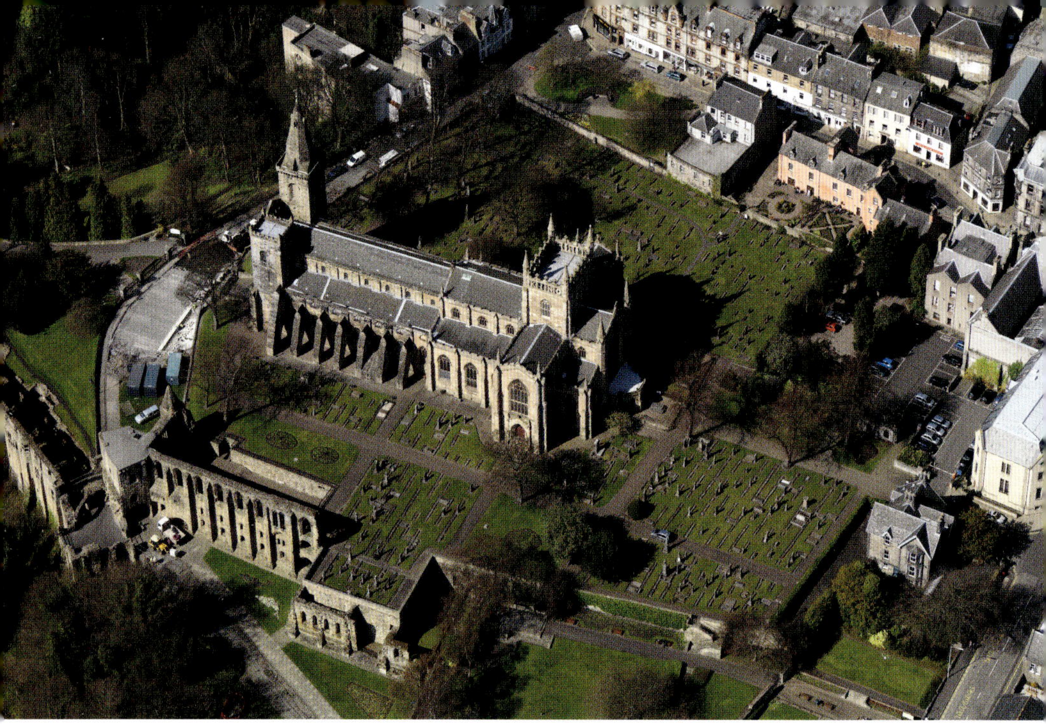

Dunfermline Abbey and Palace

After the marriage of Queen Margaret and David I in c1070, Margaret chose to commemorate the wedding, and its location, by founding the monastery which would become Dunfermline Abbey. Margaret was canonised in 1249 and her relics were held in the abbey, further reinforcing its importance. The abbey long continued to have royal connections – even after the Reformation, Anna of Denmark, wife of James VI, developed the abbey guesthouse into a luxurious palace. But once the royal couple moved to England in the early 1600s, the palace fell into disrepair.

DP043347

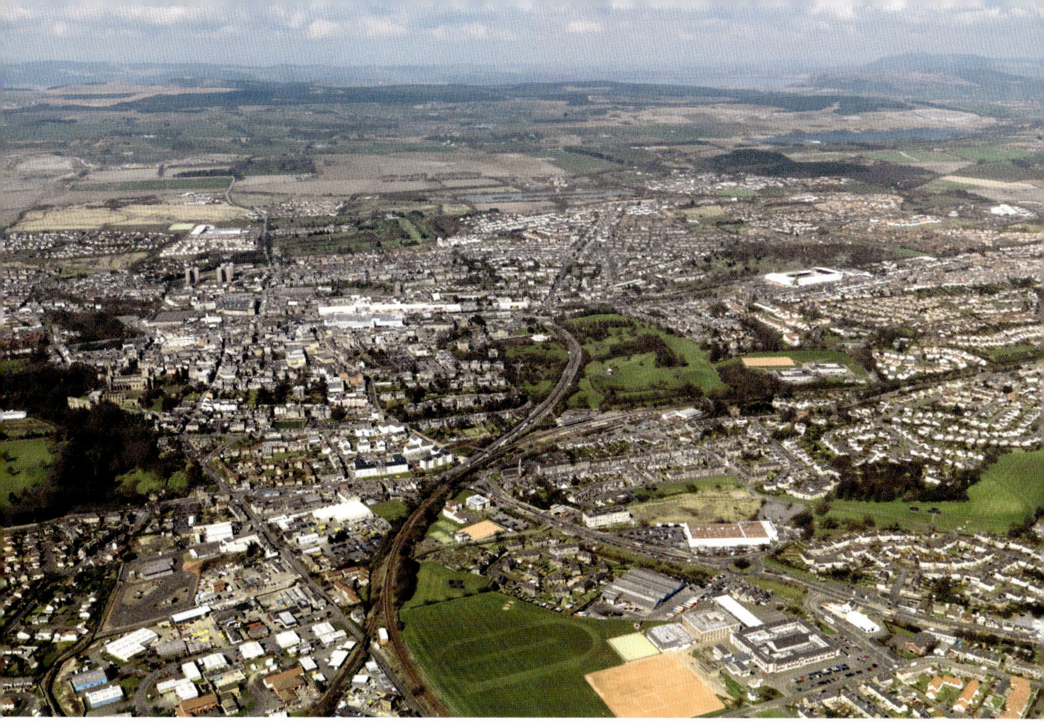

City Centre, Dunfermline

The new city of Dunfermline sweeps further and further across the landscape as residential developments continue to be grow. Yet the abbey remains, both as part of the modern city and as a legacy of royal and spiritual prestige.

DP043355

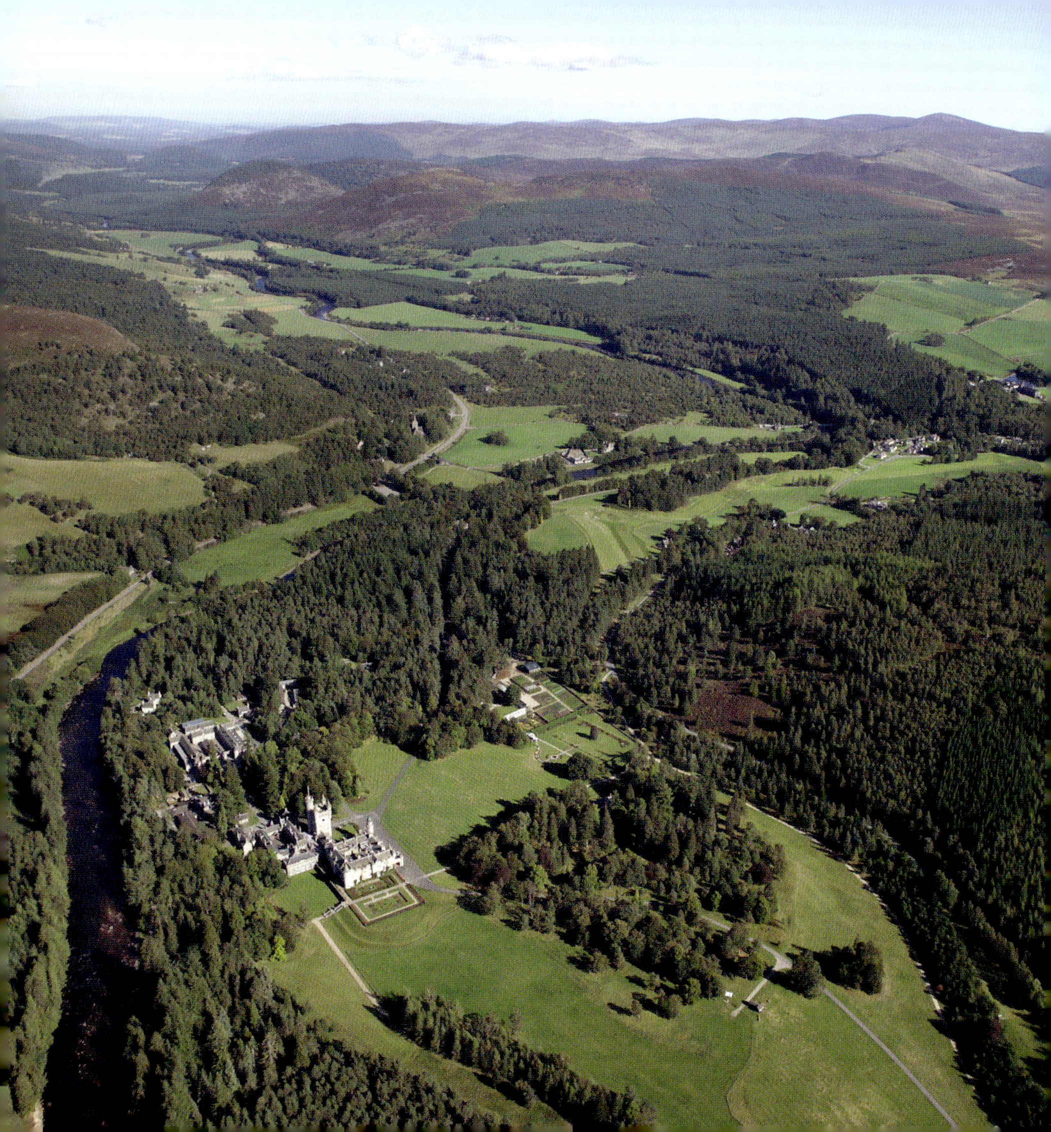

When Queen Victoria recounted in her 2 September 1869 entry for *More Leaves from the Journal of a Life in the Highlands* that 'this solitude, the romance and wild loveliness of everything here … all make beloved Scotland the proudest, finest country in the world', she was captivated by a romantic vision of Scotland. In the 1850s she and her husband Prince Albert had purchased the Balmoral Estate in Aberdeenshire, where they were able to shape part of the Highland landscape.

Literature played a role in creating the romantic picture that the royals found so appealing. The wild, mythical Scotland conjured up in the poems of Ossian, purportedly translated from Gaelic by James Macpherson, and the strong national image that was presented in the historical novels of Sir Walter Scott, created a far-reaching and enduring image of a rugged and romantic Scotland.

Today, Scotland's landscapes are iconic. Whether it is a high mountain peak, a royal estate, the depths of a loch or a beach on an uninhabited island, this is a country of contrasts to be explored.

Balmoral Castle, Aberdeenshire
Queen Victoria and Prince Albert transformed Balmoral into their principal residence in Scotland, with a new Scots Baronial castle at the heart of the grounds. This royal Highland estate popularised a romantic version of Scottishness.
DP020832

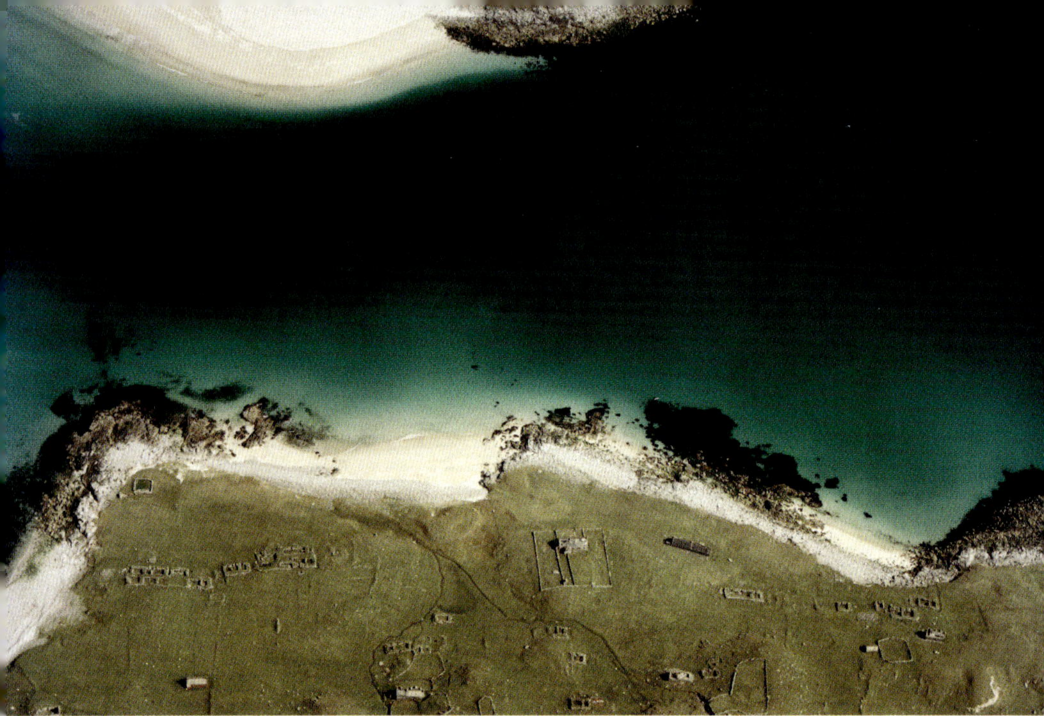

Scarp, Na h-Eileanan Siar

Two golden beaches face each other across a thin stretch of
aquamarine sea in the Western Isles. A favoured location for
settlement for thousands of years, the coastal fringe of Scarp
off the west coast of Harris was finally abandoned in the
middle of the 1100s.

SC1007626

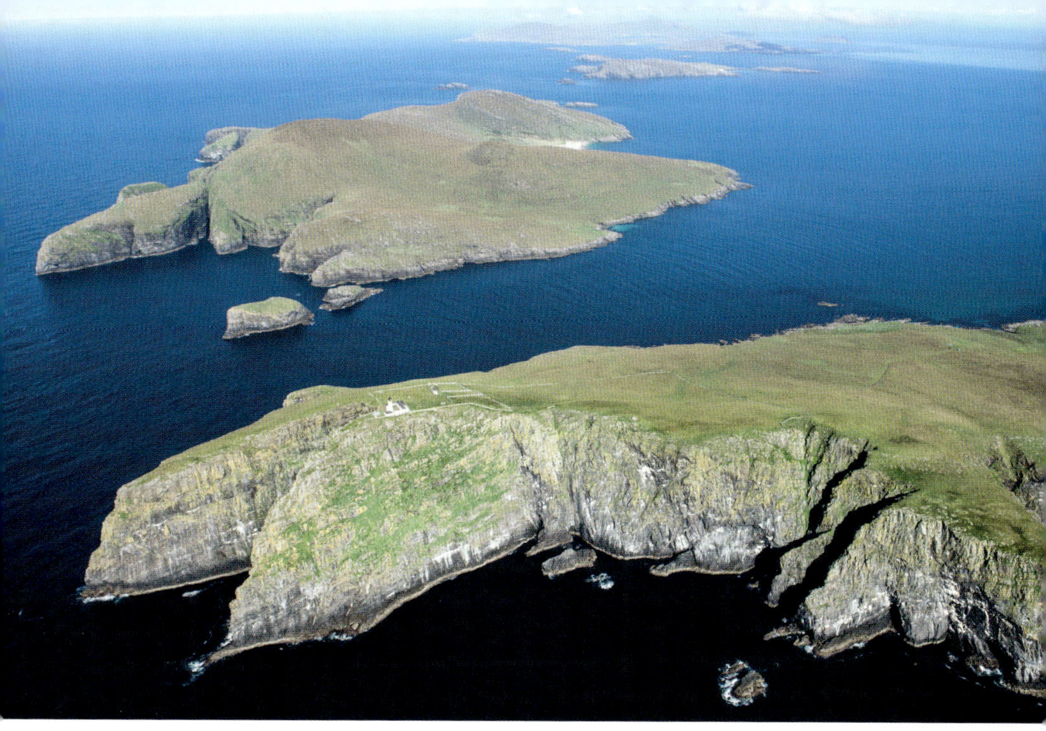

Berneray, Na h-Eileanan Siar

At the very edge of the Hebridean archipelago, the lighthouse of Barra Head on Berneray casts its light down from the cleaved rocks of the Sròn an Dùin promontory, out over the relentless surge of the Atlantic Ocean. Completed in 1833, Barra Head was the work of the renowned lighthouse designer and builder Robert Stevenson, grandfather of the famous writer Robert Louis Stevenson.

SC1056455

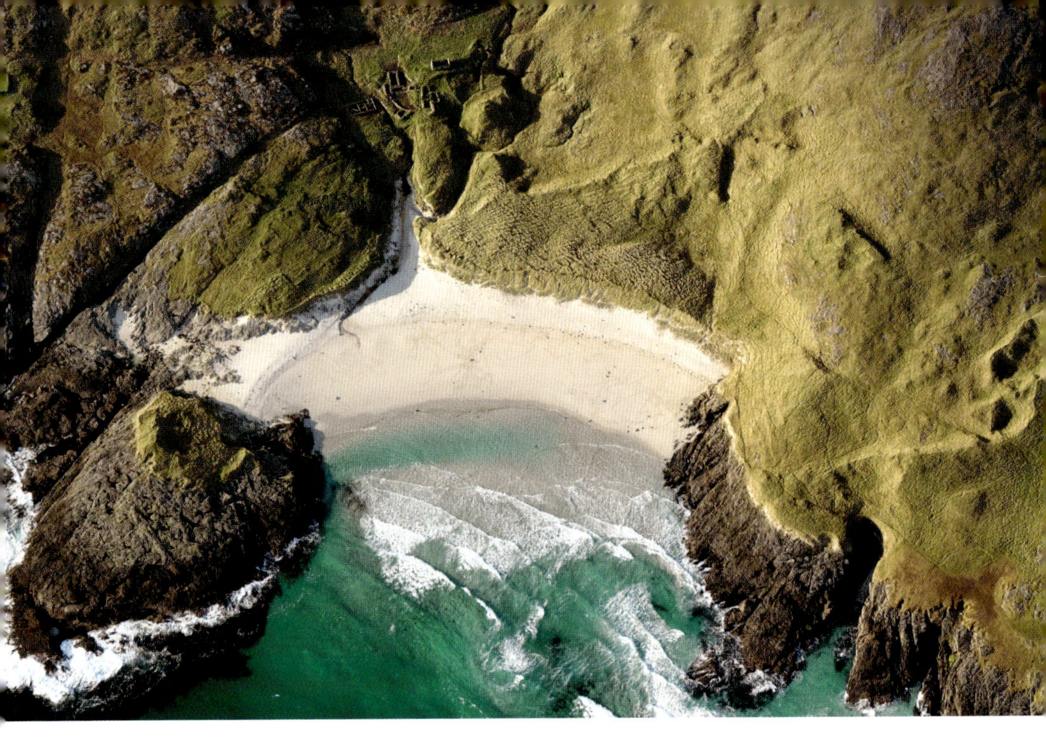

Pabbay, Na h-Eileanan Siar

A tiny cluster of roofless, ruined buildings sits at the head of Bagh Ban on the now uninhabited island of Pabbay. The winding tracks on the beach were not left by humans, but by a herd of seals that has colonised this bay.

DP109553

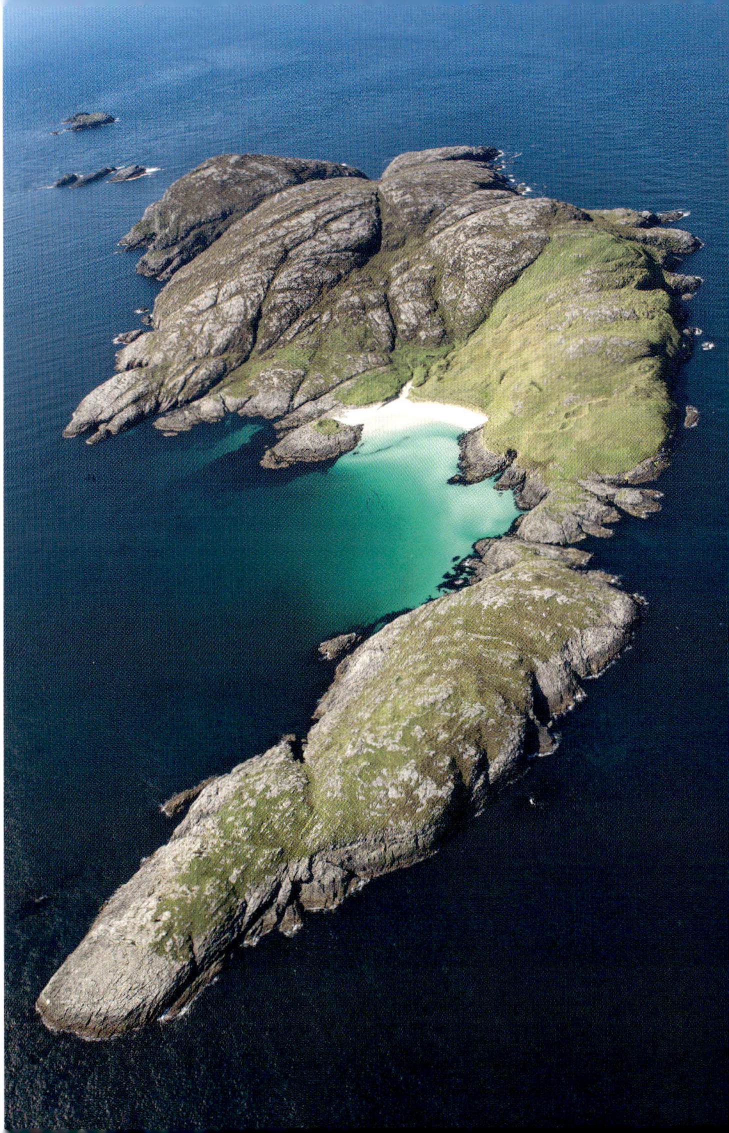

Pabbay, Na h-Eileanan Siar

One of the southernmost of the Western Isles, Pabbay measures just 3km by 1.6km. Despite its small scale, the island community had a chapel above the bay – now ruined – where a carved Pictish symbol stone was uncovered nearby.

DP221959

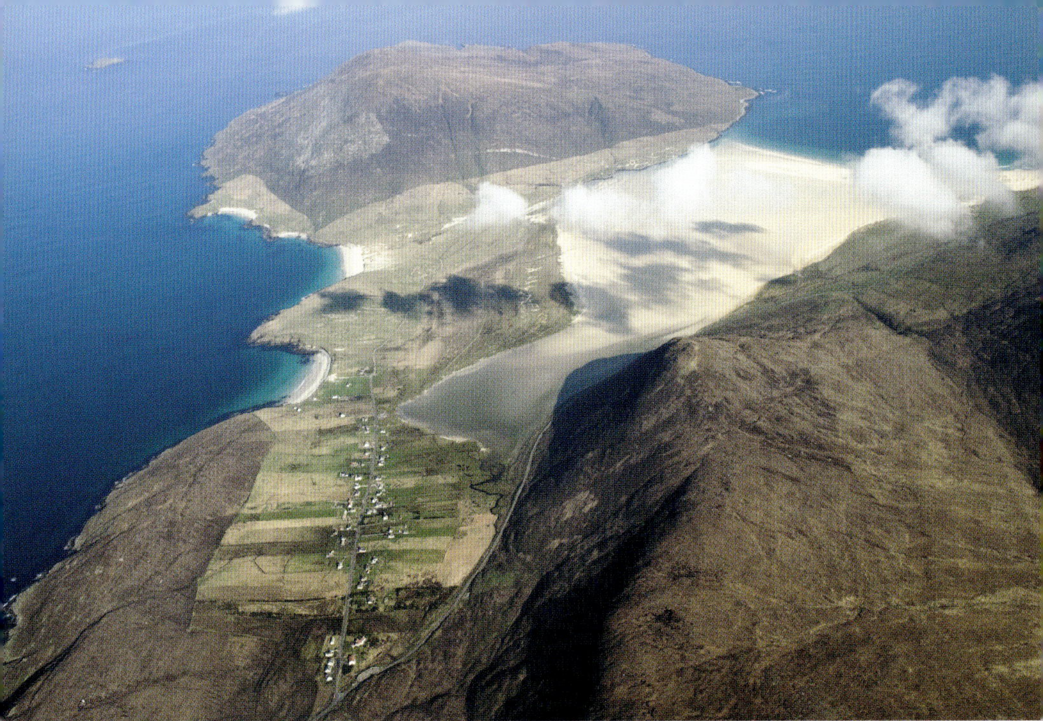

Northton, Harris, Na h-Eileanan Siar
The narrow spine of a crofting community clings to the ancient
landscape of Northton at the southern end of Harris.
DP011860

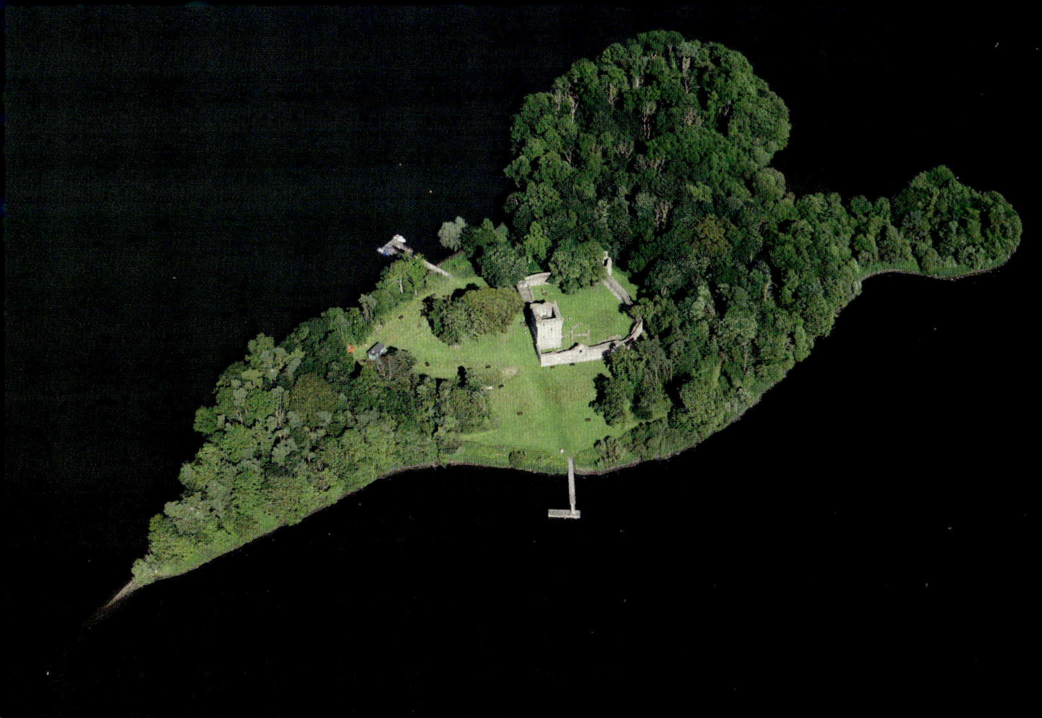

Lochleven Castle, Perth and Kinross

Lochleven Castle is famed as the prison of Mary, Queen of Scots. She was held in the castle from June 1567 until her escape in May 1568, and during these months she was forced to abdicate, passing the Crown to her infant son James VI. When Mary fled to England later that year, she was held captive once again and never returned to Scotland. After nearly 20 years as a prisoner in England on the instructions of her cousin Elizabeth I, she was executed in 1587.

DP019096

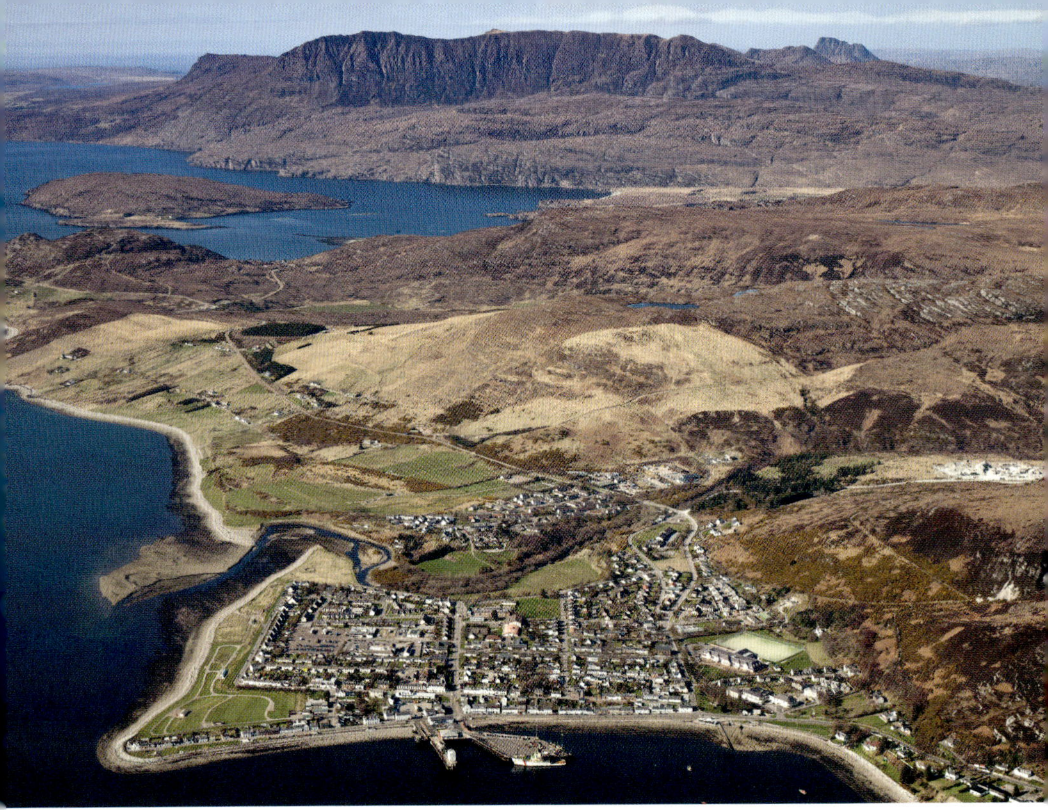

Ullapool, Highlands

Chosen as the site for a fishing village by the British Fisheries Society, construction of Ullapool began in 1788. The geometric grid of Ullapool's planned streets contrasts with the Highland landscape, rigid lines set against the curving banks of Loch Broom and the uneven heights of Ben More Coigach in the distance.

DP024758

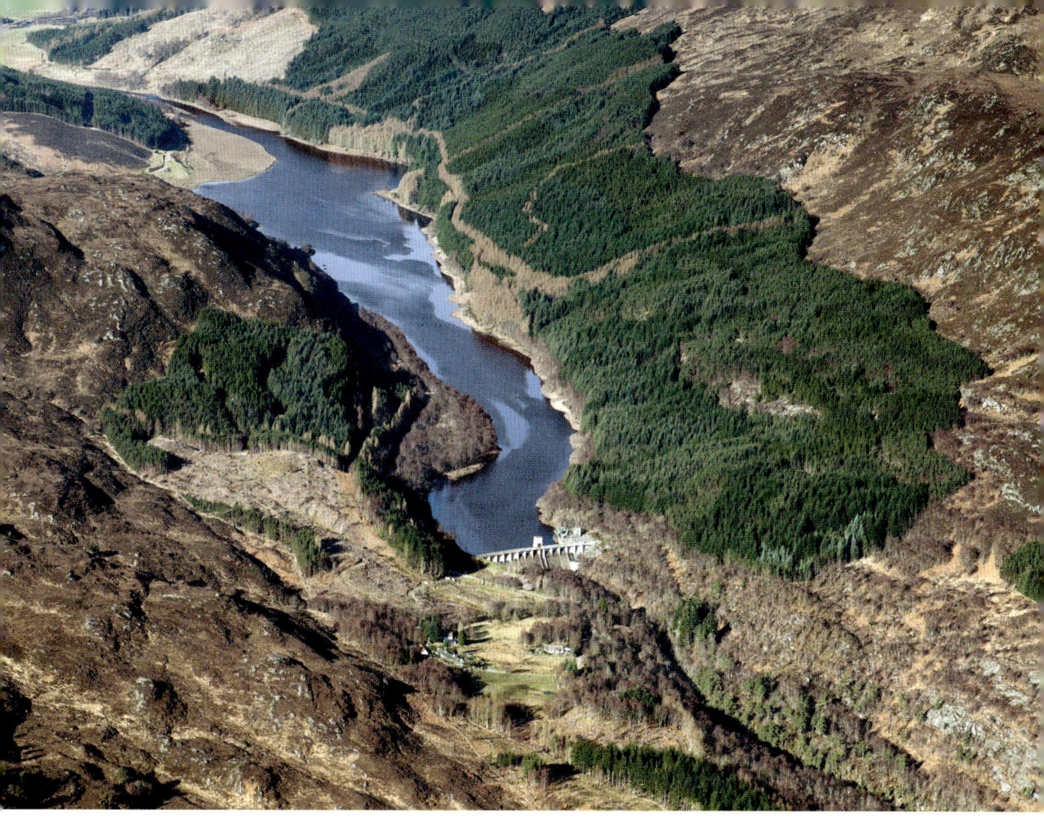

Loch Meig, Highlands

In the immediate post-war period the government aimed for
self-sufficiency, looking to substantially increase tree coverage
and farmland, and flooding entire valleys for hydroelectricity. As
part of these efforts, the construction of a massive concrete dam
systematically transformed the River Meig into Loch Meig.
DP024941

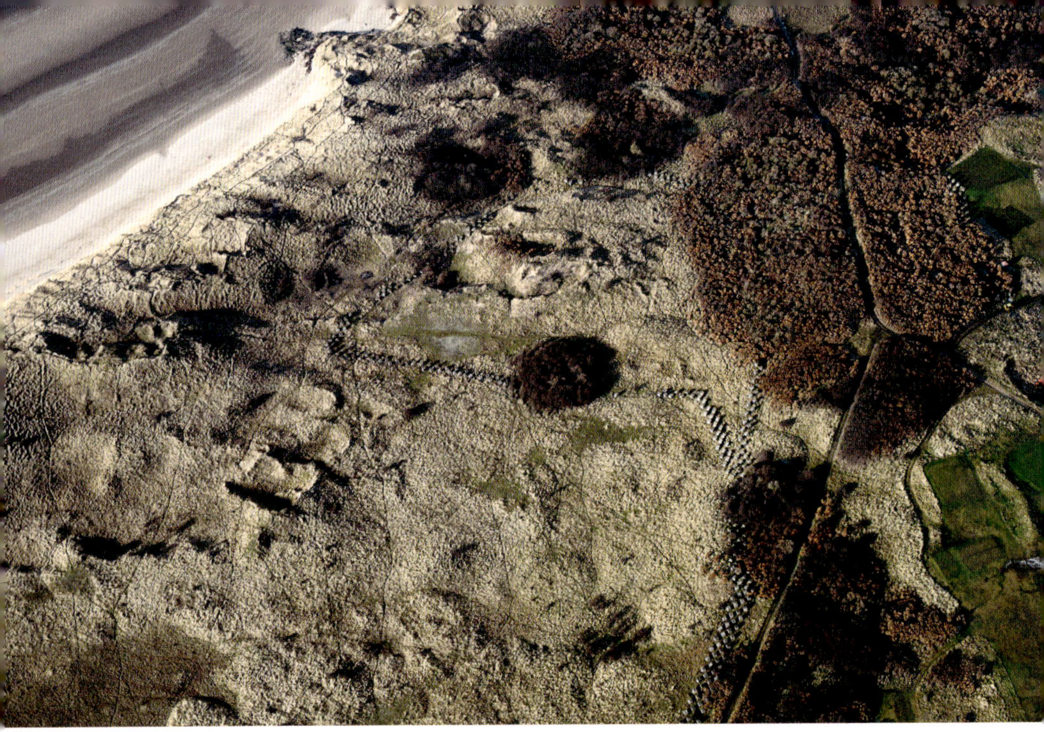

Gullane Sands, East Lothian

Anti-tank blocks form a loop in single, double and triple rows beside Gullane Sands. Now a defensive relic, these square concrete blocks are a stark legacy of the twentieth century on the coastline.

DP054857

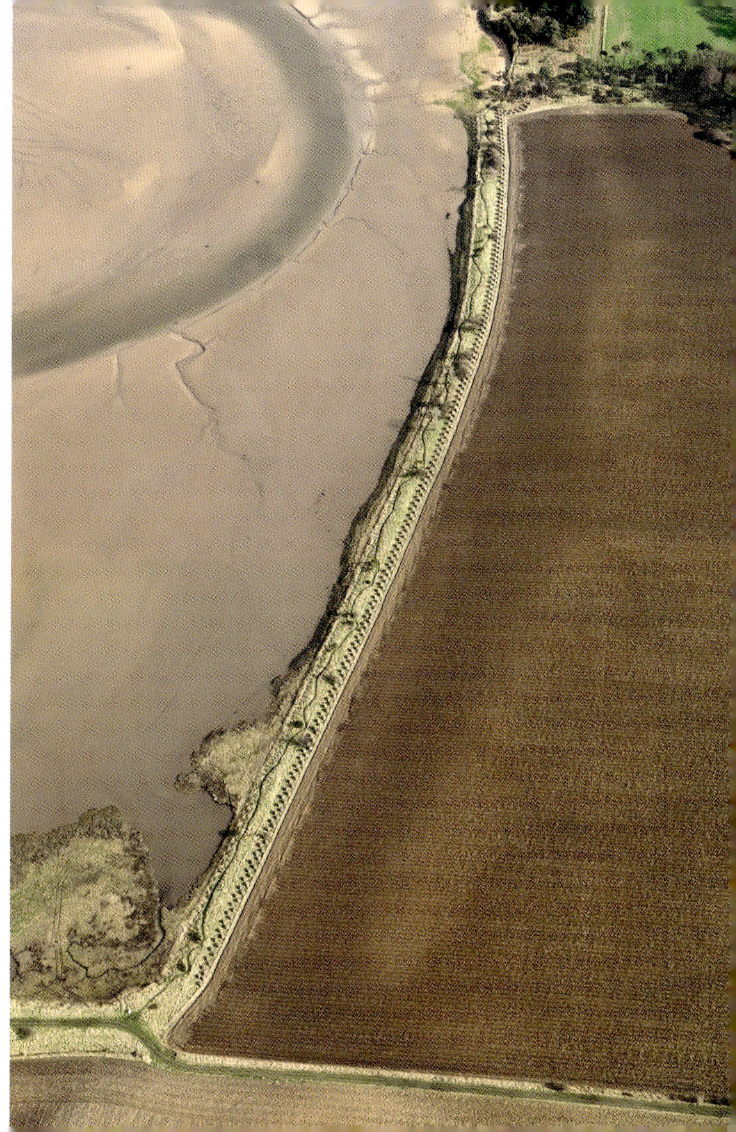

Hedderwick, East Lothian

A regimented double line of anti-tank blocks looks out across the Tyne estuary. Each cast concrete block is 1.5m in height, a weighty presence on the landscapes many decades after the final days of the Second World War.

DP058339

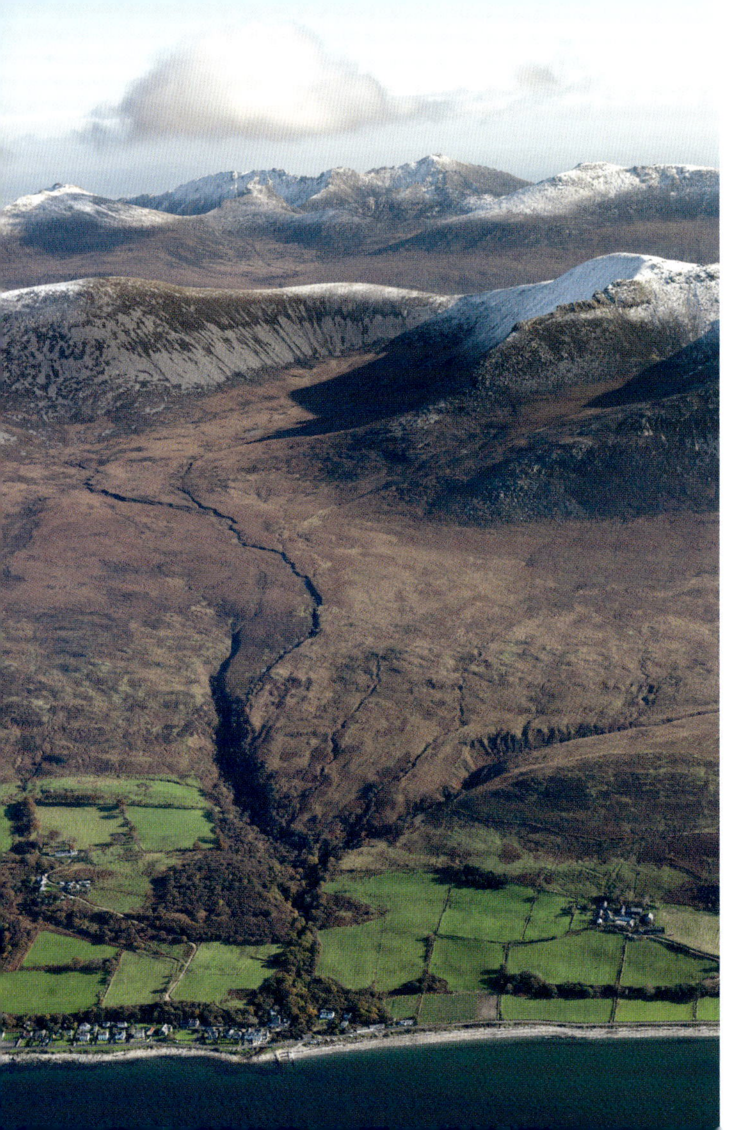

Arran, Ayrshire
A village was established on the north-west of Arran in the 1700s by cotton traders, with the fast flowing stream descending the Beinn Bharrain mountainside used to power a pirn mill – a mill which harvested the woodlands to make bobbins. In 1840, with the supply of trees exhausted, the mill was closed. Yet the village – still known as Pirnmill – has remained, stretching along this secluded stretch of Arran's coastline.
DP056902

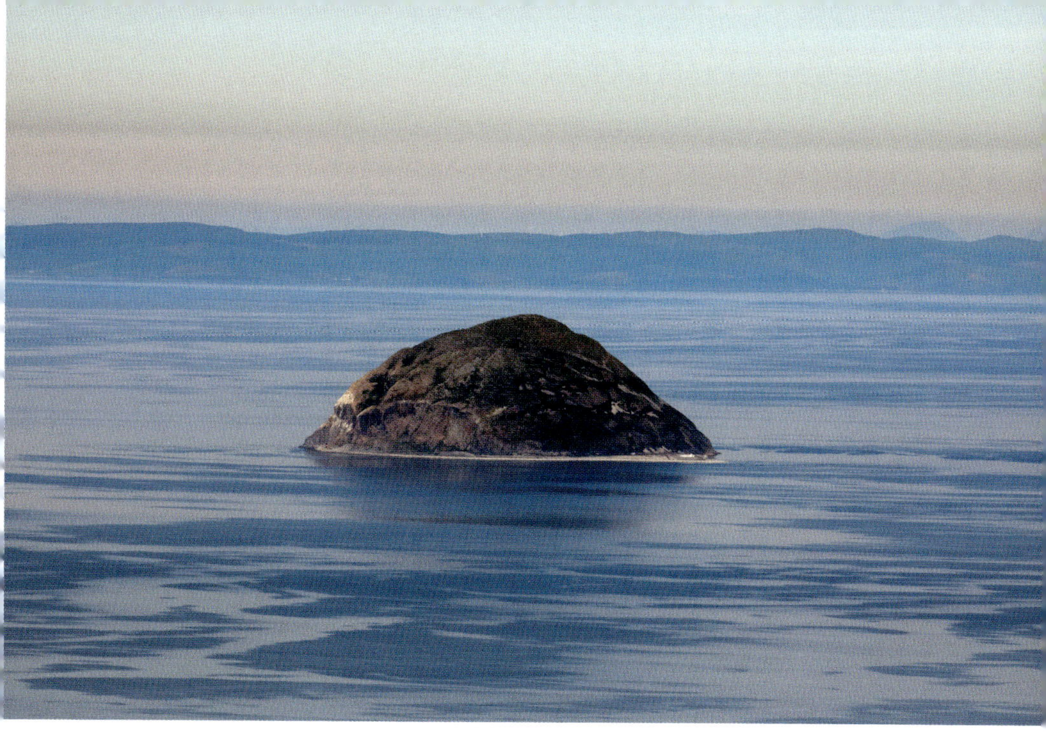

Ailsa Craig, Ayrshire

The recognisable form of Ailsa Craig emerges from the Firth of Clyde. Although the rocky island is inhabited only by wildlife today, the castle and automated lighthouse are a reminder of the reach of human influence.

DP279449

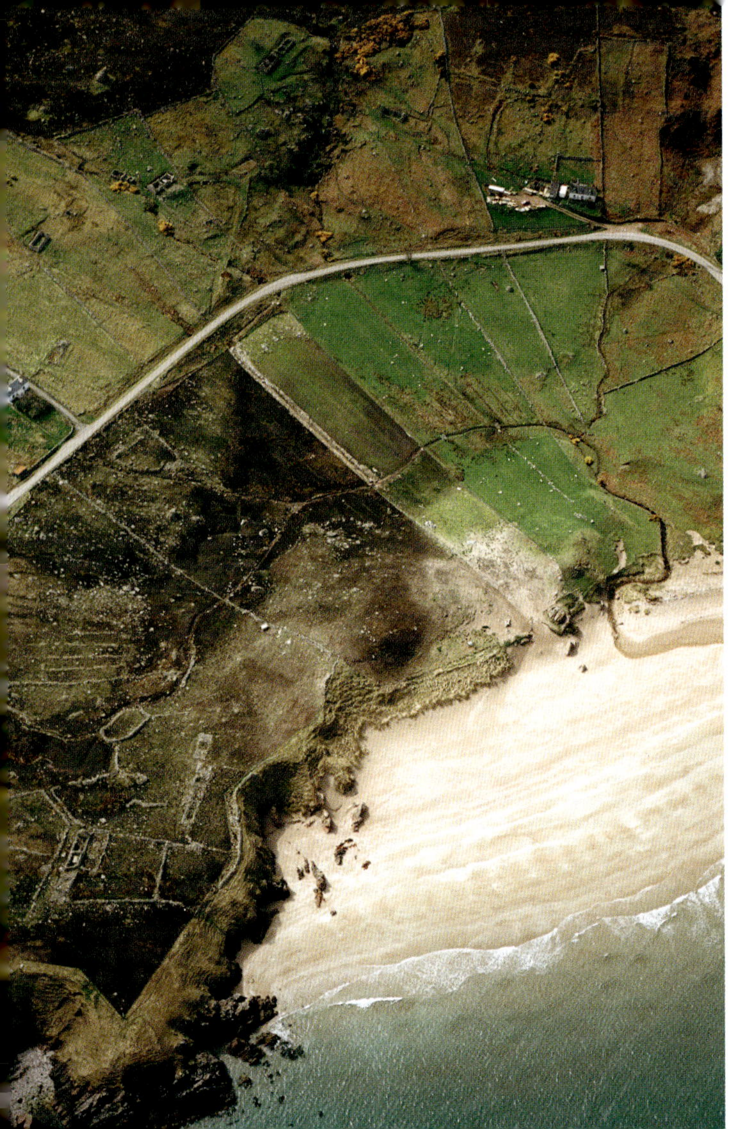

Sangobeg, Highlands
Across parts of highland Scotland a barren interior has concentrated settlement onto the coast. Here at Sangobeg, near Durness, thin crofting strips overlie the remains of earlier farms.
SC1138548

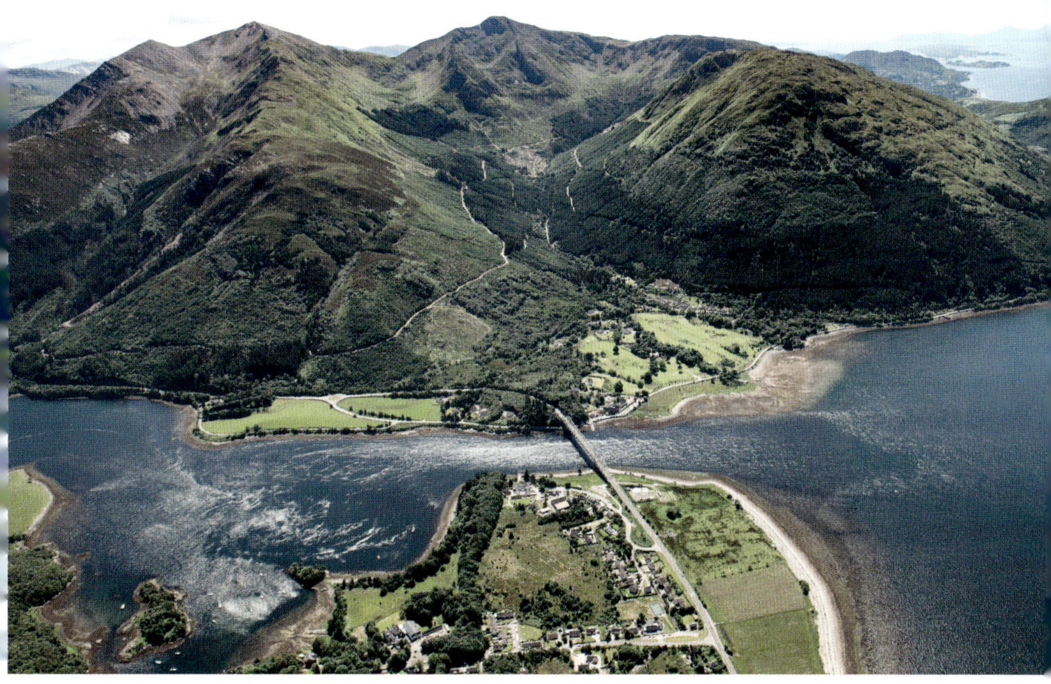

Ballachulish Bridge, Highlands

The modern A82 – passing through the high plateau of Rannoch
Moor and then dropping down through Glencoe to sea level at
Ballachulish – follows almost exactly the route laid down by engineer
Thomas Telford at the beginning of the 1800s. Telford, in turn, had
used portions of the old military roads built in the mid 1700s. The
bridge at Ballachulish is a relatively recent addition, completed in 1975
to replace the ferry crossing.

DP193658

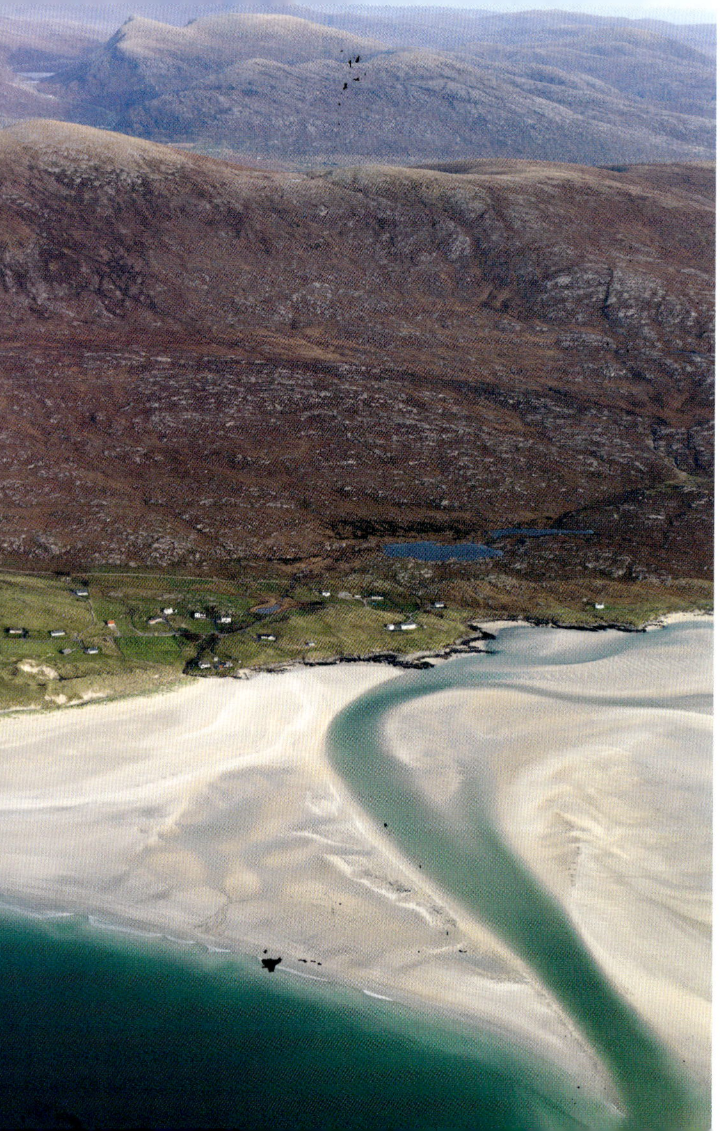

Luskentyre, Harris, Na h-Eileanan Siar

The white sands at the foot of Beinn Losgaintir are overlooked not only by the residents of Luskentyre, but by the remains of past settlements, field boundaries and agriculture.
DP110503

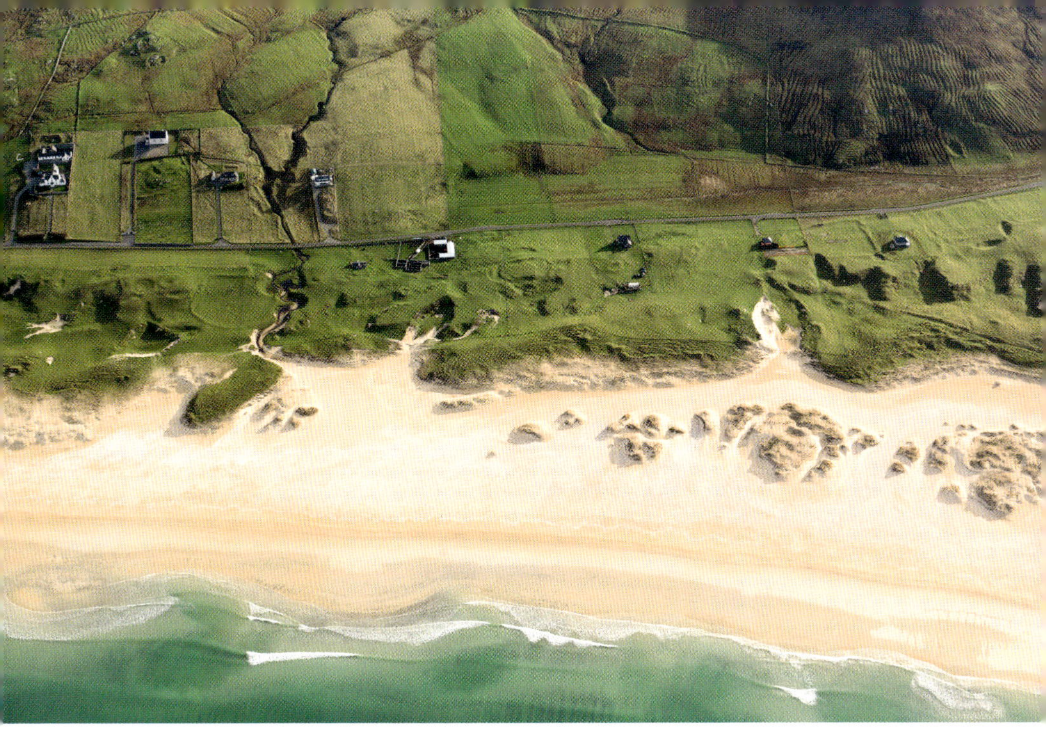

Scarastavore and Scarastabeg, Harris, Na h-Eileanan Siar
Running indiscriminately beneath new boundaries laid out by modern
farms and houses are the ditches, lines, humps and bumps left behind by
the old crofting townships of Scarastabeg and Scarastavore.
DP110509

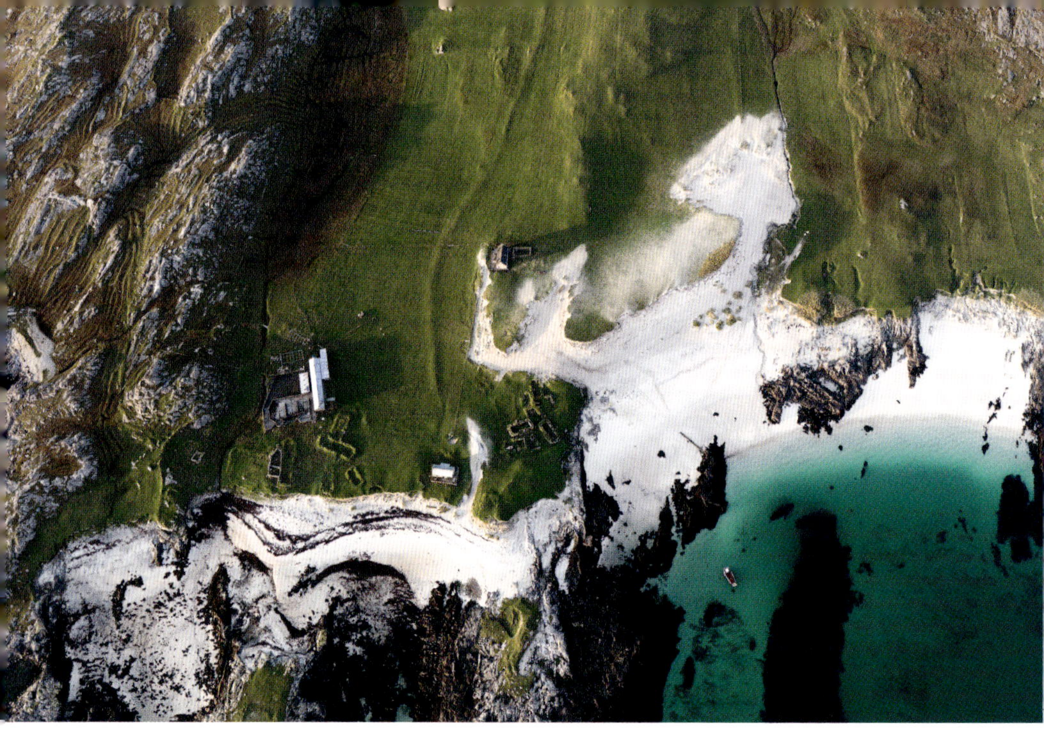

Paibeil, Taransay, Na h-Eileanan Siar

Paibeil was one of three villages on the island of Taransay,
which lies in close proximity to its larger island neighbour,
Harris. Taransay was first inhabited at least as early as AD 300,
but the whole population left in 1947. Although a handful of
families returned, by 1974 it was abandoned once again.
DP110668

**Raah, Taransay, Na
h-Eileanan Siar**
Along the coastline from
Paibeil are the remains of
Raah, another Taransay
township, surrounded
by traces of farming and
agriculture.
DP110667

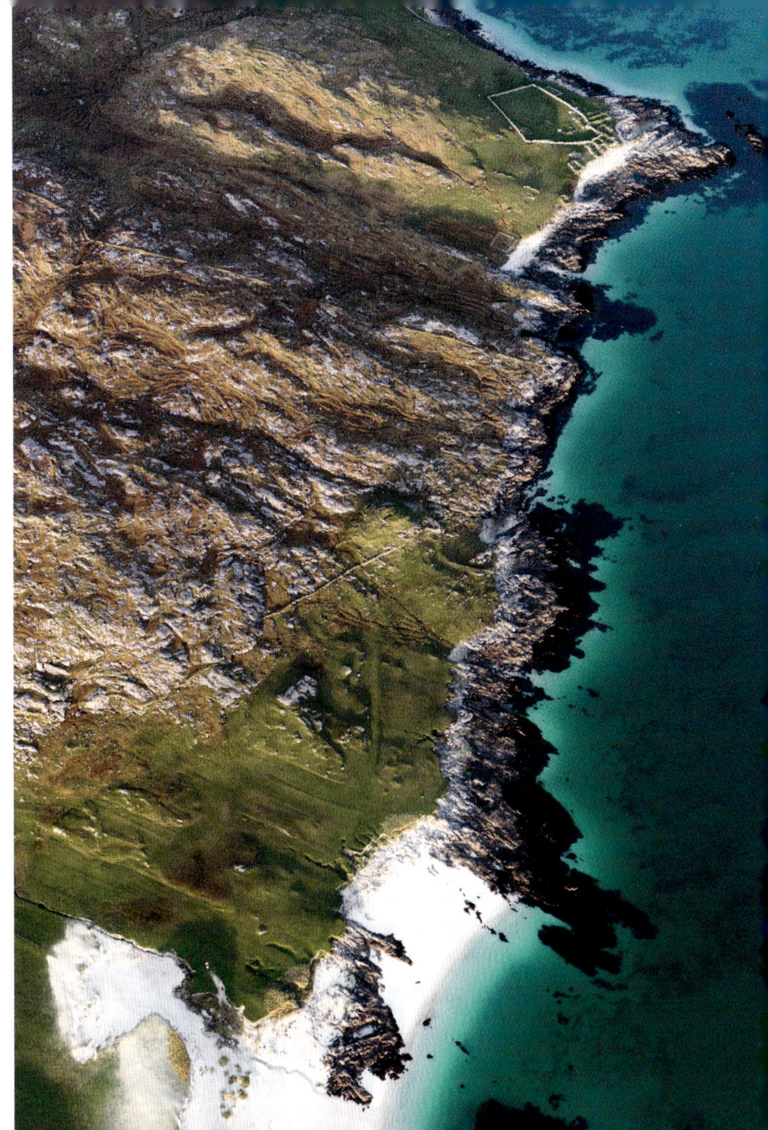

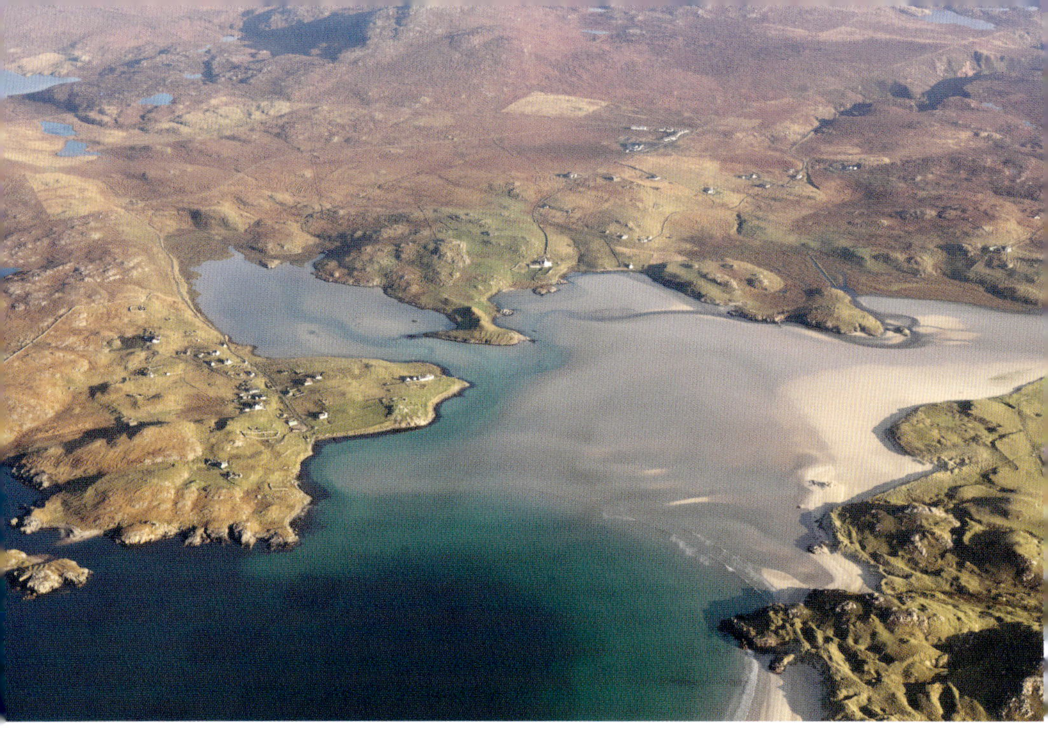

Traigh Uige, Lewis, Na h-Eileanan Siar

In 1831 a remarkable discovery was made in the sand dunes at Traigh Uige, to the right of this photograph – it was here that the Lewis chess pieces were uncovered. Believed to be of Scandinavian origin and dating to around the 1200s, these charismatic and beautifully carved characters provide an immediate connection to the past.
DP110825

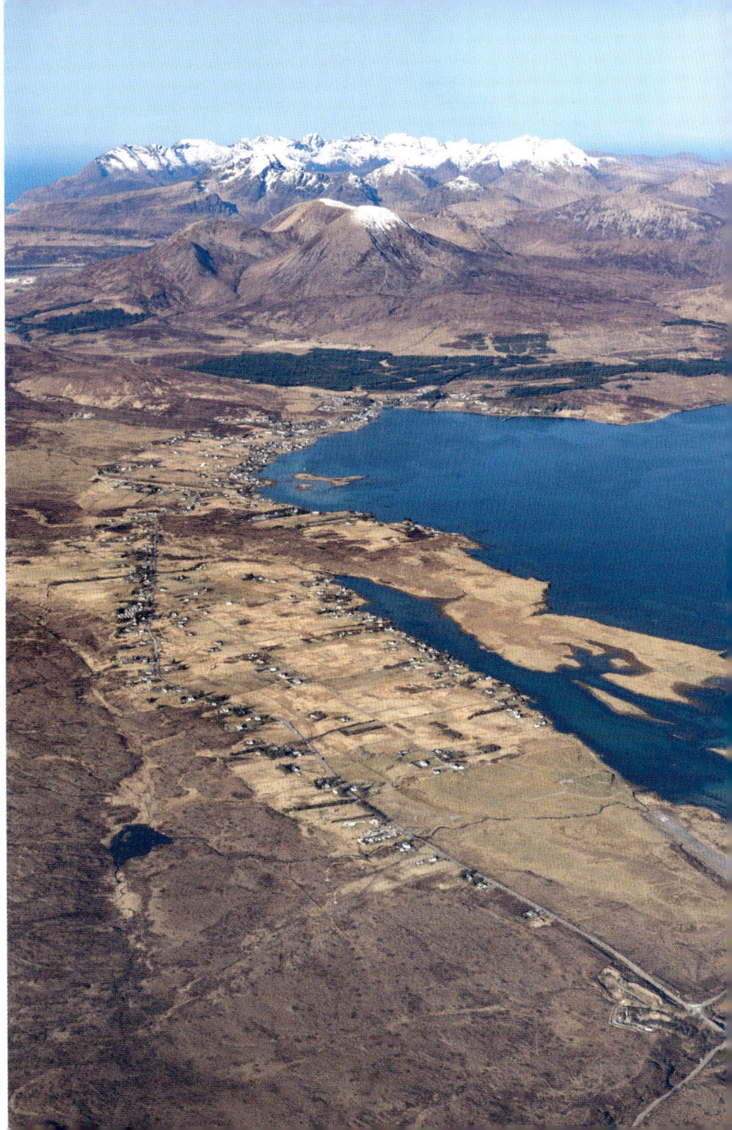

Cuillin Mountains, Skye, Highlands

Directly west of the flat coastal settlement of Broadford, the landscape of Skye rears up into the tightly packed, sharp-peaked ridges of the Cuillin Mountains.

DP156356

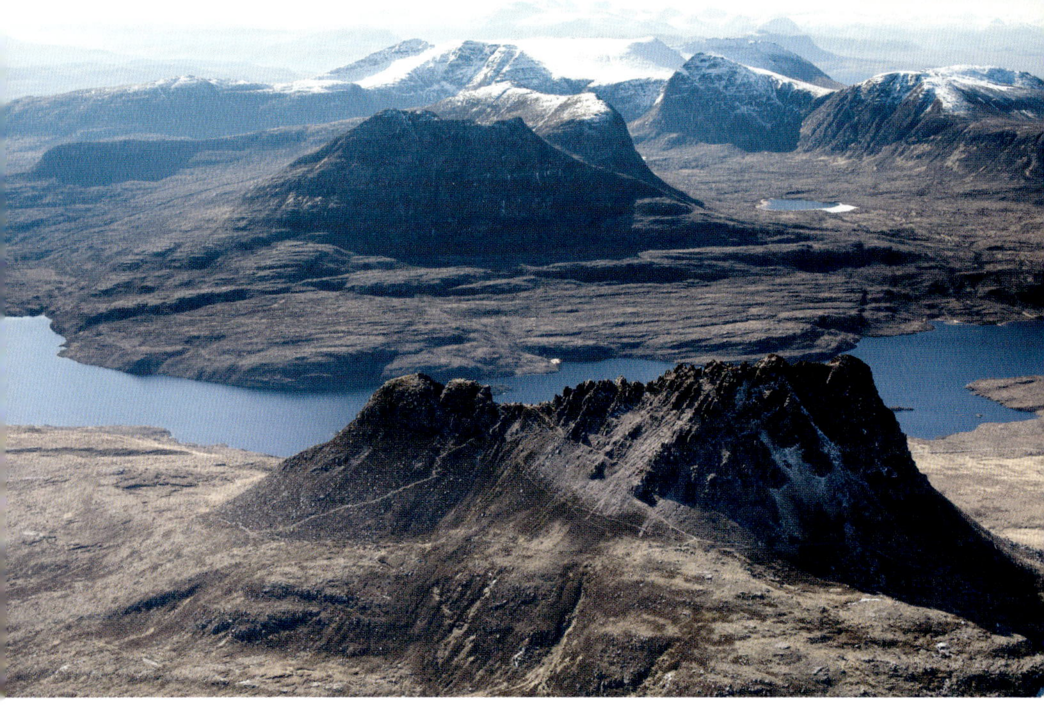

Stac Pollaidh, Highlands

Despite standing at a height of only 612 metres, Stac Pollaidh's popular
summit can only be reached by scrambling through and over rocky
pinnacles along its castellated Torridonian sandstone crest.

DP156594, DP156637

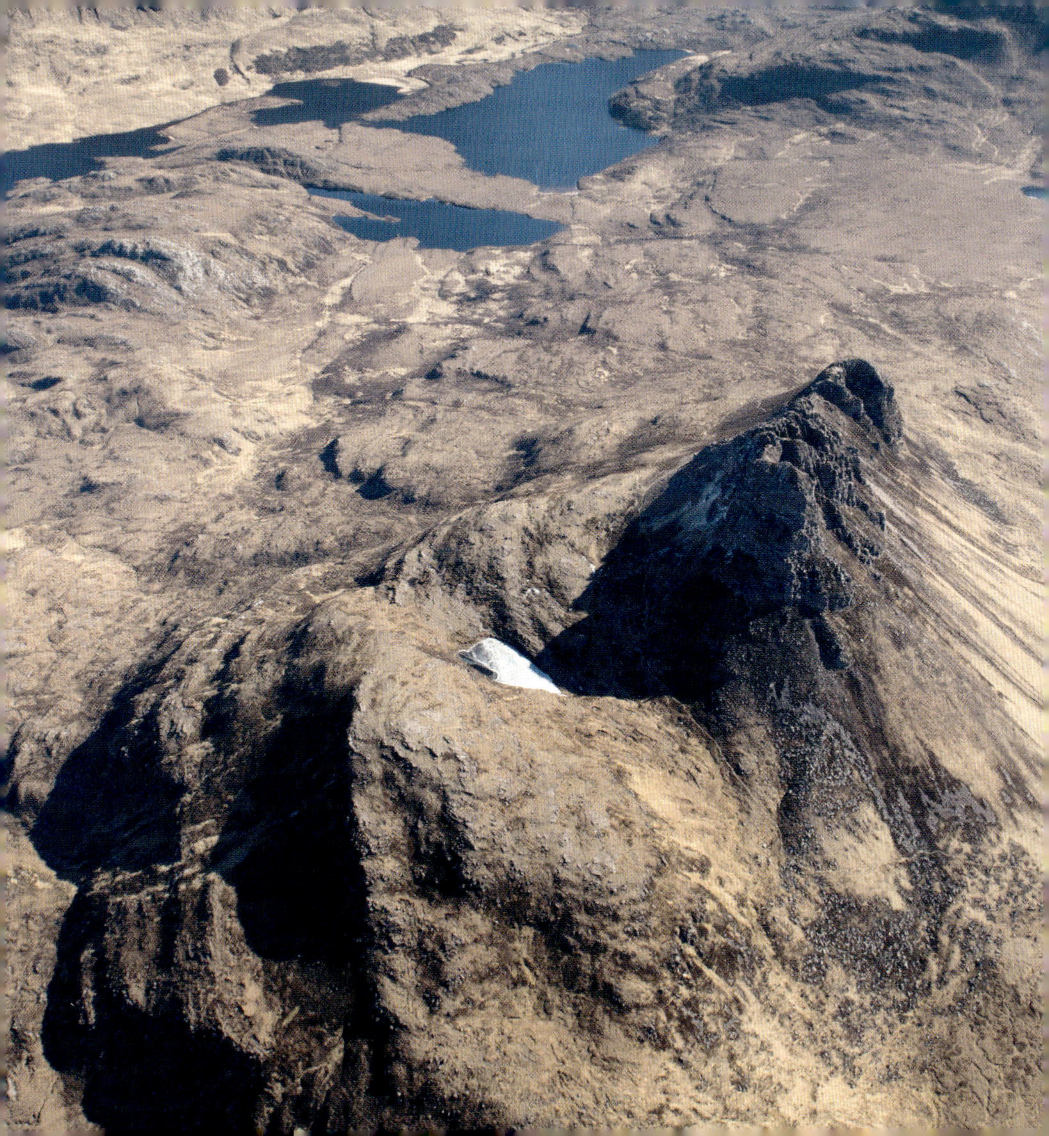

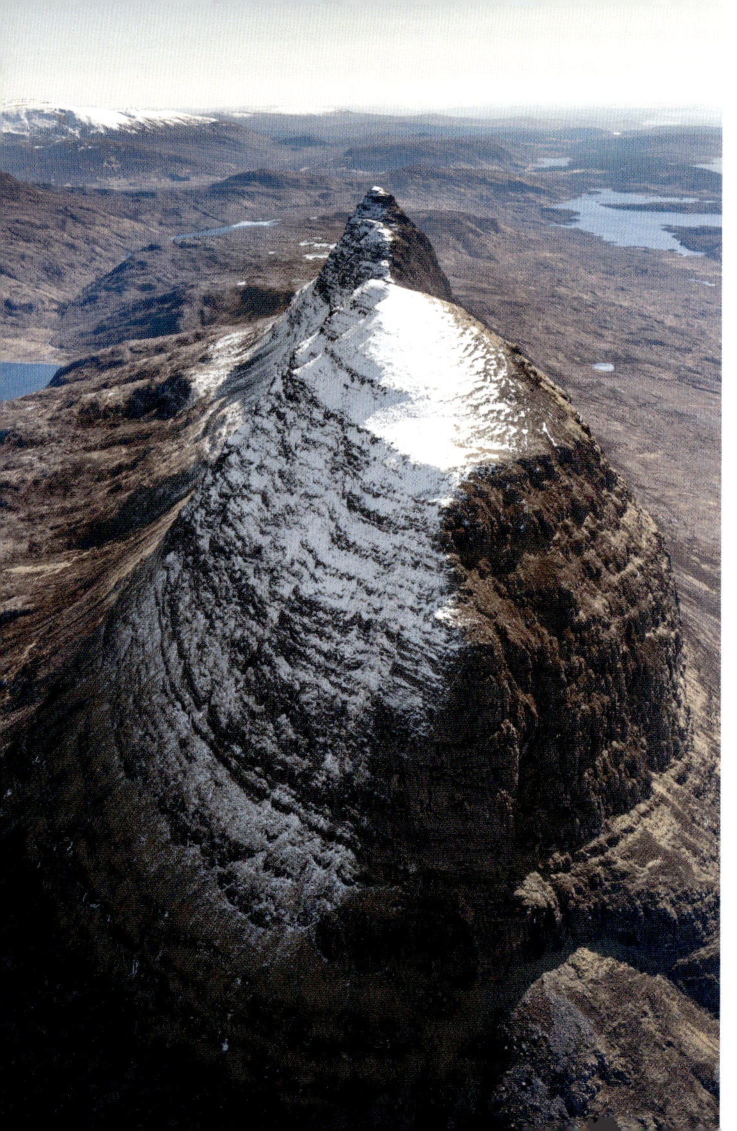

Suilven, Highlands
The ridged peak of Suilven emerges out of the rocky landscape. When the naturalist Thomas Pennant travelled through Assynt in 1772, his response was a kind of awed horror at the barrenness of the landscape: 'I never saw a country', he wrote, 'that seemed to be so torn and convulsed: the shock, whenever it happened, shook off all that vegetates.'
DP156633

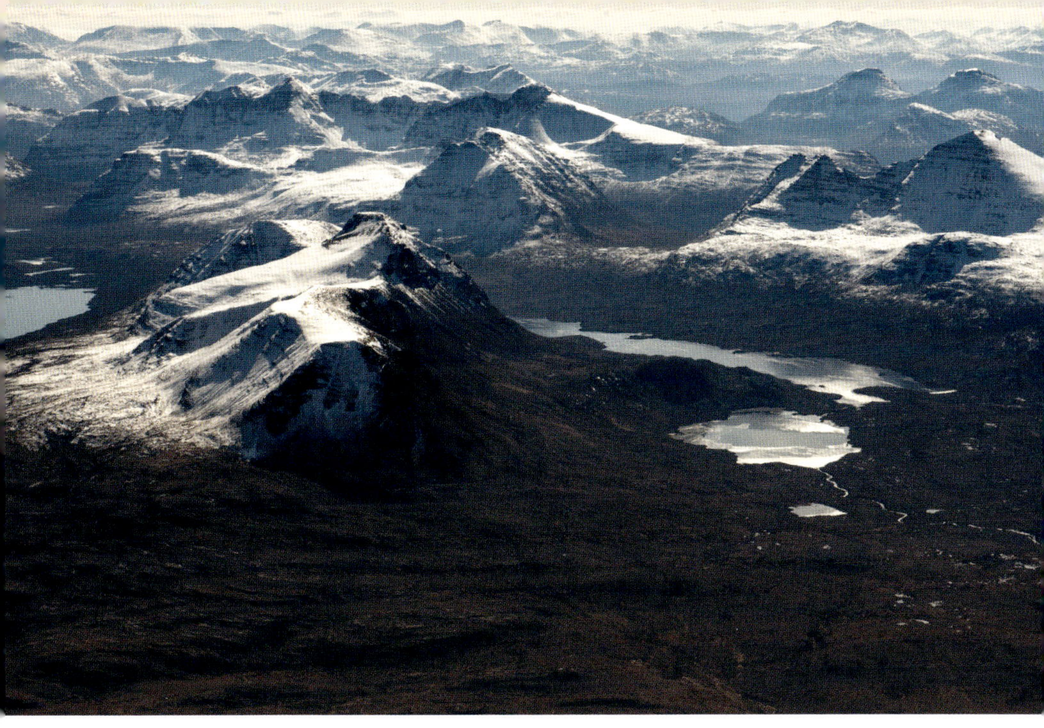

Baosbheinn, Highlands

The steep partially snow-covered slopes of Baosbheinn rise up from
the Flowerdale and Shieldaig Forests. Beyond these treeless 'forests'
lie the Torridon Hills.

DP156650

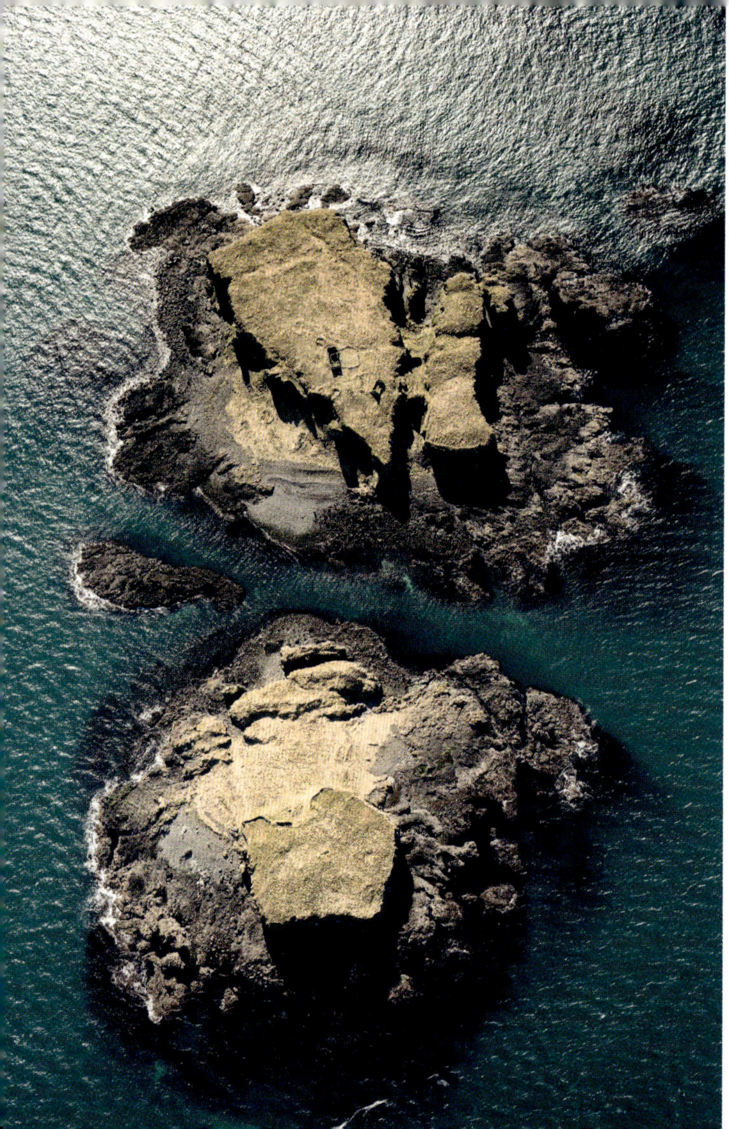

Cairnburgh Castle, Treshnish Isles, Argyll and Bute
The first mention of a fortification on this site comes from a Norse saga dating to the 1200s. It was later converted into a castle which, unusually, made use of both islands, with a courtyard, barrack block, chapel and guard-house on one island, and a second guard-house and well on the other.
DP162124

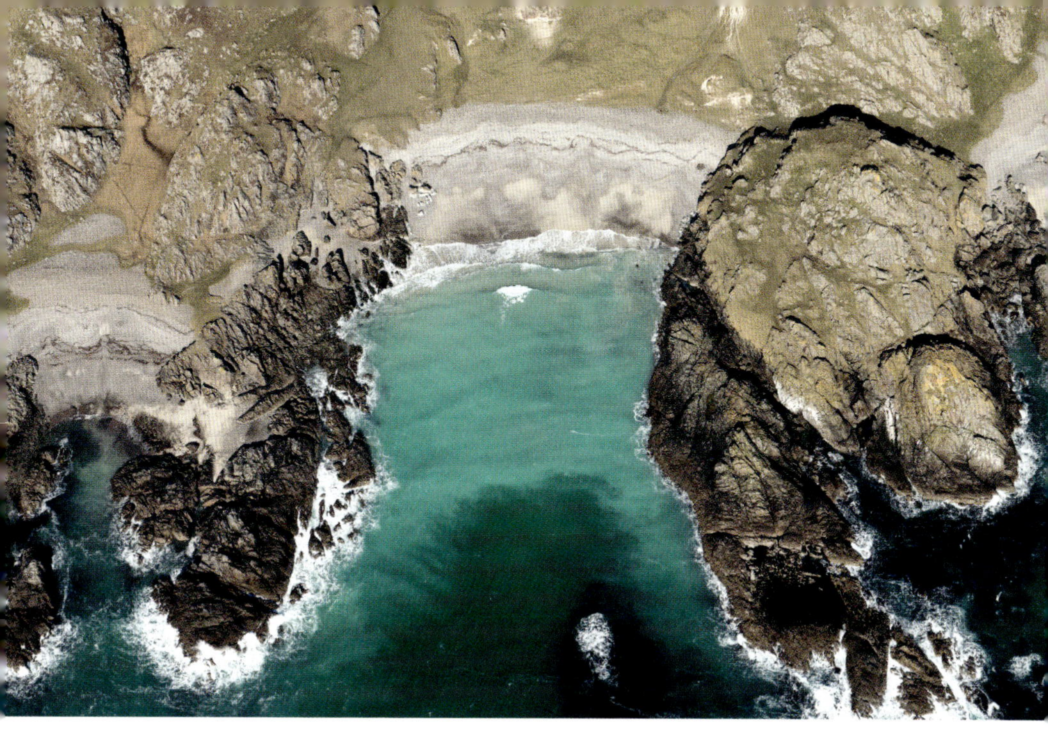

Dun Na Cleite, Tiree, Argyll and Bute

A substantial fort once rose up from the rocky headland on the right
of this photograph, making use of the site's obvious natural defences:
high sea cliffs on one side and a steep, boulder-strewn approach,
rising up to a 42m-high summit, on the other. Today the remains are
all but indistinguishable from the natural landscape.
DP162253

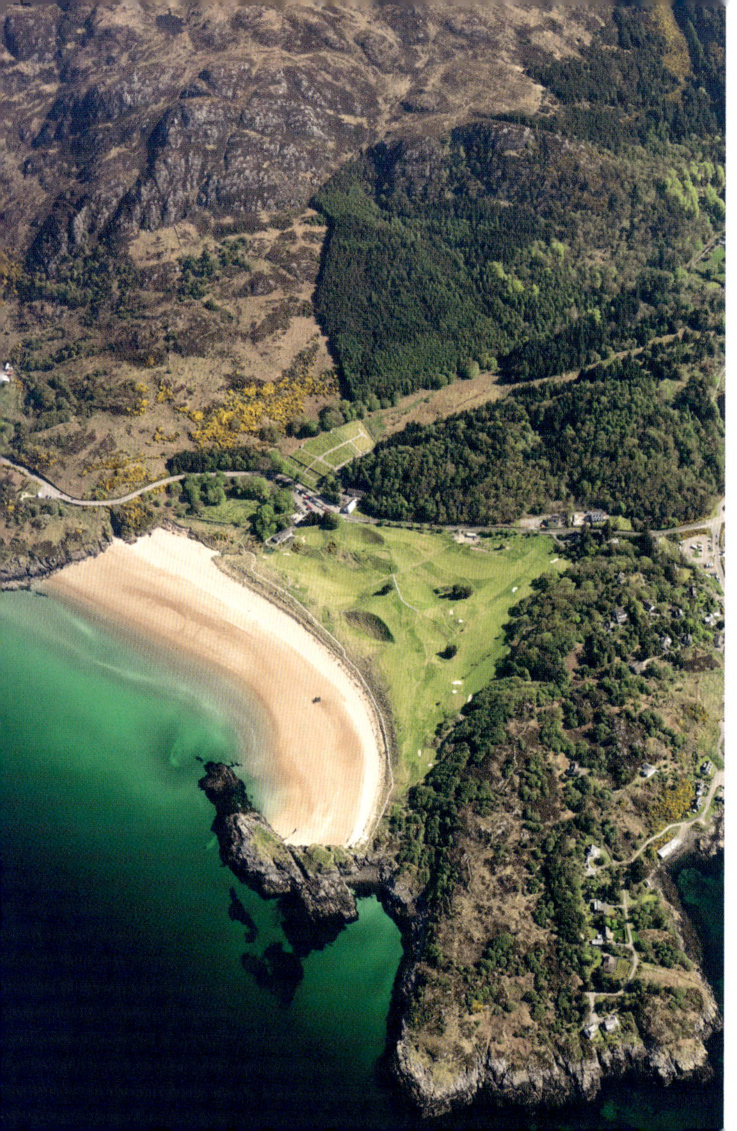

Gairloch Golf Course, Highlands

Golf, which Scotland claims to have invented, was banned by Scottish kings between 1457 and 1502 to encourage archery. But in the 1500s James IV, his granddaughter, Mary, Queen of Scots, and great-grandson, James VI, were all players. Scotland boasts some truly fabulous courses – at Gairloch you can tee off above a beautiful sandy beach with views of Skye, Harris and Lewis to the west and the Torridon mountains to the south.
DP109997

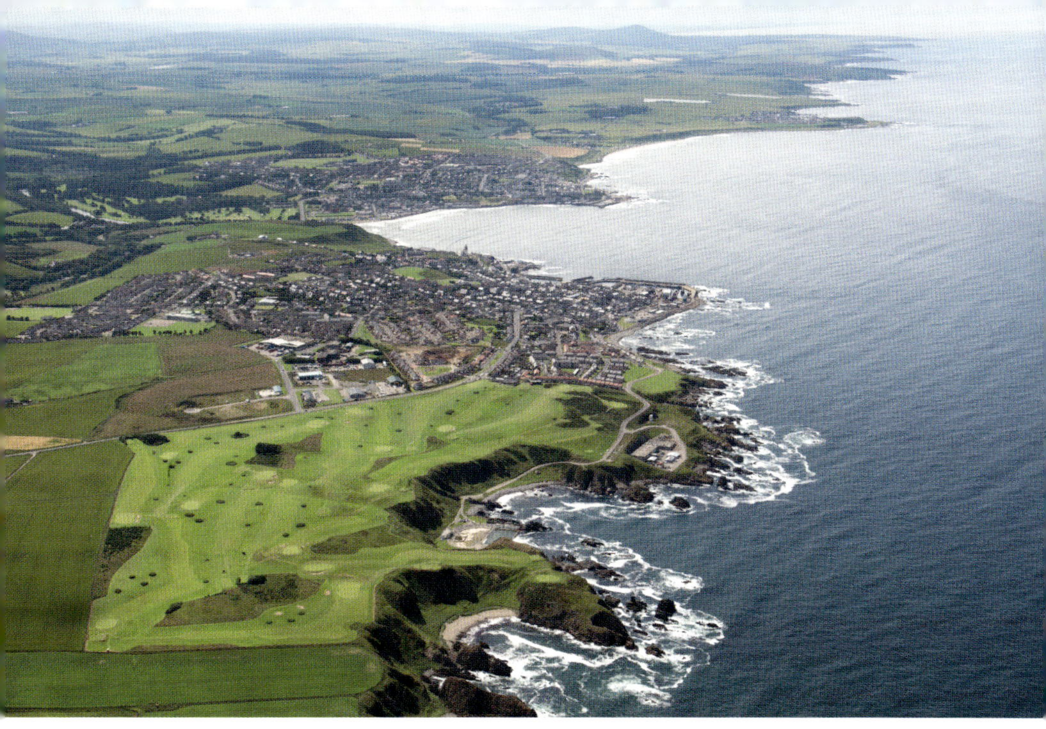

Royal Tarlair Golf Course, Aberdeenshire
This modernised early twentieth century course still retains its
notorious thirteenth hole, the 'Clivet', situated on a rocky headland.
DP193193

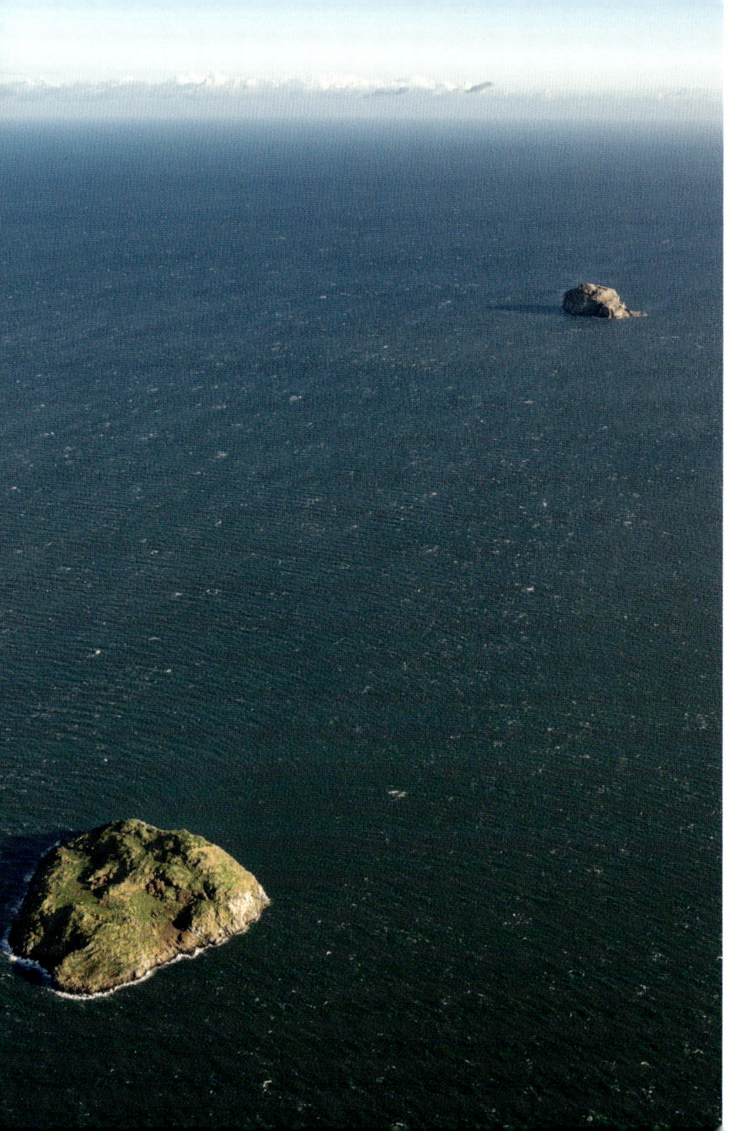

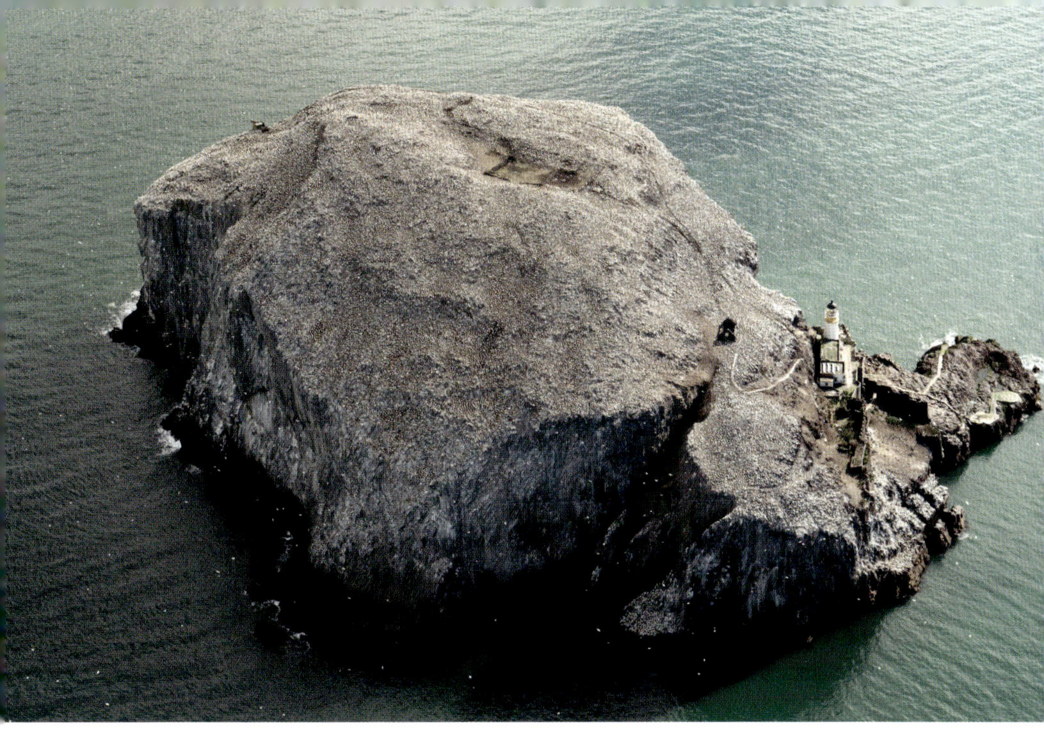

Bass Rock, East Lothian

Lying just a mile off the coast, this seemingly inhospitable chunk of volcanic rock has served many purposes over the centuries. Around the sixth century, it became a retreat for Christian hermits, and was later the site for a prominent castle. By the late 1600s it had acquired a darker purpose – as an island prison. Another change was to come, however, with the lighthouse lamp first shining in 1902, and not automated until 1988. Today the island is home to the world's largest colony of northern gannets.

DP266258, DP214002

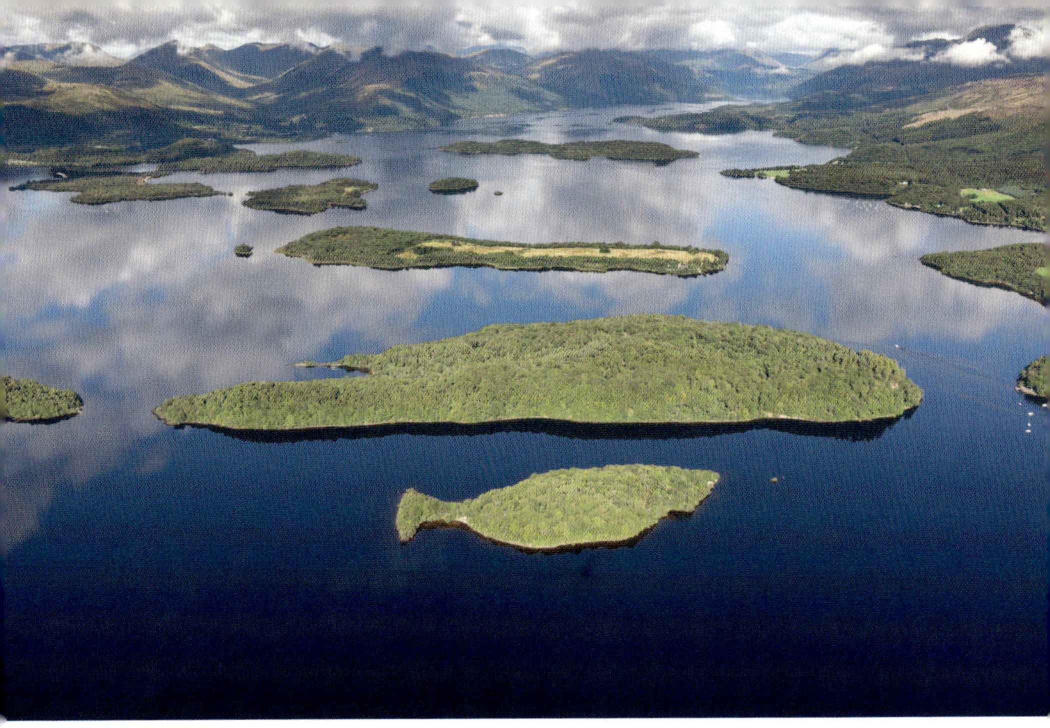

Loch Lomond, Stirling

The curious fish shape of the island of Clairinsh on Loch Lomond is an accident of nature. Surprisingly, though, the tiny islet found off its northern tip is man-made, created about 2,000 years ago to support a settlement known as a crannog. Scattered along seashores and in freshwater lochs, the remains of crannogs are visible today as rocky islets shrouded by scrubby trees.

DP221616, SC506612

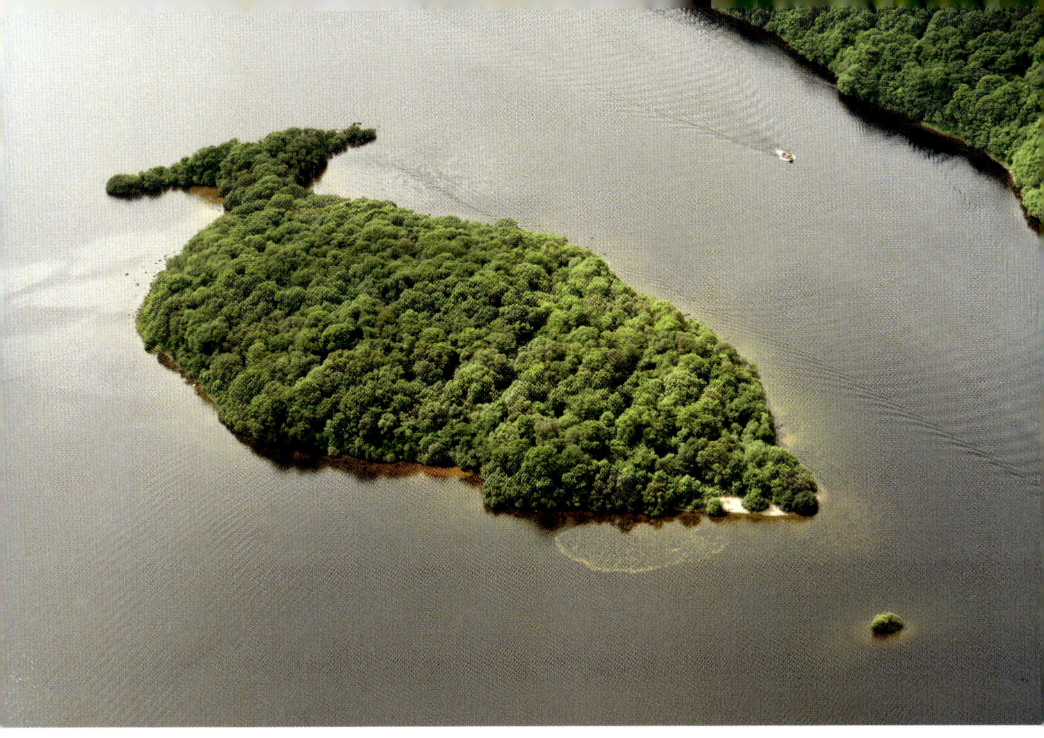

The township which runs down either side of the burn leading
to Mingulay Bay was the main area of settlement for generations.
Evidence of human habitation on the island dates back to prehistoric
times, but the last residents departed in 1912 – when the school
closed two years previously, there were only nine registered pupils.
DP221958

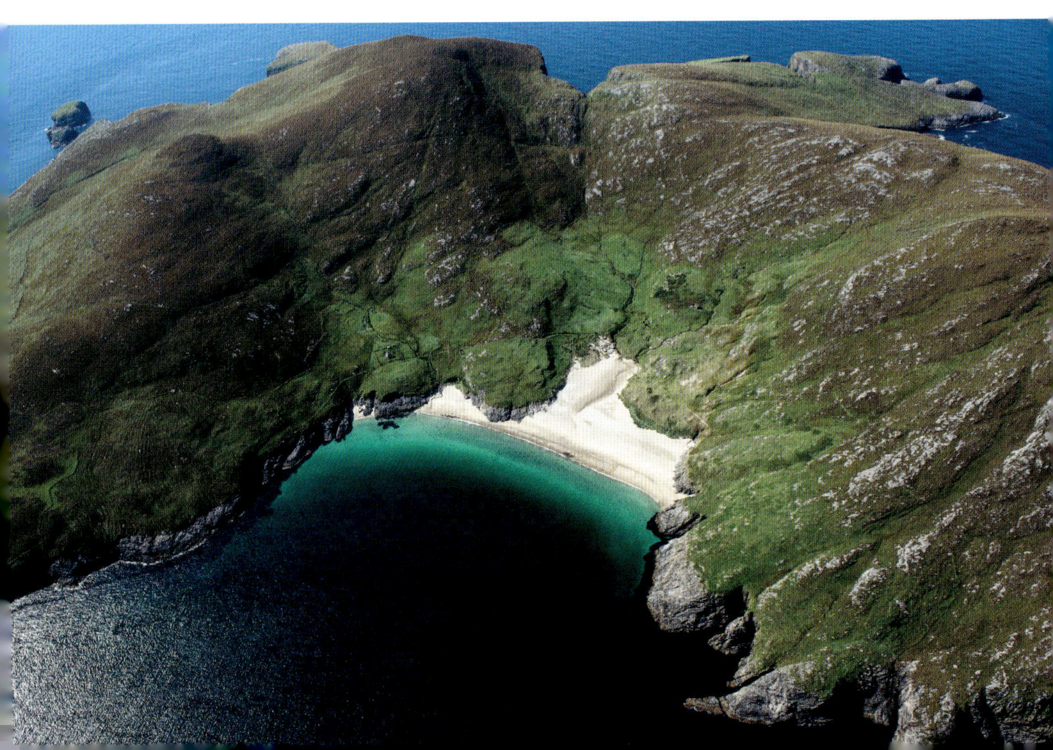

Mingulay Bay, Mingulay, Na h-Eileanan Siar

Hundreds of seals cluster on the beach and swim in the turquoise waters of Mingulay Beach. It is a reminder that what humans abandon, other species are quick to reclaim. The island also has a large seabird population, and is an important breeding ground for razorbills, guillemots and black-legged kittiwakes.
DP221841

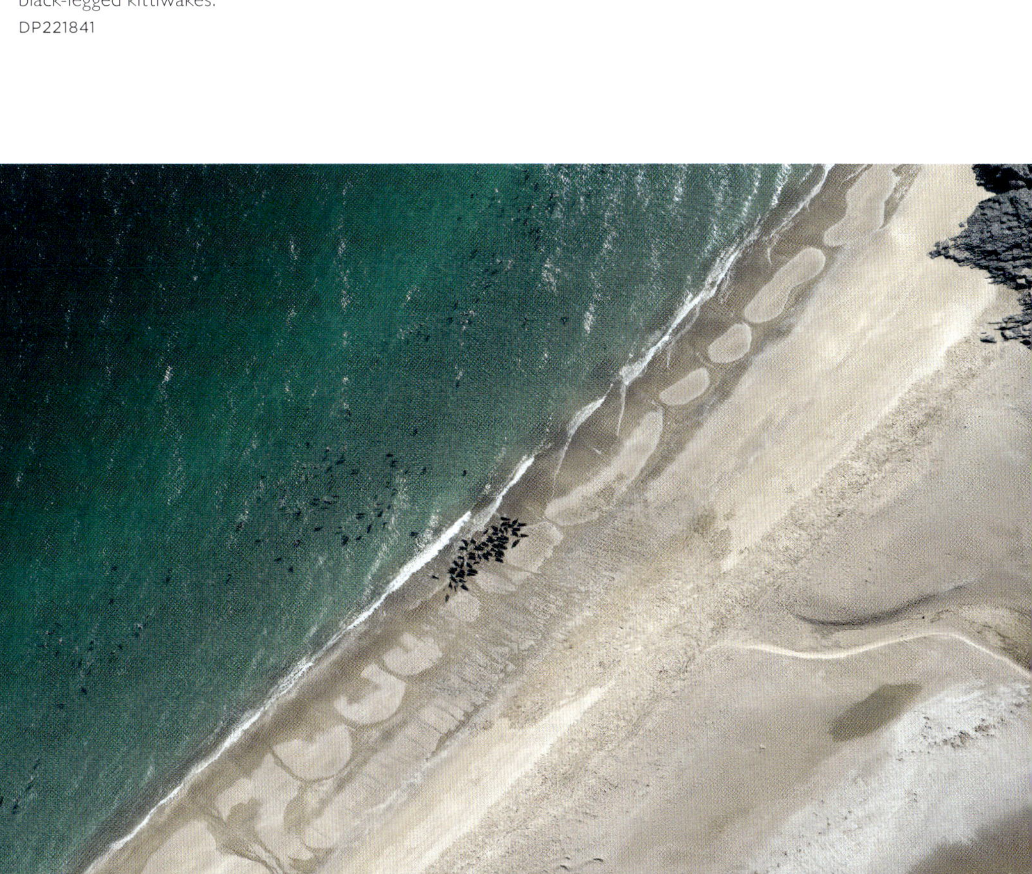

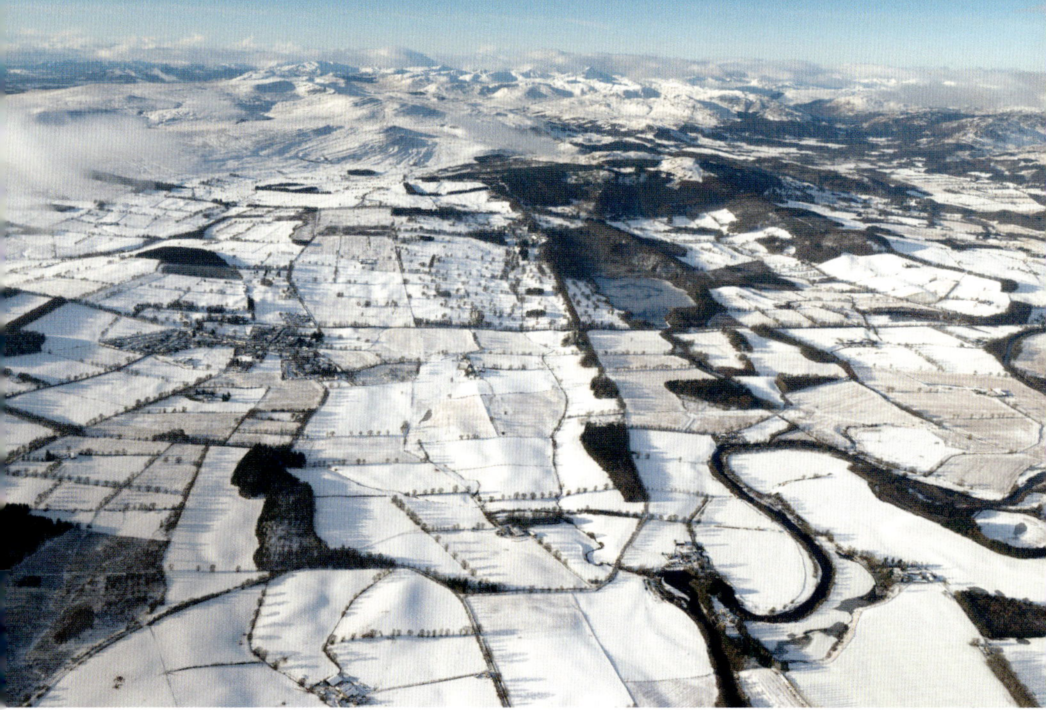

Strathearn, Perth and Kinross

This is a landscape still criss-crossed by the traces of
ancient war. A major Roman road once ran through here,
just to the south of the village of Muthill in the centre
left of the photograph. It linked defensive outposts and
temporary marching camps at nearby Strathgeath and
Innerpeffray to the massive Ardoch Fort.

DP229029

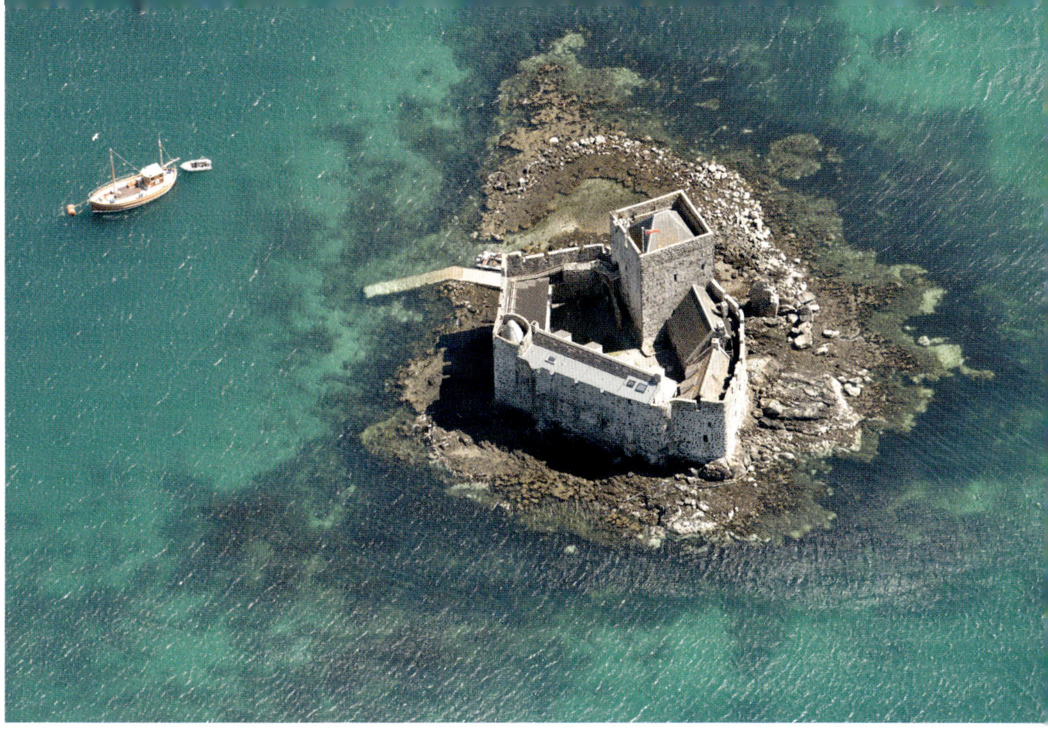

Kisimul Castle, Barra, Na h-Eileanan Siar

Kisimul Castle was the stronghold of the Macneils of Barra, a seafaring clan who claimed ancestry from Niall of the Nine Hostages, the high king of Ireland and great-grandfather of St Columba. The origins of this castle are difficult to pin down. Thought to have been built from the 1400s, it was abandoned by the 1700s. However, this was not the end of the Macneils at Kisimul – the castle was purchased and restored by the 45th Macneil Chief in the twentieth century.

DP235346

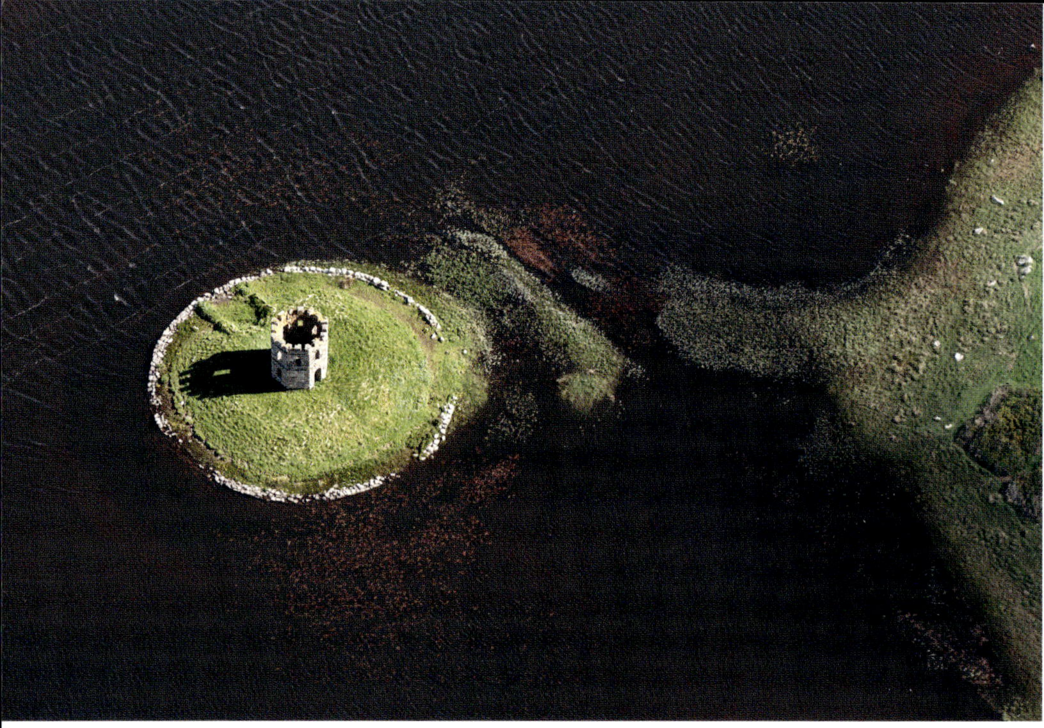

Loch Scolpaig, North Uist, Na h-Eileanan Siar

On Loch Scolpaig, a small circular island with a stone circumference
is topped by Scolpaig Tower, a folly dating to the 1800s. It is thought
that the islet had previously been the site of Dun Scolpaig, but this
earlier structure has been erased or reused in the construction of
the folly.

DP235534

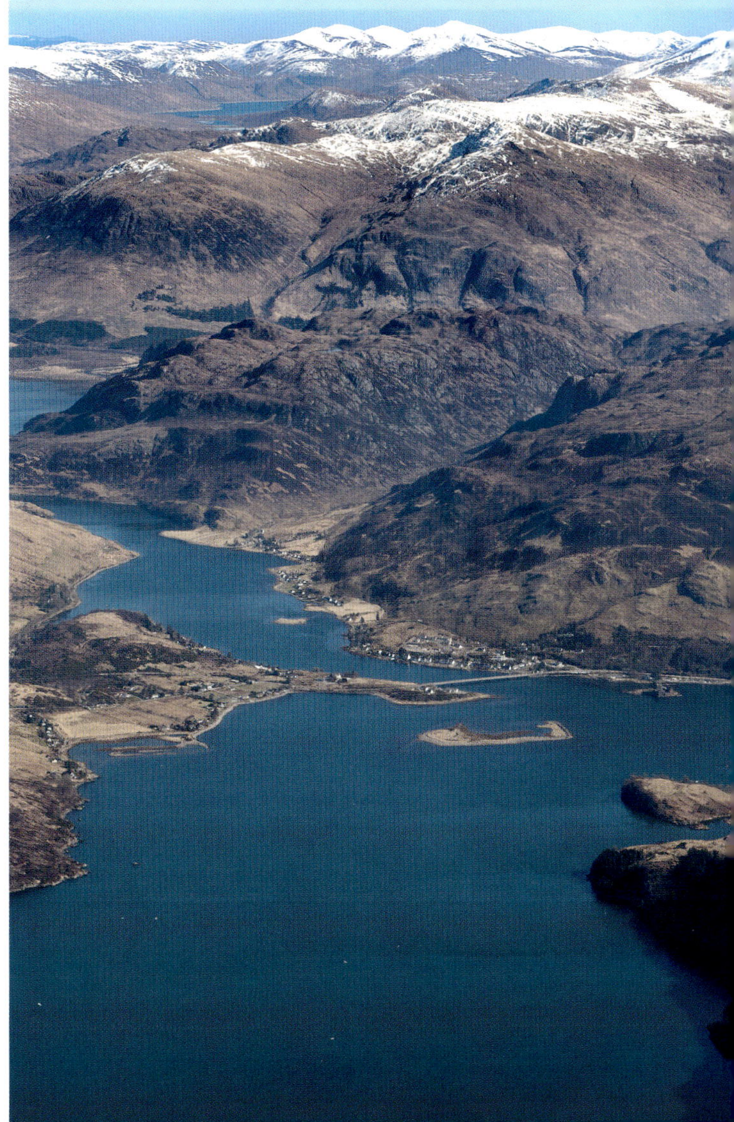

Loch Alsh, Highlands

Passing alongside Loch Duich and the famous ruin of Eilean Donan Castle, the road to Skye crosses the narrow meeting point of Loch Long and Loch Alsh via the Dornie Bridge. The present bridge dates from 1990, replacing an older bridge first constructed in 1940 – which operated a toll up until 1946.

DP156660

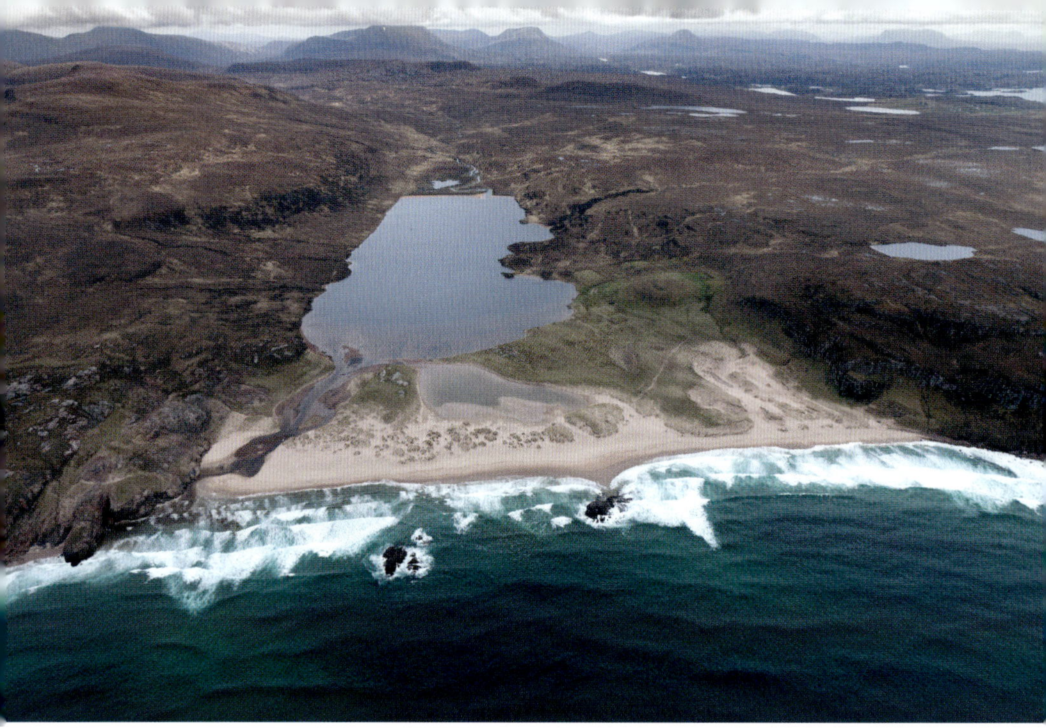

Sandwood Bay, Highlands

Sandwood Bay, just south of Cape Wrath on Scotland's north-west
coast, is one of Britain's most beautiful and haunting beaches. It is also
one of its most inaccessible – a two-hour walk once the road comes
to a dead end at Blairmore.

DP211984

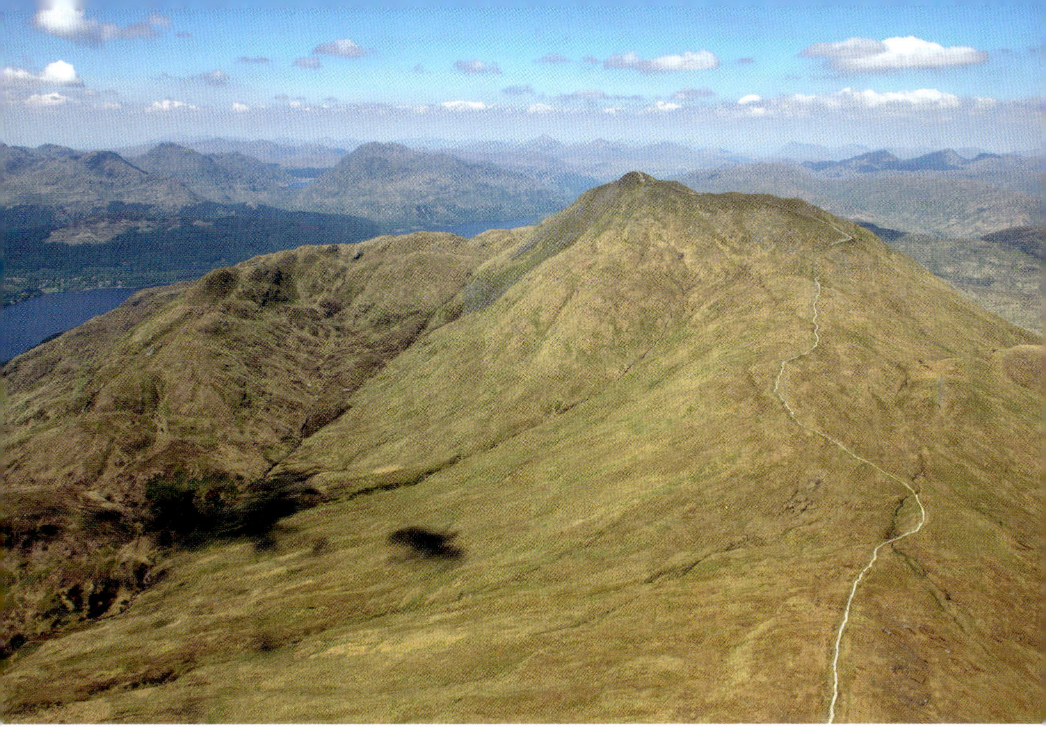

Ben Lomond, Stirling

With a summit 974m high, Ben Lomond is a munro – a classification
for Scottish mountains over 3,000ft (914.4m) – towering over the
famous shores of Loch Lomond. Thousands of walkers attempt to
reach the peak of Ben Lomond each year.

DP279046

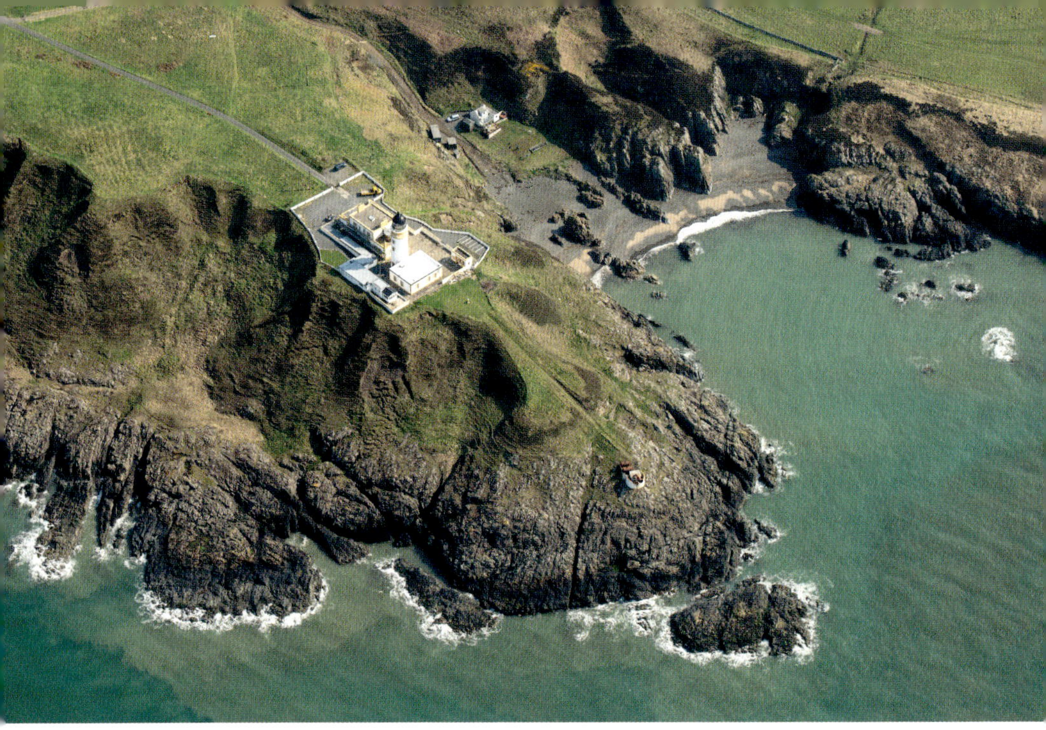

**Killantringan Lighthouse,
Dumfries and Galloway**

This lighthouse – with the old foghorn
perched on the cliff edge – was built
by DA Stevenson and first lit in 1900.
Inscribed above the door of the keeper's
cottage is the motto 'In Salutem
Omnium' – 'For the Safety of All'.
DP292514

**Inch Garvie Island and Forth Railway Bridge,
Edinburgh**

Thought to have been occupied as early as the 1400s, Inch
Garvie has been the site of a castle, a state prison, a plague
colony, a construction office for the Forth Railway Bridge,
and a First and Second World War defensive battery.
SC532491

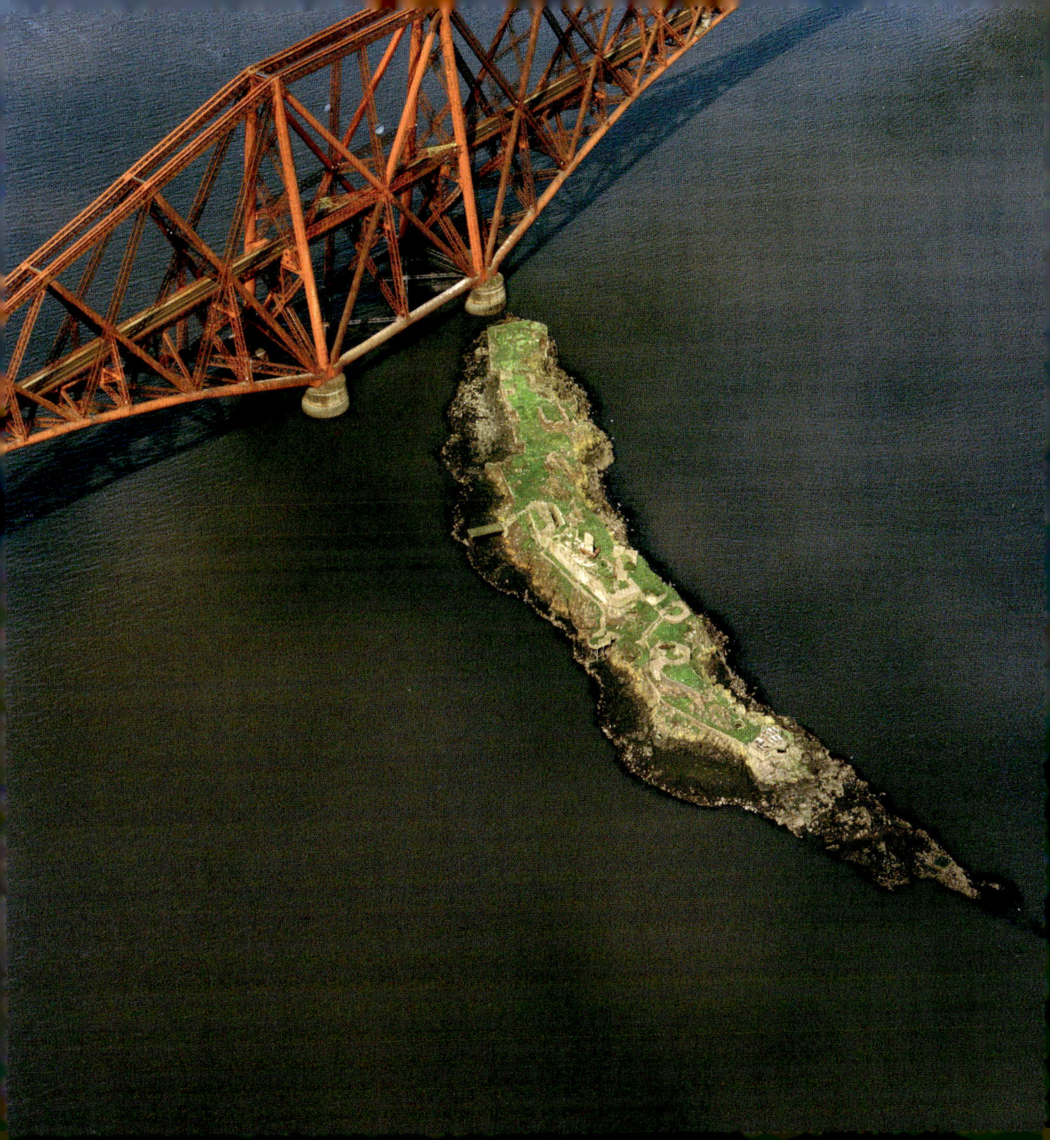

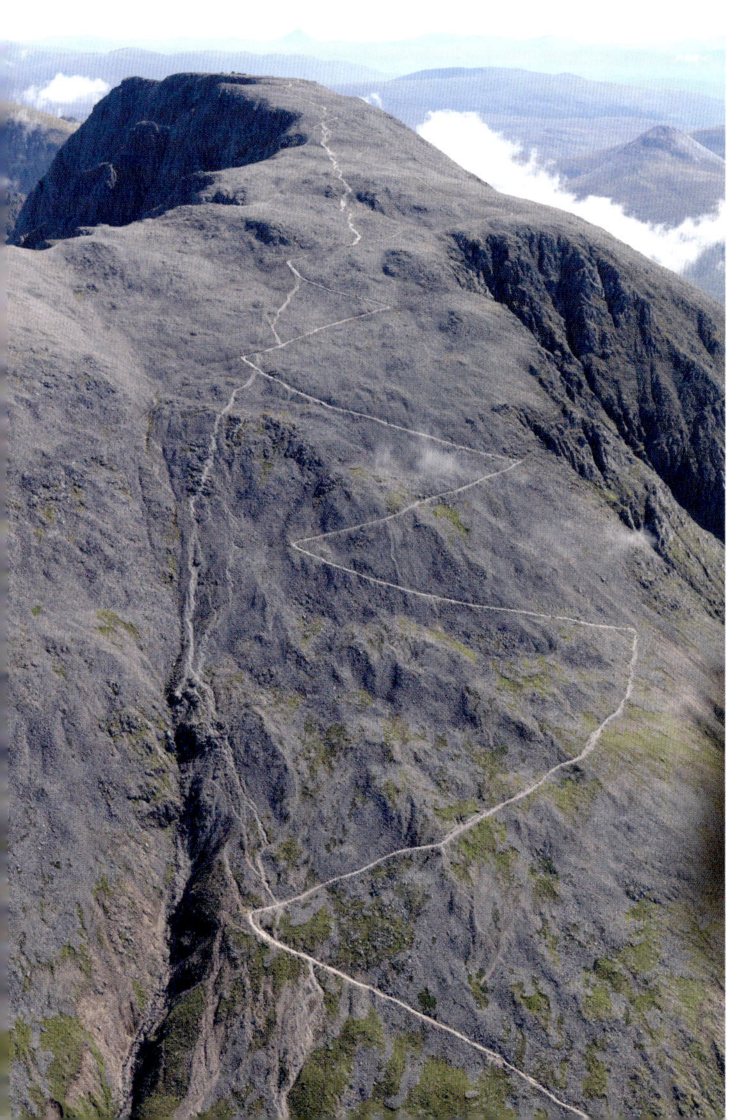

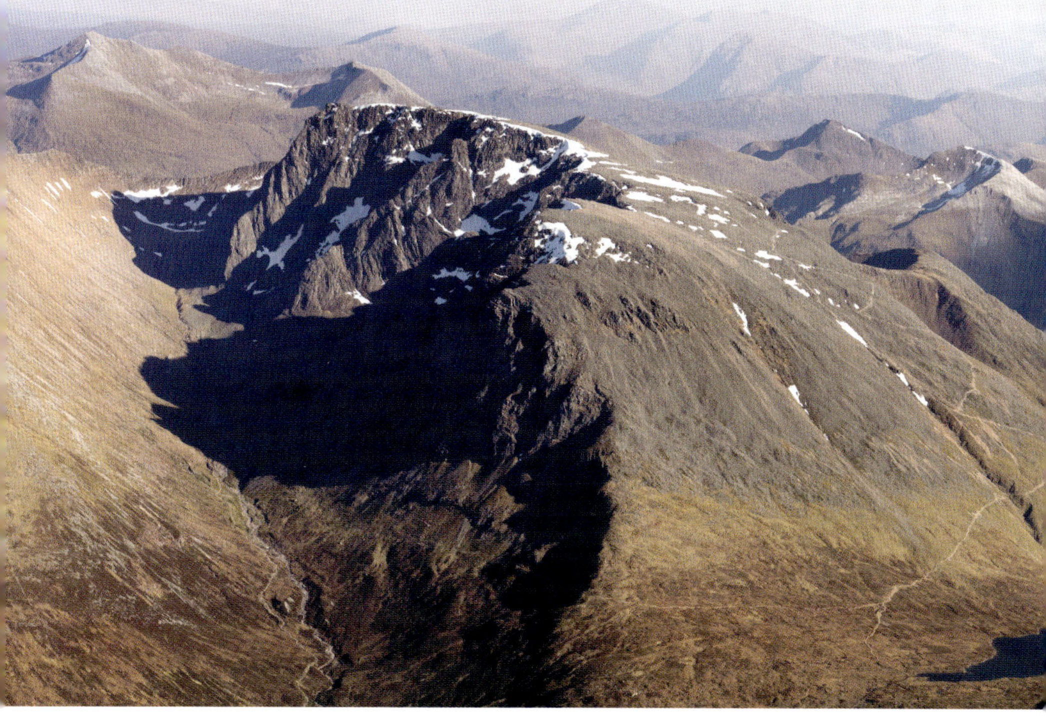

Ben Nevis, Highlands

Often capped by snow into late spring and summer, the imposing peak of Ben Nevis stands at 1,345m – the highest mountain in the UK. The ruined meteorological observatory at the summit can be reached by a long walk up the zig-zag mountain path from Glen Nevis or one of the steep climbing routes on the impressive cliffs of its north face above the Allt a Mhuilinn.
DP094871, DP111939

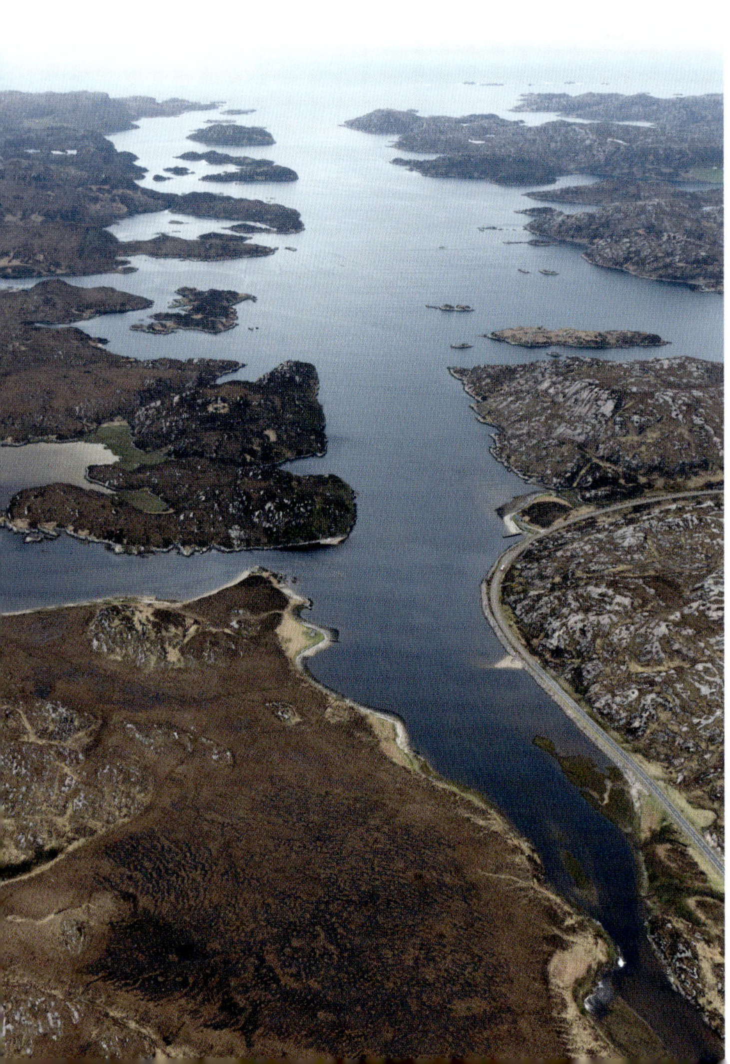

Laxford Bay, Highlands
As the A838 makes its way towards the most north-western point on the British mainland, the road passes the narrow, rocky inlet of Loch Laxford. On the right hand side of the image is a small coursed rubble pier, built in the mid 1800s. Beyond the mouth of the loch is nothing but the Atlantic Ocean.
DP211890

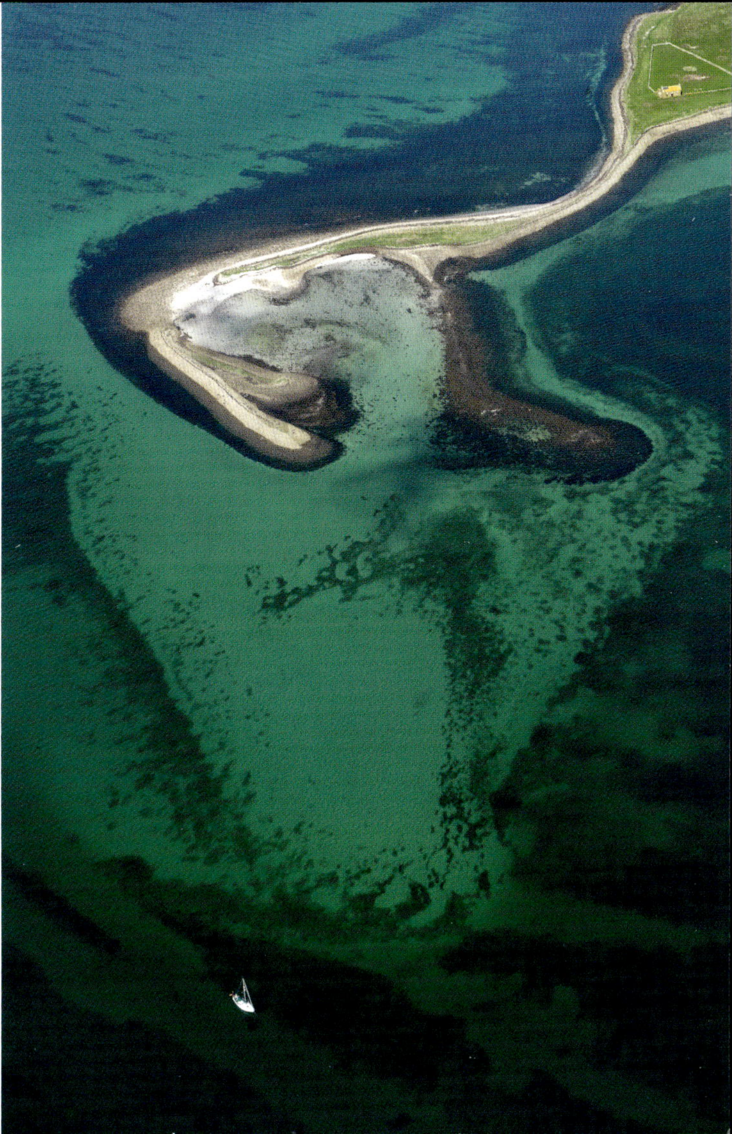

Deer Sound, Orkney

A yacht rests in the clear
waters of Deer Sound on the
west Mainland of Orkney.
Remarkably, beneath its
fibreglass hull is a drowned
landscape on which our
prehistoric ancestors once
lived and walked. Even in
this remote, secluded bay
Scotland's varied landscapes
never stop changing.
DP058592

The Grahams & The Donalds (SMC)
Rab Anderson and Tom Prentice
(Scottish Mountaineering Press, 2022)

The Munros (SMC)
Rab Anderson and Tom Prentice
(Scottish Mountaineering Press, 2021)

Scotland's Landscapes:
The National Collection of Aerial Photography
James Crawford (Historic Environment Scotland, 2014)

Victoria in the Highlands
David Duff (Frederick Muller, 1968)

Historic Scotland – Official Souvenir Guides, various titles

Clan and Castle: The Lives and Lands of Scotland's Great Families
Chris Tabraham (Historic Scotland, revised edition, 2014)

Scotland's History (Pocket HES)
Fiona Watson (Historic Environment Scotland, 2020)

A History of Scotland's Landscapes
Fiona Watson with Piers Dixon
(Historic Environment Scotland, 2018)